# TABLE OF CONTENTS

# Solutions Manual

# Investment Analysis and Portfolio Management

**Fifth Edition**

## Frank K. Reilly
University of Notre Dame

## Keith C. Brown
University of Texas at Austin

## Ladd Kochman
Kennesaw State University

**The Dryden Press**

**Harcourt Brace College Publishers**

Fort Worth   Philadelphia   San Diego   New York   Orlando   Austin   San Antonio
Toronto   Montreal   London   Sydney   Tokyo

**Cover Illustration:** Ken Reid/FPG International

*Address for Editorial Correspondence*
Harcourt Brace College Publishers, 301 Commerce Street, Suite 3700, Fort Worth, TX 76102

*Address for Orders*
Harcourt Brace & Company, 6277 Sea Harbor Drive, Orlando, FL 32887
1-800-782-4479

ISBN: 0-03-020454-2

Printed in the United States of America

7 8 9 0 1 2 3 4 5 6    0 2 3    9 8 7 6 5 4 3 2

The Dryden Press
Harcourt Brace College Publishers

# CHAPTER 1

## The Investment Setting

# Answers to Questions

1.  When an individual's current money income exceeds his current consumption desires, he saves the excess. Rather than keep these savings in his possession, the individual may consider it worthwhile to forego immediate possession of the money for a larger future amount of consumption. This trade-off of present consumption for a higher level of future consumption is the essence of investment.

    An investment is the current commitment of funds for a period of time in order to derive a future flow of funds that will compensate the investor for the time value of money, the expected rate of inflation over the life of the investment, and provide a premium for the uncertainty associated with this future flow of funds.

2.  In the 20-30 year segment, an individual would tend to be a net borrower since she is in a relatively low income bracket and has several expenditures -- automobile, durable goods, etc. In the 30-40 segment, again the individual would likely dissave since her expenditures would increase with the advent of family life, and conceivably, the purchase of a house. In the 40-50 segment, the individual would probably be a saver since income would have increased substantially with no increases in expenditures. Between the age of 50 and 60, the individual would typically be a strong saver since income would continue to increase, and by now the couple would be "empty nesters." After this, depending upon when the individual retires, the individual would probably be a dissaver as income decreases (transition from regular income to income from a pension).

3.  The difference is because of the definition and measurement of return. In the case of the *WSJ*, it only refers to the current dividend yield on common stocks versus the promised yield on bonds. In the University of Chicago studies, they are talking about the total rate of return on common stocks, which is the dividend yield plus the capital gain or loss during the period. In the long run, the dividend yield has been 4-5 percent and the capital gain has

*1 - 3*

about the same. Therefore, it is important to compare alternative investments based upon total return.

4. The variance of expected returns represents a measure of the dispersion of actual returns around the expected value. The larger the variance is, everything else remaining constant, the greater the dispersion of expectations and the greater the uncertainty or risk of the investment. The purpose of the variance is to help measure and analyze the risk associated with a particular investment.

5. An investor's required rate of return is a function of the economy's risk free rate (RFR), an inflation premium that compensates the investor for loss of purchasing power, and a risk premium that compensates the investor for taking the risk. The RFR is the pure time value of money and is the compensation an individual demands for deferring consumption. More objectively, the RFR can be measured in terms of the long-run real growth rate in the economy since the investment opportunities available in the economy influence the RFR. The inflation premium, which can be conveniently measured in terms of the Consumer Price Index, is the additional protection an individual requires to compensate for the erosion in purchasing power resulting from increasing prices. Since the return on all investments is not certain as it is with T-bills, the investor requires a premium for taking on additional risk. The risk premium can be examined in terms of business risk, financial risk, liquidity risk, exchange rate risk and country risk.

6. Two factors that influence the RFR are liquidity (i.e., supply and demand for capital in the economy) and the real growth rate of the economy. Obviously, the influence of liquidity on the RFR is an inverse relationship, while the real growth rate has a positive relationship with the RFR -- i.e., the higher the real growth rate, the higher the RFR.

It is unlikely that the economy's long-run real growth rate will change dramatically during a business cycle. However, liquidity depends upon the government's monetary policy and would change, depending upon what the government considers to be the appropriate stimulus. Besides, the demand for business loans would be greatest during the early and middle part of the business cycle.

7.	The five factors that influence the risk premium on an investment are business risk, financial risk, liquidity risk, exchange rate risk, and country risk.

	Business risk is a function of sales volatility and operating leverage, and the combined effect of the two variables can be quantified in terms of the coefficient of variation of operating earnings. Financial risk is a function of the uncertainty introduced by the financing mix. The inherent risk involved is the inability to meet future contractual payments (interest on bonds, etc.) or the threat of bankruptcy. Financial risk is measured in terms of a debt ratio (e.g., debt/equity ratio) and/or the interest coverage ratio. Liquidity risk is the uncertainty an individual faces when he decides to buy or sell an investment. The two uncertainties involved are: (1) how long it will take to buy or sell this asset, and (2) what price will be received. The liquidity risk on different investments can vary substantially (e.g., real estate vs. T-bills). Exchange rate risk is the uncertainty of returns on securities acquired in a different currency. The risk applies to the global investor or multinational corporate manager who must anticipate returns on securities in light of uncertain future exchange rates. A good measure of this uncertainty would be the absolute volatility of the exchange rate or its beta with a composite exchange rate. Country risk is the uncertainty of returns caused by the possibility of a major change in the political or economic environment of a country. The analysis of country risk is much more subjective and must be based upon the history and current environment in the country.

8.	The increased use of debt increases the fixed interest payment. Since this fixed contractual payment will increase, the residual earnings (net income) will become more variable. The required rate of return on the stock will change since the financial risk (as measured by the debt/equity ratio) has increased.

9.	According to the Capital Asset Pricing Model, all securities are located on the Security Market Line with securities' risk on the horizontal axis and securities' expected return on its vertical axis. As to the locations of the five types of investments on the line, the U.S. government bonds should be located to the left of the other four, followed by United Kingdom government bonds, low-grade corporate bonds, common stock of large firms, and common stocks of Japanese firms. U.S. government bonds have the lowest risk and required rate of return simply because they virtually have no default risk at all.

10. If a market's real RFR is 4 percent, the investor will require a 4 percent return on an investment since this will compensate him for deferring consumption. However, if the inflation rate is 5 percent, the investor would be worse off in real terms if he invests at a rate of return of 4 percent -- e.g., you would receive $104, but the cost of $100 worth of goods at the beginning of the year would be $105 at the end of the year, which means you could consume less real goods. Thus, for an investment to be desirable, it should have a return of 9.20 percent (1.04 x 1.05 - 1) or an approximate return of 9 percent (4% + 5%).

11. Both changes cause an increase in the required return on all investments. Specifically, an increase in the real growth rate will cause an increase in the economy's RFR because of a higher level of investment opportunities. In addition, the increase in the rate of inflation will result in an increase in the nominal RFR. Because both changes affect the nominal RFR, they will cause an equal increase in the required return on all investments of 5 percent.

*1 - 6*

The graph should show a parallel shift upward in the capital market line of 5 percent.

12. Such a change in the yield spread would imply a change in the market risk premium because, although the risk levels of bonds remain relatively constant, investors have changed the spreads they demand to accept this risk. In this case, because the yield spread (risk premium) declined, it implies a decline in the slope of the SML as shown in the following graph.

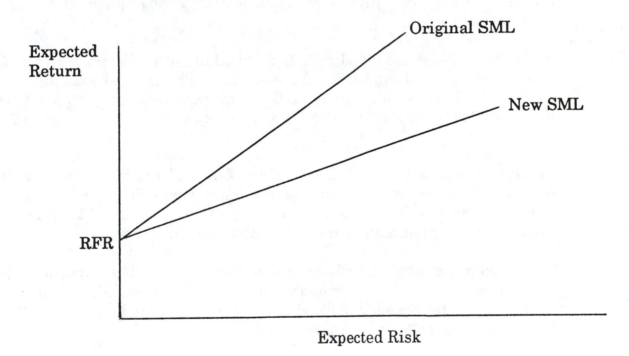

13. The ability to buy or sell an investment quickly without a substantial price concession is known as liquidity. An example of a liquid investment asset would be a United States Government Treasury Bill. A Treasury Bill can be bought or sold in minutes at a price almost identical to the quoted price. In contrast, an example of an illiquid asset would be a specialized machine or a parcel of real estate in a remote area. In both cases, it might take a considerable period of time to find a potential seller or buyer, and the actual selling price could vary substantially from expectations.

14.   Reading Reference: <u>C.F.A. Readings</u> (Fifth Edition), Rockwell Article.

14(a) Three major factors that determine an economy's long-run growth potential
are: the annual growth rate of the labor force, the annual growth rate of
man-hours worked per worker, and the annual change in worker
productivity.

The labor force is determined by the overall growth rate of the population
and the participation rate of the population, which, in turn, is influenced by
the age distribution of the population and demographics (i.e., female
participation).

In addition to how many individuals are working, it is necessary to consider
how many hours the work force is working. The general tendency is for
shorter workweeks (e.g., from 39.5 hours per week to 39.0 or lower).
Actually, this factor has tended to be a negative growth factor in terms of real
output.

Finally, in addition to the number of workers and the hours of work, it is
necessary to know the amount of production per man-hour, and this can be
influenced by a growth in productivity -- i.e., workers are able to increase
their real output per man-hour due to better machinery, etc.

14(b) The actual estimates set forth are not very important. The important factor
is a recognition of the determinants, the general direction of change, and
what affects the change. Following are the estimates by Security Pacific
Bank, but no clear "correct" answer exists:

♦   The labor force is expected to grow at about a 1.9 percent rate due to
an overall population growth of 1 percent and an increase in the
participation rate from 62 to 66 percent.

♦   The decline in the average work week is expected to continue at a rate
of about minus 0.5 percent. This is due to a preference for leisure, a
shift from agriculture and industry into services, more women and
teenagers in the labor force, and an acceptance of more flexible work
schedules and use of part-time workers.

♦   The rate of growth of productivity has gone from about 2.5 percent in
the 1950s to about 1.0 percent in the 1970s and is expected to rebound

slightly to about 1.4 percent during the next five years. This guarded optimism is due to some increase in capital investment, a turn around in the R&D expenditures, fewer government regulations that require non-productive investments, and a maturing of the labor force.

An estimation of each of the components of the composite real growth potential for the next five years is as follows:

| | |
|---|---|
| Growth of labor force | 1.9% |
| Growth of man-hours | (0.5)% |
| Productivity growth | 1.4% |
| Composite of Growth Potential | 2.8% |

(Specific numbers are not as important as the trend of changes.)

# Answers to Problems

1.  $\text{HPR} = \dfrac{\text{Ending Value of Investment (including Cash Flows)}}{\text{Beginning Value of Investment}}$

    $$= \frac{39 + 1.50}{34} = \frac{40.50}{34} = 1.191$$

    $\text{HPY} = \text{HPR} - 1 = 1.191 - 1 = .191$

2.  $\text{HPR} = \dfrac{61 + 3}{65} = \dfrac{64}{65} = .985$

    $\text{HPY} = \text{HPR} - 1 = .985 - 1 = -.015$

3.  $4,000 used to purchase 80 shares = $50 per share

    $$\text{HPR} = \frac{(59 \times 80) + (5 \times 80)}{4,000} = \frac{4,720 + 400}{4,000} = \frac{5,120}{4,000} = 1.280$$

    $\text{HPY} = \text{HPR} - 1 = 1.280 - 1 = .280$

    $$\text{HPR (Price Increase Alone)} = \frac{59 \times 80}{4,000} = \frac{4,720}{4,000} = 1.180$$

    $\text{HPY (Price Increase Alone)} = 1.180 - 1 = .180$

HPY (Price Increase Alone) $\quad= 1.180 - 1 = .180$

therefore: HPY (Total) $\quad=$ HPY (Price Increase) + HPY (Div)

$\qquad\qquad .280 \quad= .180 +$ HPY (Div)

$\qquad\qquad .10 \quad\;=$ HPY (Dividends)

4.  Annual HPR $= \quad (55 / 30)^{1/3} = 1.224$

Annual HPY $= \quad 1.224 - 1 \quad= .224$

5.  "Real" Rate of Return $= \dfrac{\text{Holding Period Return}}{1 + \text{Rate of Inflation}} - 1$

For Problem #1:  HPR $= 1.191$

at 4% inflation: $\dfrac{1.191}{1 + .04} - 1 = \dfrac{1.191}{1.04} - 1 = 1.145 - 1 = .145$

at 8% inflation: $\dfrac{1.191}{1 + .08} - 1 = \dfrac{1.191}{1.08} - 1 = 1.103 - 1 = .103$

For Problem #2:  HPR $= .985$

at 4% inflation: $\dfrac{.985}{1.04} - 1 = .947 - 1 = -.053$

at 8% inflation: $\dfrac{.985}{1.08} - 1 = .912 - 1 = -.088$

For Problem #3:  HPR $= 1.280$

at 4% inflation: $\dfrac{1.280}{1.04} - 1 = 1.231 - 1 = .231$

at 8% inflation: $\dfrac{1.280}{1.08} - 1 = 1.185 - 1 = .185$

6(a). Arithmetic Mean (AM) = $\displaystyle\sum_{i=1}^{n} \dfrac{HPY_i}{n}$

$$AM_T = \dfrac{(.19) + (.08) + (-.12) + (-.03) + (.15)}{5}$$

$$= \dfrac{.27}{5} = .054$$

$$AM_B = \dfrac{(.08) + (.03) + (-.09) + (.02) + (.04)}{5}$$

$$= \dfrac{.08}{5} = .016$$

Stock T is more desirable because the arithmetic mean annual rate of return is higher.

6(b). Standard Deviation $(\sigma) = \left(\displaystyle\sum_{i=1}^{n} P_i\,[\,R_i - E\,(R_i)\,]^2\right)^{.5}$

1 - 12

$$\Sigma_T = (.19 - .054)^2 + (.08 - .054)^2 + (-.12 - .054)^2$$
$$+ (-.03 - .054)^2 + (.15 - .054)^2$$

$$= .01850 + .00068 + .03028 + .00706 + .00922$$

$$= .06574$$

$$\sigma^2 = .06574/5 = .01315$$

$$\sigma_T = (.01314)^{.5} = .11467$$

$$\Sigma_B = (.08 - .016)^2 + (.03 - .016)^2 + (-.09 - .016)^2$$

$$+ (.02 - .016)^2 + (.04 - .016)^2$$

$$= .00410 + .00020 + .01124 + .00002 + .00058$$

$$= .01614$$

$$\sigma^2 = .01614/5 = .00323$$

$$\sigma_B = (.00323)^{.5} = .05681$$

By this measure, B would be preferable.

6(c).   Coefficient of Variation $= \dfrac{\text{Standard Deviation}}{\text{Expected Return}}$

$$CV_T = \frac{.11466}{.054} = 2.1233$$

$$CV_B = \frac{.05682}{.016} = 3.5513$$

By this measure, T would be preferable.

6(d).  Geometric Mean (GM) = $\Pi^{1/n} - 1$

where    $\Pi$ = Product of the HPRs

$GM_T$ =    $[\,(1.19)\,(1.08)\,(.88)\,(.97)\,(1.15)\,]^{1/5} - 1$

  =    $[1.26160]^{1/5} - 1$

  =    $1.04757 - 1$

  =    $.04757$

$GM_B$ =    $[\,(1.08)\,(1.03)\,(.91)\,(1.02)\,(1.04)\,]^{1/5} - 1$

  =    $[1.07383]^{1/5} - 1$

  =    $1.01435 - 1$

  =    $.01435$

Stock T has more variability than Stock B. The greater the variability of returns, the greater the difference between the arithmetic and geometric mean returns.

7.  $E(R_{LDB})$  $= (.30) (-.10) + (.10) (0.00) + (.30) (.10) + (.30) (.25)$

$= (-.03) + .000 + .03 + .075$

$= .075$

8.  $E(R_{CCC})$  $= (.05) (-.60) + (.20) (-.30) + (.10) (-.10) + (.30) (.20)$

$+ (.20) (.40) + (.15) (.80)$

$= (-.03) + (-.06) + (-.01) + .06 + .08 + .12$

$= .16$

9.  The Cheryl Computer Company presents greater risk as an investment because the range of possible returns is much wider.

10. $$\text{Rate of Inflation} = \frac{CPI_{n+1} - CPI_n}{CPI_n}$$

where CPI = the Consumer Price Index

$$\text{Rate of Inflation} = \frac{168 - 160}{160} = \frac{8}{160} = .05$$

$$\text{Real rate of return} = \frac{HPR}{1 + \text{rate of inflation}} - 1$$

$$\text{U.S. Government T-Bills} = \frac{1.055}{1.05} - 1 = 1.005 - 1 = .005$$

$$\text{U.S. Government LT bonds} = \frac{1.075}{1.05} - 1 = 1.024 - 1 = .024$$

$$\text{U.S. Common Stocks} = \frac{1.1160}{1.05} - 1 = 1.063 - 1 = .063$$

11. Nominal RFR $= (1 + .03)(1 + .04) - 1 = 1.0712 - 1 = .0712$

An approximation would be growth rate plus inflation rate or $.03 + .04 = .07$

12. Return on common stock $= (1 + .0712)(1 + .05) - 1$

$$= 1.1248 - 1 = .1248$$

An approximation would be $.03 + .04 + .05 = .12$

If investors become more risk averse, the required return will increase. Stock prices, in turn, will decline.

13.      Nominal rate on T-bills    = (1 + .03) (1 + .05) - 1
        (or risk-free rate)

$$= 1.0815 - 1 = .0815$$

An approximation would be .03 + .05 = .08

The required rate of return on common stock is equal to the risk-free rate plus a risk premium. Therefore, the approximate risk premium for common stocks implied by these data is: .14 - .0815 = .0585.

An approximation would be .14 - .08 = .06

# APPENDIX 1A

# Answers to Problems

1(a).  Expected Return =     (Probability of Return) (Possible Return)

$$E(R_{FDC}) = \sum_{i=1}^{n} P_i [R_i]$$

$$= (.25) (-.10) + (.15) (0.00) + (.35) (.10) + (.25) (.25)$$

$$= (-.025) + (.000) + (.035) + (.0625)$$

$$= .0725$$

$$\sigma^2 = \sum_{i=i}^{n} P_i [R_i - E(R_i)]^2$$

$$= (.25) (-.10 -.0725)^2 + (.15) (0.00 -.0725)^2$$
$$+ (.35) (.10 -.0725)^2 + (.25) (.25 -.0725)^2$$

$$= (.25) (.02976) + (.15) (.0053) + (.35) (.0008)$$
$$+ (.25) (.0315)$$

$$= .0074 + .0008 + .0003 + .0079$$

$$= .0164$$

$$\sigma_{FDC} = (.0164)^{.5} = .128$$

1(b).  Standard deviation can be used as a good measure of relative risk between two investments that have the same expected rate of return.

1(c).  The coefficient of variation must be used to measure the relative variability of two investments if there are major differences in the expected rates of return.

2(a).  $E(R_{TCC})$     $= (.15)(-.60) + (.10)(-.30) + (.05)(-.10)$
            $+ (.40)(.20) + (.20)(.40) + (.10)(.80)$

            $= (-.09) + (-.03) + (-.005) + .08 + .08 + .08$

            $= .115$

$\sigma^2 =$   $(.15)(-.60 - .115)^2 + (.10)(-.30 - .115)^2$
            $+ (.05)(-.10 - .115)^2 + (.40)(.20 - .115)^2$
            $+ (.20)(.40 - .115)^2 + (.10)(.80 - .115)^2$

            $= (.15)(-.715)^2 + (.10)(-.415)^2 + (.05)(-.215)^2$
            $+ (.40)(.085)^2 + (.20)(.285)^2 + (.10)(.685)^2$

            $= (.15)(.5112) + (.10)(.1722) + (.05)(.0462)$
            $+ (.40)(.0072) + (.20)(.0812) + (.10)(.4692)$

            $= .07668 + .01722 + .00231 + .00288 + .01624 + .04692$

            $= .16225$

$\sigma TCC =$       $(.16225)^{.5} = .403$

2(b).  Based on [E(Ri)] alone, Turk Computer Company's stock is preferable because of the higher return available.

2(c).  Based on standard deviation alone, the Floppy Disc Company's stock is preferable because of the greater likelihood of obtaining the expected return.

2(d).  $$CV = \frac{\text{Standard Deviation}}{\text{Expected Return}}$$

$$CV_{FDC} = \frac{.128}{.0725} = 1.77$$

$$CV_{TCC} = \frac{.403}{.115} = 3.50$$

Based on CV, Turk Computer Company's stock return has approximately twice the relative dispersion of Floppy Disc Company's stock return.

3(a).  $$AM_{US} = \frac{.063 + .081 + .076 + .090 + .085}{5}$$

$$= \frac{.395}{5} = .079$$

$$AM_{UK} = \frac{.150 + (-.043) + .374 + .192 + (-.106)}{5}$$

$$= \quad \frac{.567}{5} \quad = \quad .113$$

3(b).  The average return of U.S. Government T-Bills is lower than the average return of United Kingdom Common Stocks because U.S. Government T-Bills are riskless; therefore, their risk premium would equal 0.  The U.K. Common Stocks are subject to the following types of risk:  business risk, financial risk, liquidity risk, exchange rate risk, and (to a limited extent) country risk.

3(c).  $\text{GM} \quad = \quad \Pi^{1/n} - 1$

$\Pi_{US} \quad = \quad (1.063)\,(1.081)\,(1.076)\,()1.090)\,(1.085) \ = \ 1.462$

$\text{GM}_{US} = \quad (1.462)^{1/5} - 1 \ = \ 1.079 - 1 \ = \ .079$

$\Pi_{UK} \quad = \quad (1.150)\,(.957)\,(1.374)\,(1.192)\,(.894) \ = \ 1.611$

$\text{GM}_{UK} = \quad (1.1611)^{1/5} - 1 \ = \ 1.1 - 1 \ = \ .10$

In the case of the U.S. Government T-Bills, the arithmetic and geometric means are approximately equal (.079); therefore, the standad deviations (using E(Ri) = .079) would be equal.  The geometric mean (.10) of the U.K. Common Stocks is lower than the arithmetic mean (.113); therefore, the standard deviations will also differ.

# CHAPTER 2

## Asset Allocation

# Answers to Questions

1.  A bank's objective is to generate returns on assets that exceed its cost of funds. Banks have short-term investment horizons because: (1) they have substantial need for liquidity in order to meet withdrawal and loan demands; (2) they wish to maintain an adequate spread between interest revenue and interest expense; and (3) they offer short-term deposit accounts, thus matching maturities of their assets and liabilities. Banks are heavily regulated by numerous state and federal agencies (i.e., the Federal Reserve Board, the Comptroller of the Currency, and the Federal Deposit Insurance Corporation).

    The investment objectives and constraints for insurance companies differ depending upon type (life or non-life). A life insurance company collects premiums during a person's lifetime and makes a payment when the person dies. Therefore, cash outflows for life insurance companies are somewhat predictable based upon actuarial tables. A life insurance company's investment objective is to earn a "positive" spread. A life insurance company's investment time horizon will depend upon its specific mix of products (e.g., life insurance policies require longer-term investments, guaranteed insurance contracts (GICs) and shorter-term annuities require shorter-term investments). The investment opportunities available to life insurance companies are limited based upon acceptable risk levels (through the National Association of Insurance Commissioners). Also, insurance companies are regulated at the state level.

    Cash flows for non-life insurance companies such as property and casualty are not as predictable as in the case of life insurance companies. Therefore, these companies must maintain more liquidity due to uncertain cash outflow require-ments. Non-life insurance companies typically have shorter investment time horizons than that of life insurers. States regulate the classes and quality of investments that non-life insurance companies may hold in their portfolios.

2.  See answer to question #1 for investment objectives and constraints of an insurance company.

A defined benefit pension fund provides a stated amount of benefit to the retiree based upon the worker's salary and length of employment. The employer (company) contributes to the fund a certain amount of money each year. Under this pension plan, the retiree is guaranteed the income stream and if the fund does not have enough funds to make all guaranteed payments, the company will have to cover the "shortfall." The liquidity and investment time horizon constraints on defined benefit funds is predominantly defined by the average age of the employees. For example, if the employees are young, the liquidity requirement will be low and the investment horizon will be long-term. A defined benefit pension fund must adhere to the Employee Retirement and Income Security Act (ERISA) and investments must satisfy the "prudent man" standard.

3.   In answering this question, one assumes that the young person has a steady job, adequate insurance coverage, and sufficient cash reserves. The young individual is in the accumulation phase of the investment life cycle. During this phase, an individual should consider moderately high-risk investments, such as common stocks, because he/she has a long investment horizon and earnings ability.

4.   In answering this question, one assumes that the 63-year-old individual has adequate insurance coverage and a cash reserve. Depending on her income from social security, she may need some current income from her retirement portfolio to meet living expenses. At the same time, she will need to protect herself against inflation. Removing all her money from her company's retirement plan and investing it in money market funds would satisfy the investor's short-term current income needs. Investing in long-term investments, such as common stock mutual funds, would provide the investor with needed inflation protection.

5.   Typically investment strategies change during an individual's lifetime. In the accumulating phase, the individual is accumulating net worth to satisfy short-term needs (e.g., house and car purchases) and long-term goals (e.g., retirement and children's college needs). In this phase, the individual is willing to invest in moderately high-risk investments in order to achieve above-average rates of return.

In the consolidating phase, an investor has paid off many outstanding debts and typically has earnings which exceed expenses. In this phase, the

2 - 4

investor is becoming more concerned with long-term needs of retirement or estate planning. Although the investor is willing to accept moderate portfolio risk, he/she is not willing to jeopardize the "nest egg."

In the spending phase, the typical investor is retired or semi-retired. This investor wishes to protect the nominal value of his/her savings, but at the same time must make some investments for inflation protection.

The gifting phase is often concurrent with the spending phase. The individual believes that the portfolio will provide sufficient income to meet expenses, plus a reserve for uncertainties. If an investor believes there are excess amounts available in the portfolio, he/she may decide to make "gifts" to family or friends, institute charitable trusts, or establish trusts to minimize estate taxes.

6.     A policy statement is important for both the investor and the investment advisor. A policy statement assists the investor in establishing realistic investment goals, as well as providing a benchmark by which a portfolio manager's performance may be measured.

7.     A defined contribution pension plan differs from a defined benefit pension plan in that the former does not promise a set income stream. Under a defined contribution plan, the benefit received by the retiree (worker) is determined based upon his/her contribution to the pension fund and the rate of return earned on the invested funds. In the case of the defined contribution pension plan, the employee's retirement income is not the obligation of the employer (company); rather the responsibility rests with the worker (retiree). Defined contribution pension plans typically are more conservatively invested when compared to defined benefit pension plans. The liquidity and investment time horizon for both defined contribution and defined benefit pension funds are determined by the average age and turnover of the employees. Both types of pension plans are tax-exempt and are governed by the Employee Retirement and Income Security Act (ERISA).

(Additional discussion of defined benefit pension plans can be found in the answer to question #2.)

8.     Student Exercise

9.  Most experts recommend that about 6 month's worth of living expenses be held in cash reserves. Although these funds are identified as "cash," it is recommended that they be invested in instruments that can easily be converted to cash with little chance of loss in value (e.g., money market mutual funds, etc.).

    Most experts recommend that an individual should carry life insurance equal to 7-10 times an individual's annual salary. An unmarried individual should have coverage equal to at least 7 times salary, whereas a married individual with two children should have more coverage (possibly 9-10 times salary).

10. Married, filing jointly, $20,000 taxable income:
    Marginal tax rate   = 15%
    Taxes due           = $20,000 x .15 = $3,000

    Married, filing jointly, $40,000 taxable income:
    Marginal tax rate   = 28%
    Taxes due           = $5,535 + .28($40,000 - $36,900)
                        = $5,535 + $868 = $6,403

    Married, filing jointly, $60,000 taxable income:
    Marginal tax rate   = 28%
    Taxes due           = $5,535 + .28($60,000 - $36,900)
                        = $5,535 + $6,468 = $12,003

11. Single with $20,000 taxable income:
    Marginal tax rate   = 15
    Taxes due           = $20,000 x .15 = $3,000

    Single with $40,000 taxable income:
    Marginal tax rate   = 28%
    Taxes due           = $3,315 + .28($40,000 - $22,100)
                        = $3,315 + $5,012 = $8,327

Single with $60,000 taxable income:
Marginal tax rate $= 31\%$
Taxes due $= \$12,107 + .31(\$60,000 - \$53,500)$
$= \$12,107 + \$2,015 = \$14,122$

12(a). The investment process itself is common to all managers everywhere. Systematic exploitation of this underlying reality is as readily accomplished at a one-manager shop in which a hand-held calculator is used as it is by an industry giant employing the latest in real-time, on-line, interactive computer systems. The dynamic is there, and it is useful and fundamental.

The four key steps in the portfolio management process are:

1. Identify and specify the investor's objectives, preferences and constraints in order to develop explicit investment policies.

2. Develop and implement strategies through the choice of optimal combinations of financial and real assets in the marketplace.

3. Monitor market conditions, relative asset values and the investor's circumstances.

4. Make portfolio adjustments as appropriate to reflect significant changes in any or all of the relevant variables.

Portfolio management is a dynamic and continuous process with the four steps repeated

12(b). Objectives

**Risk:** While a need exists to protect both the corpus and the income stream against inflation, the Board of Trustees is "conservative" and spending needs are continuous while gift income is quite variable. These circumstances argue for adoption of a non-aggressive, medium-risk policy posture.

**Return:** Current income production of adequate proportions is clearly of mayor importance here, mitigated to some extent by the historical availability of gift supplements to endowment returns. A "spending rule" should be formmulated by the Board that takes inflation into account, and policy should state a preference for income over gain without, however, adopting an extreme income orientation.

Constraints

**Time Horizon:** The actual horizon is clearly a very long one (perpetual, in concept) but given the nature of the objectives it would be useful if the policy statement spoke of, say, successive 5-year planning horizons with some fairly definite 1-year sub-goals.

**Liquidity Needs:** Since gifts arc important but are quite variable as well, a 12-18 month liquidity reserve would be appropriate here to provide for spending continuity and possible emergency needs. The existence of such a reserve might allow the Board to be a bit more aggressive in its asset allocation overall.

**Tax Considerations:** Aside from meeting whatever Federal and State reporting requirements may exist, taxes are a very minor matter here and should have no effect on investment policy.

**Legal & Regulatory Requirements:** Except for required conformity with the Prudent Man Rule relating to investments, and to any human-rights type regulations that may impact policy, these considerations are minor in this case. The policy statement may wish to give some specific attention to proxy-voting and like matters.

**Unique Needs & Circumstances:** The need to satisfy a conservative Board and the wide variations in gift income must be addressed in whatever policy statement is produced. These are easily accommodated, however,-and should not disrupt normal investment action.

13(a). The advisor's statement is neither true nor false, but it expresses a viewpoint based on analysis of outcomes in a specific and rather limited time. While the evidence cited appears to support this view, such evidence is time constrained and not compelling. Accordingly, a different view may have equal validity if it is drawn from other or more extensive evidence or is consistent with a particular set of investor objectives and constraints in which a permanent non-U.S. bond portfolio would be both appropriate and desirable.

The advisor's view is drawn from examining the contribution that non-U.S. bonds can make to the risk-return profile of a broadly diversified portfolio, based on a 1973-1988 data base. His interpretation of the evidence is that only a modest reduction in portfolio risk can be achieved through non-U.S. diversification on an unhedged basis. On a hedged basis, his data suggest that, when transaction costs and other fees associated with hedging are considered, international diversification on a currency-hedged basis may be more expensive than not hedging at all.

Rather than abandon the use of non-U.S. bonds, the advisor examines the case for active management of such instruments, turning the focus away from risk control and reduction toward return enhancement opportunities. These opportunities are large but transitory. Thus, while significant opportunities exist to use non-U.S. bonds for return enhancement purposes, such opportunities are time dependent and not ongoing.

The advisor concludes that using non-U.S. bonds ought to be seen as a *tactical* move aimed at exploiting a temporary mispricing opportunity, not as a *strategic* action in which such instruments are accorded a permanent place in the portfolio for diversification or risk-reduction purposes.

If, as some evidence shows, global interest rates are now more correlated than in the past, the case for diversification as the principal reason for investing in non-U.S. bonds is weakened. Return enhancement possibilities may then become the reason the investment is considered, arising either from assuming more risk or from temporary mispricing. If such bonds are used because of their higher risk and attendant higher expected return, this decision is still strategic regarding a separate asset class. The opposite reasoning would apply if mispricing were the key decision factor.

Therefore, the reason they are to be used becomes the focal point for whether the decision is a policy one or an operating one.

13(b). There is a fundamental difference between strategic (policy level) and tactical (operating level) decision making for asset allocation.

1. **Strategic (policy level) decision making.** The board of directors is responsible for strategic decision making. Once a set of asset classes has been chosen for inclusion in the portfolio, the asset allocation decision becomes a matter of selecting an optimal set of exposures to the returns from those classes (i.e., selecting an effective asset mix). After analyzing expected outcomes

(typically done on a three-year cycle), the investor chooses the mix with range of preferred outcomes. This constitutes the policy, long-run, or strategic asset mix and specifically takes the investor's risk tolerance into account.

Strategic changes in the asset mix occur infrequently and are not based on perceptions of interim mispricing. Such changes consider the risk tolerance of the investor.

2. **Tactical (operating level) decision making.** The fund manager is responsible for making tactical decisions. Tactical asset allocation is done routinely as part of continuing asset management. Its goal is to take advantage of perceived inefficiencies in the relative prices of securities in different asset classes. Unlike the process at the strategic level, changes in the investor's risk tolerance, if any, are ignored. Risk tolerance is held constant.

Tactical changes in the asset mix are driven by predictions concerning asset returns, with or without also considering predictions relating to expected market risks and correlations.

This discussion suggests that whether to include non-U.S. bonds in the portfolio is perhaps more likely to be a strategic than a tactical decision. The "include" or "exclude" decision will have already been made at the strategic level before the tactical question of whether non-U.S. bonds are correctly priced in the markets is ever reached. That decision depends on ongoing portfolio management, not policy setting. In Donovan's context, the board, as part of its strategic planning for the pension portfolio, will make the "include" or "exclude" decision about the ongoing fundamental exposures to be included in the policy guidelines, including the decision on non-U.S. bonds. If the decision were to include them, the tactical "now or not" decision would occur downstream in the ongoing management of the portfolio and most probably would be made by the portfolio manager.

Many variations of this basic theme are possible. For example, the policy could allow but not require inclusion, leaving the "now or not" decision clearly in the hands of the tactical decision makers. The board could say "no non-U.S. bonds." The board could say that its view embraced the broadest possible definition of the fixed-income asset class, in which case non-U.S. bonds could come and go as elements in the tactical plan to maximize fixed-income asset class returns within the board's risk parameters for the total portfolio based simply on price considerations. The board could also set a target median proportion for the asset class for strategic risk control purposes and for the portfolio manager permitted to move around within the band on an opportunistic basis.

# Answers to Problems

1(a). $10,000 invest in 9 percent tax-exempt IRA (assuming annual compounding)

    in 5 years:    $10,000(FVIF @ 9%) = $10,000(1.5386) = $15,386
    in 10 years:  $10,000(FVIF @ 9%) = $10,000(2.3674) = $23,674
    in 20 years:  $10,000(FVIF @ 9%) = $10,000(5.6044) = $56,044

1(b).  After-tax yield    = Before-tax yield (1 - Tax rate)
                             = 9% (1 - .36)
                             = 5.76%

    $10,000 invest at 5.76 percent (assuming annual compounding)

    in 5 years:    $10,000(FVIF @ 5.76%) = $13,231
    in 10 years:  $10,000(FVIF @ 5.76%) = $17,507
    in 20 years:  $10,000(FVIF @ 5.76%) = $30,650

2(a). $10,000 invest in 10 percent tax-exempt IRA (assuming annual compounding)

    in 5 years:    $10,000(FVIF @ 10%) = $10,000(1.6105) = $16,105
    in 10 years:  $10,000(FVIF @ 10%) = $10,000(2.5937) = $25,937
    in 20 years:  $10,000(FVIF @ 10%) = $10,000(6.7275) = $67,275

2(b).  After-tax yield    = Before-tax yield (1 - Tax rate)
                             = 10% (1 - .15)
                             = 8.50%

    $10,000 invest at 8.50 percent (assuming annual compounding)

in 5 years:    $10,000(FVIF @ 8.50%) = $15,037
in 10 years:   $10,000(FVIF @ 8.50%) = $22,610
in 20 years:   $10,000(FVIF @ 8.50%) = $51,120


3(a).  $(.8 \times 2000)$ $(FVIFA_{40, .06})$ $=$ 1600 x 154.76   $=$ \$247,616.00
       $(.2 \times 2000)$ $(FVIFA_{40, .10})$ $=$  400 x 442.59   $=$ \$177,036.00
                                    TOTAL      $=$ \$424,652.00


3(b).  $(.5 \times 2000)$ $(FVIFA_{40, .06})$ $=$ 1000 x 154.76   $=$ \$154,760.00
       $(.5 \times 2000)$ $(FVIFA_{40, .10})$ $=$ 1000 x 442.59   $=$ \$442,590.00
                                    TOTAL      $=$ \$597,350.00


3(c).  $(.2 \times 2000)$ $(FVIFA_{40, .06})$ $=$  400 x 154.76   $=$ \$ 61,904.00
       $(.8 \times 2000)$ $(FVIFA_{40, .10})$ $=$ 1600 x 442.59   $=$ \$708,144.00
                                    TOTAL      $=$ \$770,048.00


4(a).  $(.2 \times 3000)$ $(FVIFA_{30 .07})$  $=$  600 x 94.461   $=$ \$ 56,676.60
       $(.8 \times 3000)$ $(FVIFA_{30, .10})$ $=$ 2400 x 164.49   $=$ \$394,776.00
                                    TOTAL      $=$ \$451,452.60


4(b).  $(.1 \times 3000)$ $(FVIFA_{30 .07})$  $=$  300 x 94.461   $=$ \$ 28,338.30
       $(.4 \times 3000)$ $(FVIFA_{30, .10})$ $=$ 1200 x 164.49   $=$ \$197,388.00
       $(.5 \times 3000)$ $(FVIFA_{30, .12})$ $=$ 1500 x 241.33   $=$ \$361,995.00
                                    TOTAL      $=$ \$587,721.30


4(c).  $(.1 \times 3000)$ $(FVIFA_{30 .07})$  $=$  300 x 94.461   $=$ \$ 28,338.30
       $(.9 \times 3000)$ $(FVIFA_{30, .12})$ $=$ 2700 x 241.33   $=$ \$651,591.00
                                    TOTAL      $=$ \$679,929.30


5(a).  $(.1 \times 4000)$ $(FVIFA_{25, .07})$ $=$  400 x 63.249   $=$ \$ 25,299.60
       $(.3 \times 4000)$ $(FVIFA_{25, .10})$ $=$ 1200 x 98.347   $=$ \$118,016.40
       $(.6 \times 4000)$ $(FVIFA_{25, .12})$ $=$ 2400 x 133.33   $=$ \$319,992.00
                                    TOTAL      $=$ \$463,308.00

5(b).  $(.2 \times 4000)(\text{FVIFA}_{25, .10}) = 800 \times 98.347 = \$\ 78,677.60$
       $(.3 \times 4000)(\text{FVIFA}_{25, .12}) = 1200 \times 133.33 = \$159,996.00$
       $(.5 \times 4000)(\text{FVIFA}_{25, .14}) = 2000 \times 181.87 = \$363,740.00$
       $\hphantom{(.5 \times 4000)(\text{FVIFA}_{25, .14}) = 2000 \times 181.87}$ TOTAL $= \$602,413.60$

5(c).  $(.2 \times 4000)(\text{FVIFA}_{25, .12}) = 800 \times 133.33 = \$106,664.00$
       $(.3 \times 4000)(\text{FVIFA}_{25, .14}) = 1200 \times 181.87 = \$218,244.00$
       $(.5 \times 4000)(\text{FVIFA}_{25, .16}) = 2000 \times 249.21 = \$498,420.00$
       $\hphantom{(.5 \times 4000)(\text{FVIFA}_{25, .16}) = 2000 \times 249.21}$ TOTAL $= \$823,328.00$

6(a).  $200,000 / \text{FVIFA}_{20, .06} = 200,000 / 36.786 = \$5,436.91$

6(b).  $i = .8(.06) + .2(.10) = .068$
       $200,000 / \text{FVIFA}_{20, .068} = 200,000 / 40.111 = \$4,986.14$

6(c).  $i = .2(.06) + .8(.10) = .092$
       $200,000 / \text{FVIFA}_{20, .092} = 200,000 / 52.323 = \$3,822.42$

6(d).  $200,000 / \text{FVIFA}_{20, .12} = 200,000 / 72.052 = \$2,775.76$

6(e).  $200,000 / \text{FVIFA}_{20, .16} = 200,000 / 115.380 = \$1,733.41$

# CHAPTER 3

## Selecting Investments In A Global Market

# Answers to Questions

1.   The major advantage of investing in common stocks is that generally an investor would earn a higher rate of return than on corporate bonds. Also, while the return on bonds is pre-specified and fixed, the return on common stocks can be substantially higher if the investor can pick a "winner" -- i.e., if the company's performance turns out to be better than current market expectations. The main disadvantage of common stock ownership is the higher risk. While the income on bonds is certain (except in the extreme case of bankruptcy), the return on stocks will vary depending upon the future performance of the company and could well be negative.

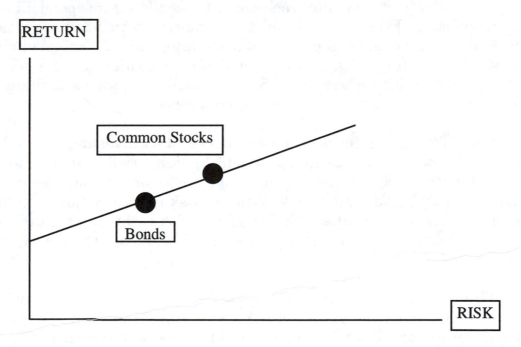

2.   The three factors are: (1) Limiting oneself to the U.S. securities market would imply effectively ignoring approximately 50% of the world securities market. While the U.S. bond market is still the dominant sector, foreign bond markets have been growing in absolute and relative size since 1969. (2) The

rates of return available on non-U.S. securities often have substantially exceeded those of U.S. securities. (3) Diversification with foreign securities reduces portfolio risk.

3. International diversification reduces portfolio risk because of the low correlation of returns among the securities from different countries. This is due to differing international trade patterns, economic growth, fiscal policies, and monetary policies among countries.

4. There are different correlations of returns between securities from the U.S. and alternate countries because there are substantial differences in the economies of the various countries (at a given time) in terms of inflation, international trade, monetary and fiscal policies and economic growth.

5. The correlations between U.S. stocks and stocks for different countries should change over time because each country has a fairly independent set of economic policies. Factors influencing the correlations include international trade, economic growth, fiscal policy and monetary policy. A change in any of these variables will cause a change in how the economies are related. For example, the correlation between U.S. and Japanese stocks will change as the balance of trade shifts between the two countries.

6. The major risks that an investor must consider when investing in any bond issue are business risk, financial risk and liquidity risk. Additional risk associated with foreign bonds, such as Japanese or German bonds, are exchange rate risk and country risk. Country risk is not a major concern for Japanese or German securities. Exchange rate risk is the uncertainty which arises from floating exchange rates between the U.S. dollar and the Japanese yen or Deutsch mark.

7. The additional risk that some investors believe international investing introduces include foreign exchange risk and country risk. For example, the domestic return on Australian bonds of 11.07 percent exceeded the U.S. return of 9.96 percent. The average foreign exchange effect of -3.13 percent, however, reduced the Australian dollar return after conversion to U.S. dollars to only 7.59 percent. (See Table 3.1)

8. There are three alternatives to direct investment in foreign stocks available to investors: (1) purchase American Depository Receipts (ADRs), (2) purchase

American shares (issued by a transfer agent), and (3) purchase international mutual funds.

9.  As opposed to corporate bonds, the interest earned on municipal bonds is exempt from taxation by the federal government and by the state that issued the bond, provided the investor is a resident of that state. Using the example presented in the text, a marginal tax rate of 30 percent means that a regular bond with an interest rate of 8 percent yields a net return after taxes of only 5.60 percent [.08 x (1 -.30)]. A tax-free bond with a 6 percent yield would be preferable.

10. The convertible bond of the growth company would have the lower yield. This is intuitive because there is a greater potential for the price of the growth company stock to increase, which would make the conversion feature of the bond extremely attractive. Thus, the investor would be willing to trade off the higher upside potential resulting from conversion for the lower yield.

11. Liquidity is the ability to buy or sell an asset quickly at a price similar to the prior price assuming no new information has entered the market. Common stocks have the advantage of liquidity since it is very easy to buy or sell a small position (there being a large number of potential buyers) at a price not substantially different from the current market price. Raw land is relatively illiquid since it is often difficult to find a buyer immediately and often the prospective buyer will offer a price that is substantially different from what the owner considers to be the true market value. A reason for this difference is that while common stock data are regularly reported in a large number of daily newspapers and several magazines and closely watched by a large number of individuals, raw land simply lacks this kind of interest. Further, the speculative nature of raw land investment calls for high risk and longer maturity before profits can be realized. Finally, the initial investment on a plot of raw land would be substantially greater than a round lot in most securities. As a result, the small investor is generally precluded from this kind of investment.

12. A stock warrant is an option issued by a corporation to buy a number of shares of the corporation's common stock at a specified price. Warrants typically have a life of several years and could even be perpetual.

A call option is similar to a stock warrant with two essential differences. One is that the call option is not issued by the corporation but by an individual who "writes" it and stands behind it. The second difference is that a call option generally has a maturity of less than a year.

13. Art and antiques are considered illiquid investments because in most cases they are sold at auctions. The implication of being traded at auctions rather than on a developed exchange is that there is tremendous uncertainty regarding the price to be received and it takes a long time to contact a buyer who offers the "right" price. Besides, many buyers of art and antiques are accumulators rather than traders and this further reduces trading.

Coins and stamps are more liquid than art and antiques because an investor can determine the "correct" market price from several weekly or monthly publications. There is no such publication of current market prices of the numerous unique pieces of art and antiques and owners are forced to rely on dealer estimates. Further, while a coin or stamp can be readily disposed of to a dealer at a commission of about 10-15 percent, the commissions on paintings range from 30-50 percent.

14. The results of Table 3.8 would tend to support adding some gold to your portfolio. The table indicates a negative correlation with U. S. stocks (-0.088) and U.S. bonds (-0.280), which implies good diversification opportunities. It should also be noted that returns on gold are highly correlated with the rate of inflation, thus providing a hedge against the depreciating value of financial assets during inflationary times. Finally, the market for gold tends to be more liquid than other real assets.

15. Table 3.9 indicates that an investment in American paintings during this period was a good investment. The average compound return of 16.20 percent was the fourth highest of all listed assets, including the S & P 500 index. In addition, the coefficient of variation (0.93) indicates a relatively small variation in returns over the 12-year period.

16. 1. Information about foreign firms is often difficult to obtain on a timely basis and, once obtained, can be difficult to interpret and analyze due to language and presentation differences.

2. Financial statements are not comparable from country to country. Different countries use different accounting principles. Even when similar accounting methods are used, cultural, institutional, political and tax differences can make cross-country comparisons hazardous and misleading.

3. Stock valuation techniques useful in the United States may be less useful in other countries. Stock markets in different countries value different attributes.

4. Smith must consider currency risk in selecting non-U.S. stocks for his portfolio.

5. Increased costs: custody, management fees, and transactions expenses are usually higher outside the United States.

17(a). Arguments in favor of adding international securities include:

1. Benefits gained from broader diversification, including economic, political and/or geographic sources.

2. Expected higher returns at the same or lower (if properly diversified) level of portfolio risk.

3. Advantages accruing from improved correlation and covariance relationships across the portfolio's exposures.

4. Improved asset allocation flexibility, including the ability to match or hedge non-U.S. liabilities.

5. Wider range of industry and company choices for portfolio construction purposes.

6. Wider range of managers through whom to implement investment decisions.

7. Diversification benefits are realizable despite the absence of non-U.S. pension liabilities.

At the same time, there are a number of potential problems associated with moving away from a domestic-securities-only orientation:

1. Possible higher costs, including those for custody, transactions, and management fees.

2. Possible reduced liquidity, especially when transacting in size.

3. Possible unsatisfactory levels of information availability, reliability, scope, timeliness and understandability.

4. Risks associated with currency management, convertibility and regulations/controls.

5. Risks associated with possible instability/volatility in both markets and governments.

6. Possible tax consequences or complications.

7. Recognition that EAFE has underperformed since 1989.

17(b). A policy decision to include international securities in an investment portfolio is a necessary first step to actualization. However, certain other policy level decisions must be made prior to implementation. That set of decisions would include:

1. What portion of the portfolio shall be invested internationally, and in what equity and fixed-income proportions?

2. Shall all or a portion of the currency risk be hedged or not?

3. Shall management of the portfolio be active or passive?

4. Shall the market exposures be country/market-wide (top-down) or company/ industry specific (bottom-up)?

5. What benchmarks shall results be judged by?

6. How will manager style be incorporated into the process?

7. How will the process reflect/resolve the important differences in orientation between the international (non U.S.) major markets and the U.S. emerging markets perspectives?

Until decisions on these additional policy-level issues have been made, implementation of the basic decision to invest internationally cannot begin.

# Answers to Problems

1. Student Exercise

2. Student Exercise

3. Student Exercise

4. Student Exercise

5(a). The arithmetic average assumes the presence of simple interest, while the geometric average assumes compounding or interest-on-interest. The geometric mean internal rate of return is a critical concept in security and portfolio selection as well as performance measurement in a multi-period framework.

5(b). Ranking is best accomplished by using the coefficient of variation (standard deviation/means, multiplied by 100):

|   |   |
|---|---|
| 1 - Real Estate | 36.9 |
| 2 - Treasury Bills | 48.9 |
| 3 - Long Government Bonds | 104.9 |
| 4 - Common Stock | 164.4 |
| 5 - Long Corp. Bond | 167.0 |

The coefficient of variation ranking methodology alternatively may be computed using the geometric mean (standard deviation – geometric mean multiplied by 100). This method provides a ranking almost identical to the prior method:

|   |   |
|---|---|
| 1 - Real Estate | 37.1 |
| 2 - Treasury Bills | 49.3 |
| 3 - Long Government Bonds | 108.3 |
| 4 - Long Corp. Bonds | 179.4 |
| 5 - Common Stocks | 191.8 |

In both cases, a lower ratio indicates a higher return for risk.

Or, a somewhat different ranking methodology utilizes Sharpe's reward for risk-taking measure using the mean return minus the risk free rate divided by the standard deviation multiplied by 100. This measure is discussed in detail in Chapter 23. The ranking using this measure would be as follows:

| | | |
|---|---|---|
| 1 - Real Estate | | 84.3 |
| 2 - Common Stocks | | 22.1 |
| 3 - Treasury Bills | | 0.0 |
| 4 - Long Gov't Bonds | | - 6.9 |
| 5 - Long Corp. Bonds | | - 8.2 |

Under this reward-for-risk ranking methodology, the higher the ratio, the higher the return per unit of risk. The arithmetic mean was used in this computation; however, the geometric mean also could be used to calculate this ranking.

5(c).  (1)  Expected mean plus or minus two standard deviations:

Arithmetic:  10.28%  +/-  16.9%(2)  =  -23.52%  to +44.08%
Geometric:   8.81%  +/-  16.9%(2)  =  -24.99%  to +42.61%

(2)  Ninety-five percent of the area under the normal curve lies between +/- two standard deviations of the mean. Since the mean minus two standard deviations (9.44 - 7.0 = 2.44) is positive, one may conclude that the probability of breaking even is greater than 98%. (Probability of more than 9.44% is .5 and two standard deviations left of the mean is 47.5%.)

5(d).  It seems at first that government bonds offer less return and more risk than real estate. However, real estate and government bonds might provide a good combination if the two do not fluctuate in a similar fashion, so that the variability of the portfolio is less than the variability of the individual investments. If the correlation coefficient applicable to this pair of investments is known and is not highly positive, the combination would be advantageous.

6(a). (1) Common Stock Risk Premium

> = Return Common Stock - Return of U.S. Gov't T-bills
> = 12.50 - 4.50
> = 8.00%

(2) Small Firms Stock Risk Premium

> = Return of Small Capitalization Common Stock
>   - Return of Total Stocks (S&P 500)
> = 14.60 - 12.50
> = 2.10%

(3) Horizon (Maturity) Premium

> = Return on Long-term Gov't Bonds
>   - Return on U.S. Gov't T-bills
> = 5.10 - 4.50
> = 0.60%

(4) Default Premium

> = Return on Long-term Corporate Bonds
>   - Return on Long-term Gov't Bonds
> = 5.80 - 5.10
> = .70%

6(b). "Real" rate of return $= \dfrac{\text{Holding Period Return}}{1 + \text{rate of inflation}} - 1$

If Inflation = 4%

U.S. T-Bills

$$\text{Real Rate of Return} = \frac{1 + .045}{1 + .04} - 1 = .0048$$

Common Stock

$$\text{Real Rate of Return} = \frac{1 + .1250}{1 + .04} - 1 = .0817$$

Long-Term Corporate Bonds

$$\text{Real Rate of Return} = \frac{1 + .058}{1 + .04} - 1 = .0173$$

Long-Term Government Bonds

$$\text{Real Rate of Return} = \frac{1 + .0510}{1 + .04} - 1 = .0106$$

Small Capitalization Common Stock

$$\text{Real Rate of Return} = \frac{1 + .1460}{+ .04} - 1 = .1019$$

3 - 12

# APPENDIX 3A

## Answers to Problems

1.  Alpha - Omega's average return    Beta Tau's average return

$$\bar{A} = \frac{(5 + 12 - 11 + 10 + 12)}{5} \qquad \bar{B} = \frac{(5 + 15 + 5 + 7 - 10)}{5}$$

$$= 28/5 = 5.6 \qquad\qquad\qquad = 22/5 = 4.4$$

| $A - \bar{A}$ | | $B - \bar{B}$ | |
|---|---|---|---|
| 5 - 5.6 = | - .6 | 5 - 4.4 = | .6 |
| 12 - 5.6 = | 6.4 | 15 - 4.4 = | 10.6 |
| -11 - 5.6 = | - 16.6 | 5 - 4.4 = | .6 |
| 10 - 5.6 = | 4.4 | 7 - 4.4 = | 2.6 |
| 12 - 5.6 = | 6.4 | -10 - 4.4 = | -14.4 |

$$COV_{AB} = \frac{(A-\bar{A})(B-\bar{B})}{N}$$

$$= \frac{(-.6)(.6)+(6.4)(10.6)+(-16.6)(.6)+(4.4)(2.6)+(6.4)(-14.4)}{5}$$

$$= \frac{-23.2}{5} = -4.64$$

*3 - 13*

2.  Calculation of Correlation Coefficient

| Observation | $i - \bar{i}$ | $(i-\bar{i})^2$ | $(j - \bar{j})$ | $(j - \bar{j})^2$ |
|-------------|---------------|-----------------|-----------------|-------------------|
| 1 | -0.6 | .36 | 0.6 | .36 |
| 2 | 6.4 | 40.96 | 10.6 | 112.36 |
| 3 | -16.6 | 275.56 | 2.6 | 6.76 |
| 4 | 4.4 | 19.36 | 0.6 | 0.36 |
| 5 | 6.4 | 40.96 | -14.4 | 207.36 |
|   |   | 377.20 |   | 327.20 |

$$\sigma_i^2 = \frac{377.2}{5} = 75.44 \qquad \sigma_j^2 = \frac{327.2}{5} = 65.44$$

$$\sigma_i = (75.44)^{.5} = 8.69 \qquad \sigma_j = (65.44)^{.5} = 8.09$$

$$r_{ij} = \frac{COV_{ij}}{\sigma_i \sigma_j} = \frac{-4.64}{(8.69)(8.09)} = -.066$$

While there is a slight negative correlation, the two securities are essentially uncorrelated.  Thus, even though the two companies produce similar products, their historical returns suggest that holding both of these securities would help reduce risk through diversification.

# CHAPTER 4

# Organization And Functioning Of Securities Markets

# Answers to Questions

1.  A market is a means whereby buyers and sellers are brought together to aid in the transfer of goods and/or services. While it generally has a physical location it need not necessarily have one. Secondly, there is no requirement of ownership by those who establish and administer the market--they need only provide a cheap, smooth transfer of goods and/or services for a diverse clientele.

    A good market should provide accurate information on the price and volume of past transactions, and current supply and demand. Clearly, there should be rapid dissemination of this information. Adequate liquidity is desirable so that participants may buy and sell their goods and/or services rapidly, at a price reflecting the supply and demand. The costs of transferring ownership and middleman commissions should be low. Finally, the prevailing price should reflect all available information.

2.  This is a good discussion question for class because you could explore with students the alternatives that are used by investors with regards to other assets such as art and antiques. Some possibilities are ads in the paper of your local community or large cities. Another obvious alternative is an auction. With an ad you would have to specify a price or be ready to negotiate with a buyer. With an auction you would be very uncertain of what you would receive. In all cases, there would be a substantial time problem.

3.  Liquidity is the ability to sell an asset quickly at a price not substantially different from the current market assuming no new information is available. A share of AT&T is very liquid, while an antique would be a fairly illiquid asset. A share of AT&T is highly liquid since an investor could convert it into cash within 1/8 of a point of the current market price. An antique is illiquid since it is relatively difficult to find a buyer and then you are uncertain as to what price the prospective buyer would offer.

4.  The primary market in securities is where new issues are sold by corporations to acquire new capital via the sale of bonds, preferred stock or common stock. The sale typically takes place through an investment banker.

The secondary market is simply trading in outstanding securities. It involves transactions between owners after the issue has been sold to the public by the company. Consequently, the proceeds from the sale do not go to the company as is the case with a primary offering. Thus, the price of the security is important to the buyer and seller.

The functioning of the primary market would be seriously hampered in the absence of a good secondary market. A good secondary market provides liquidity to an investor if he or she wants to alter the composition of his or her portfolio from securities to other assets (i.e., house, etc.). Thus, investors would be reluctant to acquire securities in the primary market if they felt they would not subsequently have the ability to sell the securities quickly at a known price.

5. An example of an initial public offering (IPO) would be a small company selling company stock to the public for the first time. By contrast, a seasoned equity refers to an established company, such as IBM, offering a new issue of common stock to an existing market for the stock. The IPO involves greater risk for the buyer because there is not an established secondary market for the small firm. Without an established secondary market the buyer incurs additional liquidity risk associated with the IPO.

6. Student Exercise

7. In competitive bid the issuer is responsible for specifying the type of security to be offered, the timing, etc. and then soliciting competitive bids from investment banking firms wishing to act as an underwriter. The high bids will be awarded the contracts. Negotiated relationships are contractual arrangements between an underwriter and the issuer wherein the underwriter helps the issuer prepare the bond issue with the understanding that they have the exclusive right to sell the issue.

8. The difference in the price of membership between the two exchanges can be explained by differences in volume and in type of instruments traded. The premium price paid for membership on the NYSE is because the NYSE is the dominant domestic market trading equity shares. Rather than engage in direct competition with the NYSE, the AMEX has become an innovative market with a strong emphasis on foreign stocks and options.

9.	One reason for the existence of regional exchanges is that they provide trading facilities for geographically local companies that do not qualify for listing on a national exchange. Second, they list national firms thus providing small local brokerage firms that are not members of a national exchange the opportunity to trade in securities that are listed on a national exchange.

	The essential difference between the national and regional exchanges is that the regional exchanges have less stringent listing requirements, thus allowing small firms to obtain listing.

10.	The OTC market is larger than the listed exchanges in terms of the number of issues traded, trading about 4,700 issues on NASDAQ compared to about 3,600 for the AMEX and NYSE combined. In sharp contrast, the NYSE is still dominant in terms of the total value of the stocks traded.

	The OTC market has greater diversity in size of issues ranging from the smallest, most unprofitable firms, to the largest companies and including U.S. government securities, banks and insurance companies. The listed exchanges, in contrast, trade only the largest companies. Again, in terms of quality, while the listed exchanges have only the large, national firms, the OTC has both these and small unprofitable ones. This difference is because of less stringent listing requirements for the NASDAQ markets and almost no requirements for non-NASDAQ OTC stocks.

11.	Level 1 provides a current quote on NASDAQ stocks for brokerage firms that are not regular OTC customers. It is a median quote that is representative of the quotes of the several market makers in the particular security. Level 2 is for serious traders who desire not only current trends but specific quotes of different market makers. This enables the broker to make a deal with the market maker offering the best price. Level 3 is for investment firms who desire all the information provided in Level 2 but also need the ability to enter their own quotes or change them relative to other market makers. NASDAQ is an electronic quotation system that serves the OTC market. It enables all quotes by all market makers to be immediately available.

12(a).	The third market is the OTC trading of exchange listed securities. It enables the non-members of the exchange to trade in exchange listed securities. Most of the large institutional favorites are traded on the third market--e.g., IBM, Xerox, General Motors.

12(b). The fourth market is the direct trading between two parties without a broker intermediary. Institutions trade in the fourth market since these trades are large volume and consequently substantial savings can be made by trading directly with a buyer, thus avoiding commissions.

13(a). A market order is an order to buy/sell a stock at the most profitable ask/bid prices prevailing at the time the order hits the exchange floor. A market order implies the investor wants the transaction completed quickly at the prevailing price. Example: I read good reports about AT&T and I'm certain the stock will go up in value. When I call my broker and submit a market buy order for 100 shares of AT&T, the prevailing asking price is 60. Total cost for my shares will be $6,000 + commission.

13(b). A limit order specifies a maximum price that the individual will pay to purchase the stock or the minimum he will accept to sell it. Example: AT&T is selling for $60--I would put in a limit buy order for one week to buy 100 shares at $59.

13(c). A short sale is the sale of stock that is not currently owned by the seller with the intent of purchasing it later at a lower price. This is done by borrowing the stock from another investor through a broker. Example: I expect AT&T to go to $48--I would sell it short at $60 and expect to replace it when it gets to $55.

13(d). A stop-loss order is a conditional order whereby the investor indicates that he wants to sell the stock if the price drops to a specified price, thus protecting himself from a large and rapid decline in price. Example: I buy AT&T at $60 and put in a stop loss at $57 that protects me from a major loss if it starts to decline.

14. The specialist acts as a broker in handling limit orders placed with member brokers. Being constantly in touch with current prices, he is in a better position to execute limit orders since it is entered in his books and executed as soon as appropriate. Second, he maintains a fair and orderly market by trading on his own account when there is inadequate supply or demand. If the spread between the bid and ask is substantial, he can place his own bid or ask in order to narrow the spread. This helps provide a continuous market with orderly price changes.

The specialist obtains income from both his functions: commissions as a broker, and outperforming the market in his dealer function using the monopolistic information he has on limit orders.

15. The Saitori members are referred to as intermediary clerks. Similar to the U.S. specialists, the Saitori members do not deal with public customers. Their duties entail matching buy and sell orders for the regular members of the Tokyo Exchange and they maintain the book for regular limit orders. Unlike the U.S. exchange specialist, the Saitori are not allowed to buy and sell for their own account and, thus, they do not have the duty or capability to ensure an orderly market.

16. Much of the change experienced on the secondary equity market can be attributed to changes occurring within the financial industry as a whole. As banks, insurance companies, investment companies and other financial service firms enter the capital markets, the volume and size of transactions continues to grow. This dominance by large institutions in the marketplace caused the following changes in the markets:

   (1)    the imposition of negotiated (competitive) commission rates
   (2)    the influence of block trades
   (3)    the impact of stock price volatility
   (4)    the development of a national market system

These changes have increased the competition among firms that trade large institutional stocks. However, there is some concern that the individual investor is being "crowded out" and that the equity market for smaller firms will also suffer. The evolving globalization of markets will also have an impact.

17. A "give-up" is the practice of the brokerage firm executing the trade paying part of the commission to other brokerage or research firms designated by the institution. Typically, these other brokerage firms provided research or sales services to the institution. These commission transfers were referred to as "soft dollars." "Give-ups" existed in the fixed commission world because brokers realized that institutions were charged more for large trades than justified by the cost.

18. The Exchange requires that the specialist have enough capital to acquire 5,000 shares of his stock. This may be inadequate with blocks of 20,000 shares being common. Even when the specialist has the capital he might be unwilling to commit himself to a large position. Holding 5,000 shares in a stock is fairly risky particularly when the market for the underlying stock is thin. The third "c," contacts, could seriously hamper the specialist especially in the light of Rule 113, which prohibits specialists from dealing directly with customers. The specialist is often compelled to contact another institution interested in buying a block of the stock. When he can't contact other potential customers he does not want to take a position in the stock.

19. A block house is a brokerage firm, either member or non-member of an exchange, which stands ready to buy or sell a block for institutions. Block houses evolved because institutions were not getting what they needed from the specialist and, hence, asked institutional brokerage firms to locate other institutions with an interest in buying or selling given blocks.

   When an institution wishes to sell a stock it typically contacts a block house, who contacts prospective institutional buyers. If the block house does not find buyers for the entire block, it buys the remainder (thus taking a position) with the hope of selling it later. Naturally, the block house assumes substantial risk on this position because of the uncertainty of subsequent price changes.

20(a). Though the exact form of the National Market System (NMS) remains nebulous, major features of such a market are:

   (1) **Centralized reporting** of all transactions regardless of where the trade took place. Currently, this exists for all NYSE stocks.

   (2) **Centralized quotation** system which would list quotes for a given stock from all market-makers on the national exchanges, the regional exchanges, and the OTC. This increased information is beneficial to the investor.

   (3) **Central limit order book (CLOB)** that contains all limit orders from all exchanges.

   (4) **Competition among market-makers** which would force dealers to offer better bids and asks, thus narrowing the bid-ask spread.

20(b). The Inter-Market Trading System (ITS) is a centralized quotation system, currently available, consisting of a central computer facility with inter-connected terminals in the participating market centers. Brokers and market-makers in each market center can indicate to those in other centers specific buying and selling commitments by way of a composite quotation display. A broker or market-maker in any market center can thus exercise his own best judgment in determining, on the basis of current quotations, where to execute a customer's orders. While ITS provides the centralized quotation system that is necessary for a National Market System (NMS), it does not have the capability for automatic execution at the best market; it is necessary to contact the market-maker and indicate that you want to buy or sell at his bid or ask. Also, it is not mandatory that a broker go to the best market to execute a customer's orders.

The data in Table 4.10 indicate significant growth in the number of issues on the system, the volume of shares traded and the size of the trades.

21. Student Exercise

# Answers to Problems

1(a).  Assume you pay cash for the stock:  Number of shares you could purchase = $40,000 – $80 = 500 shares.

    (1)  If the stock is later sold at $100 a share, the total shares proceeds would be $100 x 500 shares = $50,000. Therefore, the rate of return from investing in the stock is as follows:

$$= \frac{\$50,000 - \$40,000}{\$40,000} = 25.00\%$$

    (2)  If stock is later sold at $40 a share, the total shares proceeds would be $40 x $500 shares = $20,000.

Therefore, the rate of return from investing in the stock would be:

$$= \frac{\$20,000 - \$40,000}{\$40,000} = -50.00\%$$

1(b).  Assuming you use the maximum amount of leverage in buying the stock, the leverage factor for a 60 percent margin requirement is = 1/percentage margin requirement = 1/.60 = 5/3.  Thus, the rate of return on the stock if it is later sold at $100 a share = 25.00% x 5/3 = 41.67%.  In contrast, the rate of return on the stock if it is sold for $40 a share = -50.00% x 5/3 = -83.33%.

2(a). Since the margin is 40 percent and Lauren currently has $50,000 on deposit in her margin account, if Lauren uses the maximum allowable margin her $50,000 deposit must represent 40% of her total investment. Thus, $50,000 = .4x then x = $125,000. Since the shares are $35 each, Lauren can purchase $125,000 — $35 = 3,571 shares (rounded).

2(b). Total Profit = Total Return - Total Investment

    (1)     If stock rises to $45/share, Lauren's total return is:
             3,571 shares x $45 = $160,695.
             Total profit = $160,695 - $125,000 = $35,695

    (2)     If stock falls to $25/share, Lauren's total return is:
             3,571 shares x $25 = $89,275.

             Total loss = $89,275 - $125,000 = -$35,725.

2(c).

$$\text{Margin} = \frac{\text{Market Value - Debit Balance}}{\text{Market Value}}$$

where Market Value = Price per share x Number of shares.

Initial Loan Value = Total Investment - Initial Margin.
    = $125,000 - $50,000 = $75,000

Therefore, if maintenance margin is 30 percent:

$$.30 = \frac{(3,571 \text{ shares x Price}) - \$75,000}{(3,571 \text{ shares x Price})}$$

.30 (3,571 x Price)  = (3,571 x Price) - $75,000.
1,071.3 x Price      = (3,571 x Price) - $75,000
-2,499.7 x Price     = -$75,000
Price                = $30.00

3.    Profit = Ending Value - Beginning Value + Dividends
              - Transaction Costs - Interest

Beginning Value of Investment = $20 x 100 shares = $2,000

Your Investment = margin requirement + commission.
          = (.55 x $2,000) + (.03 x $2,000)
          = $1,100 + $60
          = $1,160

Ending Value of Investment = $27 x 100 shares
          = $2,700

Dividends = $.50 x 100 shares = $50.0

Transaction Costs  = (.03 x $2,000) + (.03 x $2,700)
(Commission)       = $60 + $81
                   = $141

Interest           = .10 x (.45 x $2,000) = $90.00

Therefore:

Profit = $2,700 - $2,000 + $50.00 - $141 - $90.00
       = $519

The rate of return on your investment of $1,160 is:

      $519/$1,160 = 44.74%

4.    Profit on a Short Sale = Beginning Value - Ending Value
              - Dividends - Transaction Costs - Interest

Beginning Value of Investment= $56 x 100 shares= $5,600
(which is sold under a short sale arrangement)

Your investment    = margin requirement + commission
                   = (.45 x $5,600) + $155
                   = $2,520 + $155
                   = $2,675

4 - 12

Ending Value of Investment    = $45 x 100 = $4,500
(Cost of closing out position)

Dividends = $2.50 x 100 shares = $250.00

Transaction Costs = $155 + $145 = $300.00

Interest = .08 x (.55 x $5,600) = $246.40

Therefore:

Profit = $5,600 - $4,500 - $250.00 - $300.00 - $246.40
               = $303.60

The rate of return on your investment of $2,675 is:

$303.60/$2,675    = 11.35%


5(a).  I am satisfied with the profit generated by the sale of my 200 shares at $40.


5(b).  <u>With</u>:       (40-25) / 25  =     60%
        <u>Without</u>:   (30-25) / 25  =     20%


6.     <u>Cash</u>:       (45-30) / 30  =    50%
      <u>Margin</u>:    Cash return x Leverage factor
                 50% x 1/.60  =    83.3%


7.     <u>Limit order @ $24</u>:    (36-24) / 24  =    50%
      <u>Market order</u>:       (36-28) / 28  =    28.6%
      <u>Limit order @ $18</u>:    No execution; no return

# CHAPTER 5

# Security-Market Indicator Series

# Answers to Questions

1. The purpose of market indicator series is to provide a general indication of the aggregate market changes or market movements. More specifically, the indicator series are used to derive market returns for a period of interest and then used as a benchmark for evaluating the performance of alternative portfolios. A second use is in examining the factors that influence aggregate stock price movements by forming relationships between market (series) movements and changes in the relevant variables in order to illustrate how these variables influence market movements. A further use is by technicians who use past aggregate market movements to predict future price patterns. Finally, a very important use is in portfolio theory, where the systematic risk of an individual security is determined by the relationship of the rates of return for the individual security to rates of return for a market portfolio of risky assets. Here, a representative market indicator series is used as a proxy for the market portfolio of risky assets.

2. A characteristic that differentiates alternative market indicator series is the sample--the size of the sample (how representative of the total market it is) and the source (whether securities are of a particular type or a given segment of the population). The weight given to each member plays a discriminatory role--with diverse members in a sample, it would make a difference whether the series is price-weighted, value-weighted, or unweighted. A final distinction could be the computational procedure used for calculating return-- i.e., whether arithmetic mean, geometric mean, etc.

3. A price-weighted series is an unweighted arithmetic average of current prices of the securities included in the sample--i.e., closing prices of all securities are summed and divided by the number of securities in the sample.

   A $100 security will have a greater influence on the series than a $25 security because a 10 percent increase in the former increases the numerator by $10 while it takes a 40 percent increase in the price of the latter to have the same effect.

4.  A value-weighted index begins by deriving the initial total market value of all stocks used in the series (market value equals number of shares outstanding times current market price). The initial value is typically established as the base value and assigned an index value of 100. Subsequently, a new market value is computed for all securities in the sample and this new value is compared to the initial value to derive the percent change which is then applied to the beginning index value of 100.

5.  Given a four security series and a 2-for-1 split for security A and a 3-for-1 split for security B, the divisor would change from 4 to 2.8 for a price-weighted series.

| Stock | Before Split Price | After Split Prices |
|-------|--------------------|--------------------|
| A | $20 | $10 |
| B | 30 | 10 |
| C | 20 | 20 |
| D | 30 | 30 |
| Total | 100/4 = 25 | 70/x = 25 |
| | | x = 2.8 |

The price-weighted series adjusts for a stock split by deriving a new divisor that will ensure that the new value for the series is the same as it would have been without the split. The adjustment for a value-weighted series due to a stock split is automatic. The decrease in stock price is offset by an increase in the number of shares outstanding.

**Before Split**

| Stock | Price/Share | # of Shares | Market Value |
|-------|-------------|-------------|--------------|
| A | $20 | 1,000,000 | $ 20,000,000 |
| B | 30 | 500,000 | 15,000,000 |
| C | 20 | 2,000,000 | 40,000,000 |
| D | 30 | 3,500,000 | 105,000,000 |
| Total | | | $180,000,000 |

The $180,000,000 base value is set equal to an index value of 100.

**After Split**

| Stock | Price/Share | # of Shares | Market Value |
|-------|-------------|-------------|--------------|
| A | $10 | 2,000,000 | $ 20,000,000 |
| B | 10 | 1,500,000 | 15,000,000 |
| C | 20 | 2,000,000 | 40,000,000 |
| D | 30 | 3,500,000 | 105,000,000 |
| Total | | | $180,000,000 |

$$\text{New Index Value} = \frac{\text{Current Market Value}}{\text{Base Value}} \times \text{Beginning Index Value}$$

$$= \frac{180,000,000}{180,000,000} \times 100$$

$$= 100$$

which is precisely what one would expect since there has been no change in prices other than the split.

6.  In an unweighted price indicator series, all stocks carry equal weight irrespective of their price and/or their value. One way to visualize an unweighted series is to assume that equal dollar amounts are invested in each stock in the portfolio, for example, an equal amount of $1,000 is assumed to be invested in each stock. Therefore, the investor would own 50 shares of a $20 stock, 100 shares of a $10 stock, and 10 shares of a $100 stock. An unweighted price index which consists of the above three stocks would be constructed as follows:

| Stock | Price/Share | # of Shares | Market Value |
|-------|-------------|-------------|--------------|
| A | $ 20 | 50 | $1,000 |
| B | 10 | 100 | 1,000 |
| C | 100 | 10 | 1,000 |
| Total | | | $3,000 |

**A 10% price increase of stock A:**

| Stock | Price/Share | # of Shares | Market Value |
|-------|-------------|-------------|--------------|
| A | $ 22 | 50 | $1,100 |
| B | 10 | 100 | 1,000 |
| C | 100 | 10 | 1,000 |
| Total | | | $3,100 |

Student must follow this procedure for GM and Coors Brewing.

**A 10% increase of stock B:**

| Stock | Price/Share | # of Shares | Market Value |
|-------|-------------|-------------|--------------|
| A | $ 20 | 50 | $1,000 |
| B | 11 | 100 | 1,100 |
| C | 100 | 10 | 1,000 |
| Total | | | $3,100 |

**A 10% increase of stock C:**

| Stock | Price/Share | # of Shares | Market Value |
|-------|-------------|-------------|--------------|
| A | $ 20 | 50 | $1,000 |
| B | 10 | 100 | 1,000 |
| C | 110 | 10 | 1,100 |
| Total | | | $3,100 |

Thus, a 10% increase of any of the three stocks would have the same impact on the total value of the index (i.e., in all cases the index increases by 3.33%). An alternative treatment is to compute percentage changes for each stock and derive the average of these percentage changes. In this case, the average would be 3.33% (10% - 0% - 0%). So, a 20% price increase of GM would be no different from a 20% price increase of Coors.

7.  Based upon the sample from which it is derived and the fact that is a value-weighted index, the Wilshire 5000 Equity Index is a weighted composite of the NYSE composite index, the AMEX market value series, and the NASDAQ composite index. We would expect it to have the highest correlation with the NYSE composite index because the NYSE has the

highest market value. The AMEX index would have the lowest correlation with the Wilshire Index.

8.   The high correlations between returns for alternative NYSE price indicator series can be attributed to the **source** of the sample (i.e. stock traded on the NYSE). The four series differ in sample size; that is, the DJIA has 30 securities, the S&P 400 has 400 securities, the S&P 500 has 500 securities, and the NYSE Composite about 2330 stocks. The DJIA differs in computation from the other series; that is, the DJIA is a price-weighted series where the other three series are value-weighted. Even so, there is strong correlation between the series because of similarity of types of companies (see Table 5.10).

9.   Table 5.12 shows that the AMEX achieved the highest average annual return with the greatest amount of variability. Economic theory would suggest that the larger companies in the NYSE Composite Index would tend to have less risk (the smallest standard of the three U.S. equity market segments) and thus a smaller return (lowest average annual price change). However, examining the coefficient of variation for the NYSE Composite (1.88), it was actually higher than the AMEX (1.82).

10.  In terms of sample size, the relationship between the Nikkei-Dow Jones Average and the Tokyo Stock Exchange Price Index is very similar to the relationship between the FT Ordinary Share Index and the FT Actuaries All Share Index. In both cases the first index serves as a smaller sample of the heaviest traded stocks included in the broader TSE and FT Actuaries All Share Index.

In terms of weight and computational procedure, both the TSE and the FT Actuaries All-Share Index are value-weighted series in which the changes of value are reported in terms of a basic index value. On the other hand, the Nikkei-Dow Jones Average is price-weighted and the FT Ordinary Share Index is an unweighted index. Both of these methods have drawbacks in that the price-weighted series is more strongly influenced by changes in high priced stocks and the unweighted FT Ordinary Share Index uses a geometric average that tends to result in a downward bias.

As a result of the different population samples, Table 5.10 illustrates that while the alternative series of each country show a high positive correlation, there is virtually no correlation between the two TSE indexes and the two indexes of the London Stock Exchange.

Likewise, there is virtually no correlation between the TSE indexes and the two NYSE indexes (DJIA and NYSE Composite). These results support the argument for diversification among countries.

11. Since the equal weighted series implies that all stocks carry the same weight, irrespective of price or value, the results indicate that on average all stocks in the index increased by 23 percent. On the other hand, the percentage change in the value of a large company has a greater impact than the same percentage change for a small company in the value weighted index. Therefore, the difference in results indicate that for this given period, the smaller companies in the index outperformed the larger companies.

12. The bond-market series are more difficult to construct due to the wide diversity of bonds available. Also bonds are hard to standardize because their maturities and market yields are constantly changing. In order to better segment the market, you could construct five possible subindexes based on coupon, quality, industry, maturity, and special features (such as call features, warrants, convertibility, etc.).

13. Since the Merrill Lynch-Wilshire Capital Markets index is composed of a distribution of bonds as well as stocks, the fact that this index increased by 15 percent, compared to a 5 percent gain in the Wilshire 5000 Index indicates that bonds outperformed stocks over this period of time.

14. The Russell 1000 and Russell 2000 represent two different population sample of stocks, segmented by size. The fact that the Russell 2000 (which is composed of the smallest 2,000 stocks in the Russell 3000) increased more than the Russell 1000 (composed of the 1000 largest capitalization U.S. stocks) indicates that small stocks performed better during this time period.

15. One would expect that the level of correlation between the various world indexes should be relatively high. These indexes tend to include the same countries and the largest capitalization stocks within each country.

# Answers to Problems

1(a).   Given a three-security series and a price change from Period T to T+1, the percentage change in the series would be 42.85 percent.

|  | Period T | Period T+1 |
|---|---|---|
| A | $ 60 | $ 80 |
| B | 20 | 35 |
| C | 18 | 25 |
| Sum | $ 98 | $140 |
| Divisor | 3 | 3 |
| Average | 32.67 | 46.67 |

$$\text{Percentage change} = \frac{46.67 - 32.67}{32.67} = \frac{14.00}{32.67} = 42.85\%$$

1(b).   **Period T**

| Stock | Price/Share | # of Shares | Market Value |
|---|---|---|---|
| A | $60 | 1,000,000 | $ 60,000,000 |
| B | 20 | 10,000,000 | 200,000,000 |
| C | 18 | 30,000,000 | 540,000,000 |
| Total | | | $800,000,000 |

**Period T+1**

| Stock | Price/Share | # of Shares | Market Value |
|---|---|---|---|
| A | $ 80 | 1,000,000 | $ 80,000,000 |
| B | 35 | 10,000,000 | 350,000,000 |
| C | 25 | 30,000,000 | 750,000,000 |
| Total | | | $1,180,000,000 |

$$\text{Percentage change} = \frac{1{,}180 - 800}{800} = \frac{380}{800} = 47.50\%$$

1(c). The percentage change for the price-weighted series is a simple average of the differences in price from one period to the next. Equal weights are applied to each price change.

The percentage change for the value-weighted series is a weighted average of the differences in price from one period T to T+1. These weights are the relative market values for each stock. Thus, Stock C carries the greatest weight followed by B and then A. Because Stock C had the greatest percentage increase and the largest weight, it is easy to see that the percentage change would be larger for this series than the price-weighted series.

2(a). **Period T**

| Stock | Price/Share | # of Shares | Market Value |
|-------|-------------|-------------|--------------|
| A | $ 60 | 16.67 | $1,000.00 |
| B | 20 | 50.00 | 1,000.00 |
| C | 18 | 55.56 | 1,000.00 |
| Total | | | $3,000.00 |

**Period T+1**

| Stock | Price/Share | # of Shares | Market Value |
|-------|-------------|-------------|--------------|
| A | $ 80 | 16.67 | $1,333.60 |
| B | 35 | 50.00 | 1,750.00 |
| C | 25 | 55.56 | 1,389.00 |
| Total | | | $4,472.60 |

$$\text{Percentage change} = \frac{4{,}472.60 - 3{,}000}{3{,}000} = \frac{1{,}472.60}{3{,}000} = 49.09\%$$

2(b).

Stock A $= \dfrac{80 - 60}{60} = \dfrac{20}{60} = 33.33\%$

Stock B $= \dfrac{35 - 20}{20} = \dfrac{15}{20} = 75.00\%$

Stock C $= \dfrac{25 - 18}{18} = \dfrac{7}{18} = 38.89\%$

Arithmetic average $= \dfrac{33.33\% + 75.00\% + 38.89\%}{3}$

$= \dfrac{147.22\%}{3} = 49.07\%$

The answers are the same (slight difference due to rounding). This is what you would expect since Part A represents the percentage change of an equal-weighted series and Part B applies an equal weight to the separate stocks in calculating the arithmetic average.

2(c). Geometric average is the nth root of the product of n items.

Geometric average $= [(1.3333)(1.75)(1.3889)]^{1/3} - 1$

$= [3.2407]^{1/3} - 1$

$= 1.4798 - 1$

$= .4798$ or $47.98\%$

The geometric average is less than the arithmetic average. This is because variability of return has a greater effect on the arithmetic average than the geometric average.


3.    Student Exercise


4(a).  DJIA $= \sum\limits_{i=1}^{30} P_{it}/D_{adj}$


### Day 1

| Company | Price/Share |
|---------|-------------|
| A | 12 |
| B | 23 |
| C | 52 |

$$\text{DJIA} = \frac{12 + 23 + 52}{3} = \frac{87}{3} = 29$$


### Day 2

| Company | (Before Split) Price/Share | (After Split) Price/Share |
|---------|-------------|-------------|
| A | 10 | 10 |
| B | 22 | 44 |
| C | 55 | 55 |

$$\text{DJIA} = \frac{10 + 22 + 55}{3} \qquad \text{DJIA} = \frac{10 + 44 + 55}{X}$$

$$= \frac{87}{3} = 29 \qquad 29 = \frac{109}{X}$$

$$X = 3.7586 \text{ (new divisor)}$$

**Day 3**

| Company | (Before Split) Price/Share | (After Split) Price/Share |
|---|---|---|
| A | 14 | 14 |
| B | 46 | 46 |
| C | 52 | 26 |

$$\text{DJIA} = \frac{14 + 46 + 52}{3.7586}$$

$$= \frac{112}{3.7586} = 29.798$$

$$\text{DJIA} = \frac{14 + 46 + 26}{Y}$$

$$= \frac{86}{Y}$$

$$Y = 2.8861 \text{ (new divisor)}$$

**Day 4**

| Company | Price/Share |
|---|---|
| A | 13 |
| B | 47 |
| C | 25 |

$$\text{DJIA} = \frac{13 + 47 + 25}{2.8861}$$

$$= \frac{85}{2.8861} = 29.452$$

**Day 5**

| Company | Price/Share |
|---|---|
| A | 12 |
| B | 45 |
| C | 26 |

$$\text{DJIA} = \frac{12 + 45 + 26}{2.8861}$$

$$= \frac{83}{2.8861} = 28.759$$

5 - 13

4(b). Since the index is a price-weighted average, the higher priced stocks carry more weight. But when a split occurs, the new divisor ensures that the new value for the series is the same as it would have been without the split. Hence, the main effect of a split is just a repositioning of the relative weight that a particular stock carries in determining the index. For example, a 10% price change for company B would carry more weight in determining the percent change in the index in Day 3 after the reverse split that increased its price, than its weight on Day 2.

4(c). Student Exercise

5(a). Base
$$\begin{aligned} &= (\$12 \times 500) + (\$23 \times 350) + (\$52 \times 250) \\ &= \$6,000 + \$8,050 + \$13,000 \\ &= \$27,050 \end{aligned}$$

Day 1
$$\begin{aligned} &= (\$12 \times 500) + (\$23 \times 350) + (\$52 \times 250) \\ &= \$6,000 + \$8,050 + \$13,000 \\ &= \$27,050 \end{aligned}$$

$Index_1 = (\$27,050/\$27,050) \times 10 = 10$

Day 2
$$\begin{aligned} &= (\$10 \times 500) + (\$22 \times 350) + (\$55 \times 250) \\ &= \$5,000 + \$7,700 + \$13,750 \\ &= \$26,450 \end{aligned}$$

$Index_2 = (\$26,450/\$27,050) \times 10 = 9.778$

Day 3
$$\begin{aligned} &= (\$14 \times 500) + (\$46 \times 175) + (\$52 \times 250) \\ &= \$7,000 + \$8,050 + \$13,000 \\ &= \$28,050 \end{aligned}$$

$Index_3 = (\$28,050/\$27,050) \times 10 = 10.370$

Day 4          = ($13 x 500) + ($47 x 175) + ($25 x 500)
               = $6,500 + $8,225 + $12,500
               = $27,225

$Index_4$      = ($27,225/$27,050) x 10 = 10.065

Day 5          = ($12 x 500) + ($45 x 175) + ($26 x 500)
               = $6,000 + $7,875 + $13,000
               = $26,875

$Index_5$      = ($26,875/$27,050) x 10 = 9.935

5(b).    The market values are unchanged due to splits and thus stock splits have no effect. The index, however, is weighted by the relative market values.

6(a).    Using Table 5.12, the arithmetic mean for the DJIA for years 1986-1995 would be calculated as:

$$\frac{22.58 + 2.26 + 11.85 + 26.96 + (-4.34) + 20.32 + 4.17 + 14.94 + 2.14 + 33.45}{10}$$

= 134.33/10 = 13.433%

6(b).    The geometric mean for the DJIA for the years 1986-1995 would be calculated as follows:

[ (1.2258) (1.0226) (1.1185) (1.2696) (.9566)

(1.2032) (1.0417) (1.1494) (1.0214) $(1.3345)]^{1/10}$ - 1

= $[3.3437]^{1/10}$ - 1

= 1.1283 - 1 = .1283 or 12.83%

The student should use this same procedure for each of the indexes. The differences between the two means illustrate the point that greater variability produces sharper differences between means.

7(a).  $\text{PWI}_0 = \dfrac{20 + 80 + 40}{3} = 46.67$

$\text{PWI}_1 = \dfrac{32 + 45 + 42}{2.143} = 55.53$

Since  $\dfrac{20 + (80/2) + 40}{x} = 46.67 \text{ and } x = 2.143$

Pct. chg.  $\dfrac{55.53 - 46.67}{46.67} = .190 \text{ or } 19.0\%$

$\text{VWI}_0 = 20 \,(100 \text{ million}) + 80 \,(2 \text{ million}) + 40 \,(25 \text{ million})$

$= 3{,}160{,}000{,}000 \,/\, 3{,}160{,}000{,}000 \quad = 1 \times 100 \quad = 100.0$

$\text{VWI}_1 = 32 \,(100 \text{ million}) + 45(4 \text{ million}) + 42(25 \text{ million})$

$= 4{,}430{,}000{,}000 \,/\, 3{,}160{,}000{,}000 = 1.402 \times 100 = 140.2$

Pct. chg.  $= \dfrac{140.2}{100.0} - 1 = .402 \text{ or } 40.2\%$

7(b).  The percent change in the value-weighted index was much larger owing to the fact that the stock with the largest market value (K) had the greatest gain (60%).

7(c).  Arithmetic:  $\dfrac{.60 + .125 + .05}{3}$  =  .258  or 25.8%

Geometric:  $[(1.60)\,(1.125)\,(1.05)]^{1/3}$  $-1$ = .236  or 23.6%

Such results may not resemble price- and value-weighted results since unweighted averages are not impacted by unusual changes in stocks with high prices or large market values.

8(a).  $100 \times [\,(1.1361)\,(1.4261) \cdots (1.1324)\,]^{1/10}$ = 167.71

8(b).  $(167.71 / 100)^{1/10} - 1$ = .053 or 5.3%

8(c).  $(167.71 / 105)$ = 1.597

$(100 / 250)$ = 0.400

Return = $(1.597 / 0.400)^{1/10} - 1$ = .149 or 14.9%

# CHAPTER 6

## Sources Of Information On Global Investments

# Answers to Questions

1.    Past data on Gross Domestic Product can be readily obtained from the *Federal Reserve Bulletin, Survey of Current Business*, and *Economic Indicators* among several other sources.

2.    Data on rates of exchange with foreign countries is available from the *Federal Reserve Bulletin* and *The Wall Street Journal* under the section "Foreign Exchange."

3.    Past data for the steel industry and the outlook for the future can be obtained from the Standard & Poor's *Industry Surveys* and trade association publications such as that of the Iron and Steel Institute. Similarly, relevant information on the automobile industry can be readily derived from the S & P *Industry Surveys* and industry magazines like *Automotive News*. The individual industry data can then be compared with national industrial production data, the latter published widely in several government publications such as the *Federal Reserve Bulletin* and the *Survey of Current Business*.

The relationship between industry and aggregate industrial production can be estimated by a regression equation – i.e., how sensitive the particular industry is to changes in the aggregate economy and its relative performance in expansions and recessions. Also, the analyst would be interested in whether the industry's output as a percent of industrial production is constant, increasing, or decreasing. Finally, you should analyze factors unique to the industry – sources of raw materials, expansion and retooling requirements, foreign demand, etc.

4.    Data on money supply (MI, M1B, M2 or M3) can be obtained from one of several government sources such as the *Federal Reserve Bulletin, Business Conditions Digest, Economic Indicators*, etc. Again, there are numerous sources for data on aggregate stock market prices, depending upon what market indicator series is being employed – i.e., *S & P Trade and Securities Statistics* for S & P series, *AMEX Fact Book* for American Exchange Series,

etc. Two general sources are the quarterly ISL books that provide data on most aggregate market series on a daily basis and *Barron's* which include daily data on a weekly basis.

5.  Information on a company listed over the counter can be obtained from annual reports of the company, 10-K reports, commercial publications such as *Value Line* (limited to large, widely-traded OTC companies), the S & P *Stock Reports* (contains 1,100 OTC stocks), the Moody's OTC *Industrial Manual* (limited to OTC industrials), and the S & P *Stock Guide*, among several other sources.

6.  There are numerous sources from which to obtain macroeconomic data for various countries. One very broad publications source would be *The Economic Intelligence Unit*, which publishes 88 separate quarterly reviews and an annual supplement covering the economic and business conditions and outlook for 160 countries. The review considers the economy, trade and finance, trends in investment and consumer spending, along with information pertaining to the political environment. Another good source would be the *US Institutional Trade Administration, International Economic Indicators*. This quarterly publication of the US Government Printing Office contains comparative economic indicators and trends in the U.S. and its seven principal industrial competitors. Information includes trade indicators, price indicators, finance indicators, labor indicators, and general indicators. The primary sources of data are also listed if more information is needed.

    Two sources of industry information could include the MSCI that provides monthly publications concerning valuation data on individual stocks and world industries and various industry publications that will include up-to-date global information on the particular industry. The best source for company data would be the specific company's annual report. Among other information, this source provides the name of a contact person from which you can get additional information. Another good source would be *Moody's International Manual* which provides financial information on about 3,000 major foreign corporations.

7.  *Barron's* would be a good publication to have. It is a weekly publication that typically contains four articles on topics of interest to investors. In addition, it has the most complete weekly listing of prices and quotes for all financial

markets. It provides weekly data on individual stocks and the latest information on earnings and dividends. Finally, there is an extensive statistical section with detailed information on stock market behavior for the past week. *The Outlook* is another publication to which investors could subscribe. It contains advice on the general market environment and also has features on specific groups of stocks or industries. Additionally, it contains weekly figures for 88 industry groups and other market statistics. With regard to international markets, *The Financial Times* provides information similar to *The Wall Street Journal*. However, it goes much further in that it includes a true world perspective on the financial news. Also, *Equities International* emphasizes major trends and events in countries around the world. It includes a complete listing of stock market indicator series for major global markets.

8.   S & P *Trade and Securities Statistics* is a service of Standard & Poor's which includes a basic set of historical data on various economic and security price series and a monthly supplement that updates the series for the recent period. There are two major sets of data: 1] the business and financial section, which includes long-term statistics on trade, banking, industry, prices, agriculture, and financial trends; and 2] the security price index record sections that contain historical data for all of the Standard & Poor's stock price series. The *Industry Survey* is the major publication containing information on a number of industries. Coverage for all the industries is divided into a current analysis and a basis analysis.

Two publications contain substantial information about individual stocks. *Moody's International Manual* covers industrial companies listed on the NYSE and AMEX, as well as companies listed on regional exchanges. There is also a section on international industrial firms. The second one is The Value Line Investment Survey, which is published in two parts. Part one contains basic historical information on about 1.700 companies, as well as a number of analytical measures of earnings stability, growth rates, and a common safety factor. It also includes extensive two-year projections for each firm and three-year estimates of performance. The second volume is a weekly service that provides general investment advice and recommends individual stocks for purchase or sale.

9.   Student Exercise

# CHAPTER 7

## Efficient Capital Markets

# Answers to Questions

1. There are several reasons why one would expect capital markets to be efficient, the foremost being that there are a large number of independent, profit-maximizing investors engaged in the analysis and valuation of securities. A second assumption is that new information comes to the market in a random fashion; and the numerous profit-maximizing investors adjust security prices rapidly to reflect this new information. Thus, price changes would be independent and random. Finally, because stock prices reflect all information, one would expect prevailing prices to reflect "true" current value.

   Capital markets as a whole are generally expected to be efficient, but the markets for some securities might not be as efficient as others. Recall that markets are expected to be efficient because there are a large number of investors who receive new information and analyze its effect on security values. If there is a difference in the number of analysts following a stock and the volume of trading, one could conceive of differences in the efficiency of the markets. For example, new information regarding actively traded stocks such as IBM and Exxon is well publicized and numerous analysts evaluate the effect. Therefore, one should expect the prices for these stocks to adjust rapidly and fully reflect the new information. On the other hand, new information regarding a stock with a small number of stockholders and low trading volume will not be as well publicized and few analysts follow such firms. Therefore, prices may not adjust as rapidly to new information and the possibility of finding a temporarily undervalued stock are also greater. Some also argue that the size of the firms is another factor to differentiate the efficiency of stocks. Specifically, it is believed that the markets for stocks of small firms are less efficient than that of large firms.

2. The weak-form efficient market hypothesis contends that current stock prices reflect all available market information including the historical sequence of prices, price changes, and any volume information. The implication is that there should be no relationship between past price changes and future price changes. Therefore, any trading rule that uses past market data alone should be of little value.

7 - 3

The two groups of tests of the weak-form EMH are (1) statistical tests of independence and (2) tests of trading rules. Statistical tests of independence can be divided further into two groups: the autocorrelation tests and the runs tests. The autocorrelation tests are used to test the existence of significant correlation, whether positive or negative, of price changes on a particular day with a series of consecutive previous days. The runs tests examine the sequence of positive and negative changes in a series and attempt to determine the existence of a pattern. For a random series one would expect $1/3(2n - 1)$ runs, where n is the number of observations. If there are too few runs (i.e., long sequences of positive changes or long sequences of negative changes), the series is not random, i.e., you would not expect a positive change to consistently follow a positive change and a negative change consistently after a negative change. Alternatively, if there are too many runs (+-+-+-+- etc.), again the series is not random since you would not expect a negative change to consistently follow a positive change.

In the trading rule studies, the second major set of tests, investigators attempted to examine alternative technical trading rules through simulation. The trading rule studies compared the risk-return results derived from the simulations, including transaction costs, to results obtained from a simple buy-and-hold policy.

3.    The semistrong-form efficient market hypothesis contends that security prices adjust rapidly to the release of all new public information and that stock prices reflect all public information. The semistrong- form goes beyond the weak-form because it includes all market and also all nonmarket public information such as stock splits, economic news, political news, etc.

Using the organization developed by Fama, studies of the semistrong-form EMH can be divided into two groups:

A.    Studies which attempt to predict futures rates of return using publicly available information (goes beyond weak-form EMH). These studies involve either time-series analysis of returns or the cross-section distribution of returns.

B.    Event studies examine abnormal rates of return surrounding specific events or items of public information. These studies determine whether it is possible to make average risk-adjusted profits by acting after the information is made public.

4. Abnormal rate of return is the amount by which a security's return differs from the expected rate of return based upon the market's rate of return and the security's relationship with the market.

5. The CAPM is grounded in the theory that investors demand higher returns for higher risks. As a result of risks specific to each individual security, the announcement of a significant economic event will tend to affect individual stock prices in either a greater or less direction than the market as a whole. Fama, Fisher, Jensen, and Roll portrayed this unique relationship of stock returns and market return for a period prior to and subsequent to a significant economic event as follows:

$$R_{it} = a_i + B_i \, R_{mt} + e$$

where

$R_{it}$    = the rate of return on security i during period t

$a_i$    = the intercept or constant for security in the regression

$B_i$    = the regression slope coefficient for security i
         equal to $cov_{im}/\sigma_m^2$

$R_{mt}$   = the rate of return on a market index during period t

$e$       = a random error that sums to zero

As an example of how one would derive abnormal risk-adjusted returns for a stock during a specific period, assume the following values for a firm:

$$a_i = .01 \text{ and } B_i = 1.40$$

If the market return ($R_{mt}$) during the specified period was 8 percent, the expected return for stock i would be:

$$
\begin{aligned}
E(R_{it}) \quad &= .01 + 1.4(.08) \\
&= .01 + .112 \\
&= .122
\end{aligned}
$$

The fact that this is the expected value, implies that the actual value will tend to deviate around the expected value. We will define the abnormal return ($AR_{it}$) as the actual return minus the expected return. In keeping with our example, if the actual return for the stock during this period were 10 percent, the abnormal return for the stock during the period would be

$$
\begin{aligned}
AR_{it} \quad &= .10 - .122 \\
&= -.022
\end{aligned}
$$

Thus, the stock price reacted to the economic event in a manner that was 2.2 percent less than expected where expectations were based upon what the aggregate market did and the stock's relationship with the market. This abnormal return surrounding an economic event can be used to determine the effect of the event on the individual security.

6.   First, only use information or data that is publicly available at the time of the decision. As an example, if you use information that is typically not available until six weeks after a period and you assume you have it four weeks after, your investment results should be superior because you implicitly have prior information. Second, take account for all transactions costs for the trading rule. This is important because almost all trading rules involve more transactions than a buy-and-hold policy and if you don't consider this, it will bias the results against buy-and-hold. Third, be sure to adjust all results for the risk involved because many trading rules will tend to select high risk stocks that will have higher returns.

7.   A number of studies have examined the adjustment of stock prices to major world events. These studies analyzed the effect of several unexpected world events on stock prices--namely, whether prices adjusted before or during the announcement or after it. The results consistently showed that the adjustments took place between the close of the previous day and the opening of the subsequent day. Notably, an investor could not derive above average profits from transacting after the news became public, thus supporting the semistrong-form EMH.

8.   In the early 1970s, several studies were performed that examined quarterly earnings reports. The results of the studies provided evidence against the semistrong-form EMH. Specifically, buying a stock after a report of unexpected higher quarterly earnings was profitable. Generally, the abnormal return for the stock occurred 13 or 26 weeks following the earnings announcement and reflected the size of the unanticipated earnings change.

9.   Studies on market efficiency are considered to be dual tests of the EMH and the CAPM. These tests involve a joint hypothesis because they consider not only the efficiency of the market, but also are dependent on the asset pricing model that provides the measure of risk used in the test. For example, if a test determines that it is possible to predict future differential risk-adjusted returns, the results could either have been caused by the market being inefficient or because the risk measure is bad thereby providing an incorrect risk-adjusted return.

10.  The strong-form efficient market hypothesis asserts that stock prices fully reflect all information, whether public or otherwise. It goes beyond the semistrong-form because it requires that no group of investors have a monopolistic access to any information. Thus, the strong-form efficient market hypothesis calls for perfect markets in which all information is available to everyone at the same time.

11.  The strong-form efficient market hypothesis goes beyond the semistrong-form in that it calls for perfect markets --i.e., no group of investors have a monopolistic access to information. Thus, tests for the strong-form efficient market hypothesis would center around examining whether any group has a monopolistic access to information and can consistently obtain above average profits by using it. Four groups of investors have been featured in these tests--corporate insiders, the stock exchange specialist, security analysts and professional money managers.

12.  In the early 1970s, a study by the Securities and Exchange Commission found that by having access to the limit order books as his source of monopolistic information, coupled with low transactions costs, the stock market specialist consistently obtains above average returns. This is evidence against the strong-form hypothesis because this group apparently has a monopoly source of information and uses it to derive above normal returns.

13. Studies by several authors examined the risk-adjusted performance of professional money managers for various periods and found support for the strong-form efficient market hypothesis. For example, a historical study of mutual fund money managers found that on a risk adjusted basis, only about one-third of the funds outperformed the market. More recent studies have also generally provided similar results on performance.

14. The basic premise of technical analysis is that the information dissemination process is slow--thus the adjustment of prices is not immediate but forms a pattern. This view is diametrically opposed to the concept of efficient capital markets, which contends that there is a rapid dissemination process and, therefore, prices reflect all information. Thus, there would be no value to technical analysis because technicians act after the news is made public which would negate its value in an efficient market.

15. The proponents of fundamental analysis advocate that at one point in time there is a basic intrinsic value for the aggregate stock market, alternative industries, and individual securities and if this intrinsic value is substantially different from the prevailing market value, the investor should make the appropriate investment decision. In the context of the efficient market hypothesis, however, if the determination of the basic intrinsic value is based solely on historical data, it will be of little value in providing above average returns. Alternatively, if the fundamental analyst makes superior projections of the relevant variables influencing stock prices then, in accordance with the efficient market hypothesis, he could expect to outperform the market. The implication is that even with an excellent valuation model, if you rely solely on past data you cannot expect to do better than a buy-and-hold policy.

16. To be superior in an efficient market the analyst must be aware of the relevant variables influencing stock prices, and be able to consistently project these accurately. If the analyst does not have access to inside information and lacks superior analytical ability, there is little likelihood of obtaining above average returns consistently.

To establish the superiority of an analyst it is appropriate to examine the performance of numerous buy and sell recommendations by the analyst over a period of time relative to a randomly selected sample of stocks in the same risk class. To be superior the analyst must consistently perform better than the random selection. Consistency is emphasized because on average you would expect random selection to outperform the market about half the time.

17. Superior analysts should concentrate their efforts in the second tier of stocks, because they do not receive the attention given the top-tier stocks. Also these analysts should pay attention to BV/MV ratios and the size of the firms. Analysts should concentrate their efforts on these securities, since they are more likely to yield abnormal returns.

18. The major efforts of the portfolio manager should be directed toward determining the risk preferences of his clients and offering, accordingly, a portfolio approximating the risk and return desires of the clientele. Given evidence of the stationarity of beta for a portfolio, this would not be a difficult task. Further, the level of risk can be controlled by committing a portion of the portfolio to a risk free asset and changing this proportion from time to time in accordance with the client's risk preferences.

    Second, the portfolio manager should attempt to achieve complete diversification--eliminate all unsystematic risk. Thus, the portfolio should be highly correlated with the market portfolio of risky assets.

    Finally, it is important to minimize transactions costs -- minimize taxes for the client, minimize commissions by reducing trading turnover, and minimize liquidity costs by only trading currently liquid stocks.

19. Index funds are security portfolios specially designed to duplicate the performance of the overall security market as represented by some selected market index series. The first group of index funds was created in the early 1970s because people started realizing that capital markets are efficient and it is extremely difficult to be a superior analyst. Thus, instead of trying to outperform the market, a large amount of money should be managed "passively" so that the investment performance simply matches that achieved by the aggregate market and costs are minimized so as not to drop returns below the market.

    An abundance of research has revealed that the performance of professional money managers is not superior to the market, and often has been inferior. This is precisely what one would expect in an efficient capital market. Thus, rather than expending a lot of effort in selecting a portfolio, the performance of which may turn out to be inferior to the market, it is contended by some that portfolios should be designed to simply match the market. If you match the market and minimize transactions costs you will beat two-thirds of the institutional portfolio managers on average. The index funds are intended to match the market and minimize costs as suggested above. Thus, they are consistent with the EMH.

20. The portfolio manager should continue to allow his two superior analysts to make investment recommendations for some proportion of the portfolio, making sure that their recommendations are implemented in a way that would conform to the risk preference of the client. They should also be encouraged to concentrate their efforts in the second tier of stocks, because the second tier is probably not as efficient as the top tier (because of lower trading volume) and the possibility of finding a temporarily undervalued security is greater. On the other hand, the portfolio manager should encourage the average and inferior analysts to direct their efforts to matching the performance of the aggregate market. As a result, the overall performance of the portfolio should be superior to the average market performance.

21. Despite Hawawini's acknowledgment that the European markets are smaller and less active than U.S. markets, one should not be surprised by the finding that European and U.S. markets have a similar level of efficiency. Two trends that tend to promote efficiency are the increasing size of the European equity market as a percentage of the world equity market, and the tendency for portfolio managers to increase the global diversification of their portfolios through investing in various countries' securities. Each of these trends implies that there are a large number of independent, profit-maximizing investors in the European equity markets, promoting efficiency through continuous analyses of new information.

22. Both autocorrelation tests and "runs" tests can be used as tests of the weak-form EMH for the Japanese stock market. Each of these tests checks for independence between stock price changes over time. The *Wall Street Journal* lists stock prices for the Tokyo market on a daily basis, and serves as an easy source from which to get the required data. It is also possible to do this analysis for individual stocks using prices for Japanese stocks listed in the WSJ or for some ADRs listed on the NYSE or AMEX.

23(a). The notion that stock prices already reflect all available information is referred to as the <u>efficient market hypothesis (EMH)</u>. It is common to distinguish among three versions of the EMH: the weak, semi-strong, and strong forms. These versions differ by their treatment of what is meant by "all available information".

The weak-form hypothesis asserts that stock prices already reflect <u>all information that can be derived from studying past market trading data</u>. Therefore, "technical analysis" and trend analysis, etc., are fruitless pursuits. Past stock price6 are publicly available and virtually costless to obtain. If such data ever conveyed reliable signals about future stock performance, all investors would have learned to exploit such signals.

The semi-strong form hypothesis states that <u>all publicly-available information</u> about the prospects of a firm must be reflected already in the stock's price. Such information includes, <u>in addition to past prices</u>, all fundamental data on the firm, its products, its .management, its finances, its earnings, etc., that can be found in public information sources.

The strong-form hypothesis states that stock prices reflect <u>all information</u> relevant to the firm, <u>even including information available only to company</u> <u>"insiders."</u> This version is an extreme one. Obviously, some "insiders" do have access to pertinent information long enough for them to profit from trading on that information before the public obtains it. Indeed, such trading -- not only by the "insiders" themselves, but also by relatives and/or associates -- is illegal under rules of the SEC.

For the weak-form or the semi-strong forms of the hypothesis to be valid does not require the strong-form version to hold. If the strong-form version was valid, however, both the semi-strong and the weak-form versions of efficiency would also be valid.

23(b). Even in an efficient market, a portfolio manager would have the important role of constructing and implementing an integrated set of steps to create and maintain appropriate combinations of investment assets. Listed below are the necessary steps in the portfolio management process:

1) Counseling the client to help the client to determine appropriate objectives and identify and evaluate constraints. The portfolio manager together with the client should specify and quantify risk tolerance, required rate of return,

time horizon, taxes considerations, the form of income needs, liquidity, legal and regulatory constraints, and any unique circumstances that will impact or modify normal management procedures/goals.

2) Monitoring and evaluating capital market expectations. Relevant considerations, such as economic, social, and political conditions/expectations are factored into the decision making process in terms of the expected risk/reward relationship for the various asset categories. Different expectations may lead the portfolio manager to adjust a client's systematic risk level even if markets are efficient.

3) The above steps are decisions derived from/implemented through portfolio policy and strategy setting. investment policies are set and implemented through the choice of optimal combinations of financial and real assets in the marketplace -- i.e., asset allocation. Under the assumption of a perfectly efficient market, stocks would be priced fairly, eliminating any added value by specific security selection. It might be argued that an investment policy which stresses diversification is even more important in an efficient market context because the elimination of specific risk becomes extremely important.

4) Market conditions, relative asset category percentages, and the investor's circumstances are monitored.

5) Portfolio adjustments are made as a result of significant changes in any or all relevant variables.

24(a). The fundamental impact of the Fama and French research is to challenge the validity of the Capital Asset Pricing Model (CAPM). Specifically, they found little relation between beta and average stock returns over the 50year period 1941-1990 (although there were some sub-periods when a positive relationship was indicated).

To isolate the "pure" impact of beta, Fama and French evaluated the joint roles of beta, size, earnings/price, leverage, and book-to-market over a broad range of large- and small-capitalization stocks from 1963-1990. They found no relation between beta and average return over this period; on the other hand, a combination of book-to-market and size factors did explain differences in those average returns.

Max's attractive results for his low price/cash flow strategy might have arisen from (1) a bias toward small stocks—as a result of equal-weighting the stocks in the portfolio—and (2) a value bias, which might more realistically be reflecting low price/book relationships.

If asset pricing is rational and the Fama and French research is valid, performance (i.e., returns) should be evaluated by comparing average returns for a portfolio to a benchmark comprised of similar size and book-to-market characteristics, not by reference to beta.

Also, Abel points out that an extension to the CAPM, the consumption CAPM, predicts a much lower equity risk premium compared to what has actually occurred. This suggests that the predictive ability of the CAPM, and hence the validity of beta, is questionable.

24(b). Many studies have been done on single-factor models, including such factors as size, price/earnings, beta, "neglect," day-of-the-week, etc., all of which have been referred to as "naive" anomalies. Often, the results have been taken as strong evidence of market inefficiencies and the opportunity to create attractive investment management products. However, these simple variable effects are not independent; rather, there may be a complex web of interrelationships underlying a host of different variables.

As computer power has become more available and databases more extensive, researchers have been able to test several variables simultaneously, rather than just one variable in isolation, often using a multiple regression framework. Using such techniques, they have been able to disentangle the observed effects and to isolate the "pure" and independent impacts of each variable. Jacobs and Levy, for example, studied a total of 25 separate anomaly measures, together with industry effects, and did so simultaneously.

As a single-factor study, Max's price/cash flow results merely indicate a naive anomaly, one which may simply be a proxy for other, more significant underlying factors. To make them credible would require further research using a more robust model design to see if the results hold up. An example of a similar situation is found in the Jacobs and Levy work, where a simple price/cash flow screen is found to produce an illusory anomaly: its naive results were completely dissipated in the pure form test.

24(c). A number of problems exist with respect to Max's test design, including:

1. <u>Survivorship Bias</u> - Max used the **current** list of S&P 600 Index companies rather than the list as it existed at the start of each test year. Thus, he failed to account for companies that may have left the list during the backtest period due to bankruptcy (affecting his negative returns) or that may have been merged out of existence (affecting his positive returns).

2. <u>Look-ahead Bias</u> - It is not clear that Max used only that information that was available to all investors at the time that the ranking process implied it was. For example, a company's 1983 cash flow would not have been known until many weeks or several months after the end of 1983, not at actual year end when price data was available.

3. <u>Improper Reference Portfolio</u> - Max compared an equal-weighted. stock portfolio to the capitalization-weighted S&P 500 Index.

4. <u>Ignoring the Real World</u> - There is no indication that Max took account of such real-world factors tending to reduce realized returns as turnover, commissions, market impact, implementation shortfalls or fees. In combination, these cost-producing factors could well have significantly lowered—or even eliminated—the potential for excess returns.

5. <u>Time Period</u> - Five years may be too short of a time to have back tested the model.

6. <u>Holdout Sample</u> - Max apparently found the anomaly by looking over the past five years of data. He should use a different time period as a holdout sample to test his model.

7. <u>Inappropriate Sampling</u> - TMP's investment philosophy is to utilize small capitalization stocks. The occurrence of an anomaly across the S&P 500 may be irrelevant to TMP because it may not occur in their investment universe.

8. <u>Market Efficiency</u> - Although the anomaly occurred in the past, it may not occur in the future. Buying activity by TMP and other money managers who have discovered this anomaly may drive the price of low price-to-cash-flow stocks up, causing the abnormal returns to dissipate.

9. <u>Data Mining</u> - Max may have investigated hundreds of potential anomalies and found a few that worked. Hence, Max might be guilty of "data mining." To prevent this, Max should start out with a theory of why an anomaly might occur and use the data to test that theory.

25(a). Efficient market hypothesis (EMH) states that a market is efficient if security prices immediately and fully reflect all available relevant information. Efficient means informationally efficient, not operationally efficient. Operational efficiency deals with the cost of transferring funds. If the market fully reflects information, the knowledge of that information would not allow anyone to profit from it because stock prices already incorporate the information.

1. **Weak** form asserts that stock prices already reflect all information that can be derived by examining market trading data such as the history of past prices and trading volume.

*Empirical evidence supports the weak-form.*
A strong body of evidence supports weak-form efficiency in the major U.S. securities markets. For example, test results suggest that technical trading rules do not produce superior returns after adjusting for transactions costs and taxes.

2. **Semi-strong** form says that a firm's stock price already reflects all publicly available information about a firm's prospects. Examples of publicly available information are annual reports of companies and investment advisory data.

*Empirical evidence mostly supports the semi-strong form.*
Evidence strongly supports the notion of semi-strong efficiency, but occasional studies (e.g., those identifying market anomalies including the small-firm effect and the January effect) and events (e.g., stock market crash of October 19, 1987) are inconsistent with this form of market efficiency. Black suggests that most so-called "anomalies" result from data mining.

3. **Strong** form of the EMH holds that current market prices reflect all information, whether publicly available or privately held, that is relevant to the firm.

*Empirical evidence does not support the strong form.*
Empirical evidence suggests that strong-form efficiency does not hold. If this form were correct, prices would fully reflect all information, although a corporate insider might exclusively hold such information. Therefore, insiders could not earn excess returns. Research evidence shows that corporate officers have access to pertinent information long enough before public release to enable them to profit from trading on this information.

25(b). **Technical analysis** in the form of charting involves the search for recurrent and predictable patterns in stock prices to enhance returns. The EMB implies that this type of technical analysis is without value. If past prices contain no useful information for predicting future prices, there is no point in following any technical trading rule for timing the purchases and sales of securities. According to weak-form efficiency, no investor can earn excess returns by developing trading rules based on historical price and return information. A simple policy of buying and holding will be at least as good as any technical procedure. Tests generally show that technical trading rules do not produce superior returns after making adjustments for transactions costs and taxes.

**Fundamental analysis** uses earnings and dividend prospects of the firm, expectations of future interest rates, and risk evaluation of the firm to determine proper stock prices. The EMH predicts that *most* fundamental analysis is doomed to failure. According to semi-strong-form efficiency, no investor can earn excess returns from trading rules based on any publicly available information. Only analysts with unique insight receive superior returns. Fundamental analysis is no better than technical analysis in enabling investors to capture above-average returns. However, the presence of many analysts contributes to market efficiency.

In summary, the EMH holds that the market appears to adjust so quickly to information about individual stocks and the economy as a whole that no technique of selecting a portfolio—using either technical or fundamental analysis—can consistently outperform a strategy of simply buying and holding a diversified group of securities, such as those making up the popular market averages.

25(c). Portfolio managers have several roles or responsibilities even in perfectly efficient markets. The most important responsibility is to:

1. **Identify the risk/return objectives for the portfolio given the investor's constraints,** In an efficient market, portfolio managers are responsible for tailoring the portfolio to meet the investor's needs rather than to beat the market, which requires identifying the client's return requirements and risk tolerance. Rational portfolio management also requires examining the investor's constraints, such as liquidity, time horizon, laws and regulations, taxes, and such unique preferences and circumstances as age and employment.

Other roles and responsibilities include:

2. **Developing a well-diversified portfolio with the selected risk level.** Although an efficient market prices securities fairly, each security still has firm-specific risk that portfolio managers can eliminate through diversification. Therefore, rational security selection requires selecting a well-diversified portfolio that provides the level of systematic risk that matches the investor's risk tolerance.

3. **Reducing transaction costs with a buy-and-hold strategy.** Proponents of the EMH advocate a passive investment strategy that does not try to find under- or overvalued stocks. A buy-and-hold strategy is consistent with passive management. Because the efficient market theory suggests that securities are fairly priced, frequently buying and selling securities, which generate large brokerage fees without increasing expected performance, makes little sense. One common strategy for passive management is to create an index fund that is designed to replicate the performance of a broad-based index of stocks.

4. **Developing capital market expectations.** As part of the asset-allocation decision, portfolio managers need to consider their expectations for the relative returns of the various capital markets to choose an appropriate asset allocation.

5. **Implement the chosen investment strategy and review it regularly for any needed adjustments.** Under the EMH, portfolio managers have the responsibility of implementing and updating the previously determined investment strategy for each client.

25(d). Whether active asset allocation among countries could consistently outperform a world market index depends on the degree of international market efficiency and the skill of the portfolio manager. Investment professionals often view the basic issue of international market efficiency in terms of cross-border financial market *integration* or *segmentation*. An integrated world financial market would achieve international efficiency in the sense that arbitrage across markets would take advantage of any new information throughout the world In an efficient integrated international market, prices of all assets would be in line with their relative investment values.

Some claim that international markets are not integrated, but segmented. Each national market might be efficient, but factors might prevent international capital flows from taking advantage of relative mispricing among countries. These factors include psychological barriers, legal restrictions, transaction costs, discriminatory taxation, political risks, and exchange risks.

Markets *do not* appear fully integrated or fully segmented. Markets may or may not become more correlated as they become more integrated since other factors help to determine correlation. Therefore, the degree of international market efficiency is an empirical question that has not yet been answered.

# Answers to Problems

1.    $Ar_{it} = R_{it} - R_{mt}$

      $AR_{Bt} = 11.5 - 4.0$

           $= 7.5$

      $AR_{Ft} = 10.0 - 8.5$

           $= 1.5$

      $AR_{Tt} = 14.0 - 9.6$

           $= 4.4$

      $AR_{Ct} = 12.0 - 15.3$

           $= -3.3$

      $AR_{Et} = 15.9 - 12.4$

           $= 3.5$

2.    $Ar_{it} = R_{it} - (BETA)(R_{mt})$

      $AR_{Bt} = 11.5 - .95(4.0)$

           $= 7.7$

      $AR_{Ft} = 10.0 - 1.25(8.5)$

           $= -.625$

$$AR_{Tt} = 14.0 - 1.45(9.6)$$

$$= .08$$

$$AR_{Ct} = 12.0 - .75(15.3)$$

$$= .525$$

$$AR_{Et} = 15.9 - (-.3)(12.4)$$

$$= 19.62$$

3.     The reason for the difference in each case is due to the implications of BETA. BETA determines how the stock will move in relation to movements in the market.

Considering stock C, a one percent change in the market return will result in a .75 percent change in stock C's return. Therefore, comparing the abnormal return for stock C, the value becomes positive in Problem 2. Conversely, the 1.25 percent change expected by stock F, for every 1 percent change in the market, resulted in the abnormal return moving from positive to negative.

Stock E should move opposite the market because of the negative beta value. Thus, stock E has a very large abnormal return.

For stocks B and T, the positive abnormal returns remain positive but do change in value.

4.

$$\text{Stock C} = \frac{47 - 43 + 1.50}{43} = 12.79\%$$

$$\text{C-match} = \frac{24 - 22 + 1.00}{22} = 13.64\%$$

$$\text{Stock R} = \frac{73 - 75 + 2.00}{75} = 0\%$$

$$\text{R-Match} = \frac{38 - 42 + 1.00}{42} = -7.14\%$$

$$\text{Stock L} = \frac{34 - 28 + 1.25}{28} = 25.89\%$$

$$\text{L-Match} = \frac{16 - 18 + 1.00}{18} = -5.55\%$$

$$\text{Stock W} = \frac{57 - 52 + 2.00}{52} = 13.46\%$$

$$\text{W-Match} = \frac{44 - 38 + 1.50}{38} = 19.74\%$$

$$\text{Stock S} = \frac{68 - 63 + 1.75}{63} = 10.71\%$$

$$\text{S-Match} = \frac{34 - 32 + 1.00}{32} = 9.37\%$$

Yes, this individual would be considered a superior analyst on balance. She has outperformed three of the five randomly selected stocks and her average return for the five stocks was 12.57% versus 6.01% for the five randomly selected stocks of equal risk. A wider selection of stocks would create a more accurate picture.

5.    Student Exercise

# CHAPTER 8

## <u>An Introduction To Portfolio Management</u>

# Answers to Questions

1.  Investors hold diversified portfolios in order to reduce the variance of the portfolio, which is considered a measure of risk of the portfolio. A diversified portfolio should accomplish this because the returns for the alternative assets should not be correlated so the variance of the total portfolio will be reduced.

2.  The covariance is equal to $E[(R_i - E(R_i))(R_j - E(R_j))]$ and indicates the absolute amount of comovement between two series. If they constantly move in the same direction, it will be a large positive value and vice versa. Covariance is important in portfolio theory because the variance of a portfolio is a combination of individual variances and the covariances among all assets in the portfolio. It is also shown that in a portfolio with a large number of securities, the variance of the portfolio becomes the average of all the covariances.

3.  Similar assets like common stock or stock for companies in the same industry (e.g., auto industry) will have high positive covariances because the sales and profits for the firms are being influenced by common factors since their customers and suppliers are the same. Because their profits and risk factors move together, you should expect the stock returns to likewise move together and have high covariance. The returns from different assets will not have as much covariance because the returns will not be as correlated. This is even more so for investments in different countries where the returns and risk factors are very unique.

4.  The covariance between the returns of asset i and j is affected by the variability of these two returns. Therefore, it is difficult to interpret the covariance figures without taking into account the variability of each return series. In contrast, the correlation coefficient is obtained by standardizing the covariance for the individual variability of the two return series, that is, $r_{ij} = cov_{i,j}/(\sigma_i \sigma_j)$.

    Thus, the correlation coefficient can only vary in the range of -1 to +1. A value of +1 would indicate a perfect linear positive relationship between $R_i$ and $R_j$.

5.　The efficient frontier has a curvilinear shape because if the set of possible portfolios of assets is not perfectly correlated, the set of relations will not be a straight line, but curved, depending on the correlation. The lower the correlation, the more curved.

6.

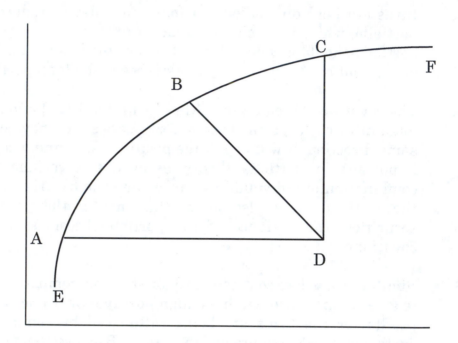

*Expected Rate of Return*

*Expected Risk (σ of return)*

A portfolio dominates another portfolio if 1) it has a higher expected return than another portfolio with the same level of risk, 2) a lower level of expected risk than another portfolio with equal expected return, or 3) a higher expected return and lower expected risk than another portfolio. For example, portfolio B dominates D by the first criteria; A dominates D by the second; and C dominates D by the third.

The Markowitz efficient frontier is simply a set of portfolios that is not dominated by any other portfolio; namely, those lying along the segment E-F.

7.  The necessary information for the program would be:

    A.  The expected rate of return
    B.  The expected variance of return
    C.  The expected covariance of return with every other feasible stock under consideration.

8.  Investors' utility curves are important because they indicate the desired tradeoff by investors between risk and return. Given the efficient frontier, they indicate which portfolio is preferable for the given investor. Notably, because utility curves differ, one should expect different investors to select different portfolios on the efficient frontier.

9.  The optimal portfolio for a given investor is the point of tangency between his set of utility curves and the efficient frontier. This will most likely be a diversified portfolio because almost all the portfolios on the frontier are diversified except for the two end points – the minimum variance portfolio and the maximum return portfolio. These two could be significant.

10. The utility curves for an individual specify the trade-offs he/she is willing to make between expected return and risk. These utility curves are used in conjunction with the efficient frontier to determine which particular efficient portfolio is the best for a particular investor. Two investors will not choose the same portfolio from the efficient set unless their utility curves are identical.

11. Student Exercise

# Answers to Problems

1.  $[E(R_i)]$ for Lauren Labs:

| Probability | Possible Returns | Expected Return |
|:-----------:|:----------------:|:---------------:|
| 0.10 | -0.20 | -0.0200 |
| 0.15 | -0.05 | -0.0075 |
| 0.20 | 0.10 | 0.0200 |
| 0.25 | 0.15 | 0.0375 |
| 0.20 | 0.20 | 0.0400 |
| 0.10 | 0.40 | 0.0400 |
| | $E(R_i) =$ | 0.1100 |

2.

| Stock | Market Value | Weight $(W_i)$ | Expected Security Return $(R_i)$ | Expected Portfolio Return $W_i \times R_i$ |
|-------|:-----------:|:-----:|:-----:|:-----:|
| Phillips | $15,000 | .16 | 0.14 | .0224 |
| Ford | 17,000 | .18 | -0.04 | -.0072 |
| Inter. Paper | 32,000 | .34 | 0.18 | .0612 |
| Apple | 23,000 | .24 | 0.16 | .0384 |
| Walgreen's | 7,000 | .08 | 0.05 | .0040 |
| | $94,000 | | $E(R_{port}) =$ | .1188 |

3.

| Month | Microsoft $(R_i)$ | General Electric $(R_j)$ | $R_i - E(R_i)$ | $R_j - E(R_j)$ | $[R_i - E(R_i)] \times [R_j - E(R_j)]$ |
|---|---|---|---|---|---|
| 1 | -.04 | .07 | -.057 | .06 | -.0034 |
| 2 | .06 | -.02 | .043 | -.03 | -.0013 |
| 3 | -.07 | -.10 | -.087 | -.11 | .0096 |
| 4 | .12 | .15 | .103 | .14 | .0144 |
| 5 | -.02 | -.06 | -.037 | -.07 | .0026 |
| 6 | .05 | .02 | .033 | .01 | .0003 |
| Sum | .10 | .06 | | | .0222 |

3(a). $E(R_i) = .10 / 6 = .017$      $E(R_j) = .06 / 6 = .01$

3(b). $\sigma_i = \sqrt{.0257 / 6} \quad = \quad \sqrt{.0043} \quad = \quad .0654$

$\sigma_j = \sqrt{.04120 / 6} \quad = \quad \sqrt{.006867} \quad = \quad .0829$

3(c). $COV_{ij} \quad = \quad 1/6 \ (.0222) \quad = \quad .0037$

3(d).

$r_{ij} \quad = \quad \dfrac{.0037}{(.0654)\ (.0829)}$

$= \quad \dfrac{.0037}{.0054}$

$= \quad .685$

4.  $E(R_1)$      =    .15          $E(\sigma_1)$ =      .10          $W_1$    =      .5

    $E(R_2)$      =    .20          $E(\sigma_2)$ =      .20          $W_2$    =      .5

    $E(R_{port})$ =    .5 (.15) + .5 (.20) =      .175

    If $r_{1,2}$  =    .40

    $\sigma_p$    =    $\sqrt{(.5)^2 (.10)^2 + (.5)^2 (.20)^2 + 2(.5)(.5)(.10)(.20)(.40)}$

                  =    $\sqrt{.0025 + .01 + .004}$

                  =    $\sqrt{.0165}$

                  =    .12845

    If $r_{1,2}$  =    -.60

    $\sigma_p$    =    $\sqrt{(.5)^2 (.10)^2 + (.5)^2 (.20)^2 + 2(.5)(.5)(.10)(.20)(-.60)}$

                  =    $\sqrt{.0025 + .01 + (-.006)}$

                  =    $\sqrt{.0065}$

                  =    .08062

The negative correlation curtails risk without sacrificing return.

5. For all values of $r_{1,2}$:

$$E(R_{port}) = (.6 \times .10) + (.4 \times .15) = .12$$

$$\sigma_{port} = \sqrt{(.6)^2 (.03)^2 + (.4)^2 (.05)^2 + 2 (.6) (.4) (.03) (.05) (r_{1,2})}$$

$$= \sqrt{.000324 + .0004 + .00072 (r_{1,2})}$$

$$= \sqrt{.000724 + .00072 (r_{1,2})}$$

5(a). $\sqrt{.000724 + .00072(1.0)} = \sqrt{.001444} = .0380$

5(b). $\sqrt{.000724 + .00072(.75)} = \sqrt{.001264} = .0356$

5(c). $\sqrt{.000724 + .00072(.25)} = \sqrt{.000904} = .0301$

5(d)             $\sqrt{.000724 + .00072(.00)} = \sqrt{.000724} = .0269$

5(e)             $\sqrt{.000724 + .00072(-.25)} = \sqrt{.000544} = .0233$

5(f)             $\sqrt{.000724 + .00072(-.75)} = \sqrt{.000184} = .0136$

5(g).            $\sqrt{.000724 + .00072(-1.0)} = \sqrt{.000004} = .0020$

6(a).   $E(R_p) =$      $(1.00 \times .12) + (.00 \times .16) = .12$

        $\sigma_p$    $=$     $\sqrt{(1.00)^2 (.04)^2 + (.00)^2 (.06)^2 + 2(1.00)(.00)(.04)(.06)(.70)}$

                $=$     $\sqrt{.0016 + 0 + 0} = \sqrt{.0016} = .04$

6(b).   $E(R_p) =$      $(.75 \times .12) + (.25 \times .16) = .13$

        $\sigma_p$    $=$     $\sqrt{(.75)^2 (.04)^2 + (.25)^2 (.06)^2 + 2 (.75) (.25) (.04) (.06) (.70)}$

                $=$     $\sqrt{.0009 + .000225 + .00063} = \sqrt{.001755} = .0419$

6(c).  $E(R_p) =$   $(.50 \times .12) + (.50 \times .16) = .14$

$\sigma_p =$  $\sqrt{(.50)^2 (.04)^2 + (.50)^2 (.06)^2 + 2 (.50) (.50) (.04) (.06) (.70)}$

$=$  $\sqrt{.0004 + .0009 + .00084}$   $=$   $\sqrt{.00214} = .0463$

6(d).  $E(R_p) =$   $(.25 \times .12) + (.75 \times .16)$   $=$   $.15$

$\sigma_p =$  $\sqrt{(.25)^2 (.04)^2 + (.75)^2 (.06)^2 + 2 (.25) (.75) (.04) (.06) (.70)}$

$=$  $\sqrt{.0001 + .002025 + .00063}$   $=$   $\sqrt{.002755} = .0525$

6(e).  $E(R_p) =$   $(.05 \times .12) + (.95 \times .16)$   $=$   $.158$

$\sigma_p =$  $\sqrt{(.05)^2 (.04)^2 + (.95)^2 (.06)^2 + 2 (.05) (.95) (.04) (.06) (.70)}$

$=$  $\sqrt{.000004 + .003249 + .00015960} = \sqrt{.0034126} = .0584$

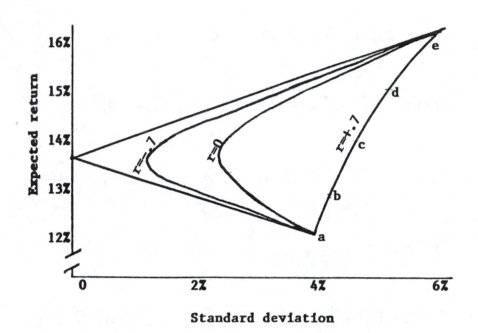

7.

| Month | DJIA $(R_1)$ | S&P $(R_2)$ | AMEX $(R_3)$ | Nikkei $(R_4)$ | $R_1-E(R_1)$ | $R_2-E(R_2)$ | $R_3-E(R_3)$ | $R_4-E(R_4)$ |
|---|---|---|---|---|---|---|---|---|
| 1 | .03 | .02 | .04 | .04 | .00167 | .00333 | .01333 | .00833 |
| 2 | .07 | .06 | .10 | -.02 | .05667 | .04333 | .07333 | -.05167 |
| 3 | -.02 | -.01 | -.04 | .07 | -.03333 | -.02667 | -.06667 | .03883 |
| 4 | .01 | .03 | .03 | .02 | -.00333 | .01333 | .00333 | -.01167 |
| 5 | .05 | .04 | .11 | .02 | .03667 | .02333 | .08333 | -.01167 |
| 6 | -.06 | -.04 | -.08 | .06 | -.07333 | -.05667 | -.10667 | .02833 |
| Sum | .08 | .10 | .16 | .19 | | | | |

7(a). $E(R_1) = \dfrac{.08}{6} = .01333$      $E(R_2) = \dfrac{.10}{6} = .01667$

$E(R3) = \dfrac{.16}{6} = .02667$      $E(R4) = \dfrac{.19}{6} = .03167$

7(b). $\Sigma_1 = (.01667)^2 + (.05667)^2 + (-.03333)^2 + (-.00333)^2 +$

               $(.03667)^2 + (-.07333)^2$

     $= .00028 + .00321 + .00111 + .00001 + .00134 + .00538$

     $= .01133$

$\sigma_1^2 = .01133/6 = .00189$

$\sigma_1 = \sqrt{.00189} = .04345$

$\Sigma_2 = (-.00333)^2 + (.04333)^2 + (-.02667)^2 + (.01333)^2 + (.02333)^2 +$

               $(-.05667)^2$

     $= .00001 + .00188 + .00071 + .00018 + .00054 + .00321$

     $= .00653$

$\sigma_2^2 = .00653 / 6 = .00109$

$\sigma_2 = \sqrt{.00109} = .03299$

$\Sigma_3$ = $(.01333)^2 + (.07333)^2 + (-.06667)^2 + (.00333)^2 + (.08333)^2 + (-.10667)^2$

= $.00018 + .00538 + .00444 + .00001 + .00694 + .01138$

= $.02833$

$\sigma_3^2$ = $.02833 / 6$ = $.00472$

$\sigma_3$ = $\sqrt{.00472}$ = $.06870$

$\Sigma_4$ = $(.00833)^2 + (-.05167)^2 + (.03833)^2 + (-.01167)^2 + (.02833)^2$

= $.00007 + .00267 + .00147 + .00014 + .00014 + .00080$

= $.00529$

$\sigma_4^2$ = $.00529 / 6$ = $.00088$

$\sigma_4$ = $\sqrt{.00088}$ = $.02970$

7(c). $COV_{1,2}$ = $\dfrac{.00006 + .00246 + .00089 - .00004 + 00086 + .00416}{6}$

= $.00839 / 6$ = $.00140$

$COV_{2,3}$ = $\dfrac{.00004 + .00318 + .00178 + .00004 + .00194 + .00604}{6}$

= $.01302 / 6$ = $.00217$

$$COV_{2,4} = \frac{.00003 - .00224 - .00102 - .00016 - .00027 - .00161}{6}$$

$$= -.00527 / 6 = -.00088$$

$$COV_{3,4} = \frac{.00011 - .00379 - .00256 - .00004 - .00097 - .00302}{6}$$

$$= -.01027 / 6 = -.00171$$

7(d).  $$R_{1,2} = \frac{.00140}{(.04345)\ (.03299)} = .98$$

$$R_{2,3} = \frac{.00217}{(.03299)\ (.06870)} = .96$$

$$R_{2,4} = \frac{.00088}{(.03299)\ (.02970)} = -.90$$

$$R_{3,4} = \frac{-.00171}{(.06870)\ (.02970)} = -.84$$

$$SD_{2,3} = \sqrt{.5^2(.03299)^2 + .5^2(.06870)^2 + 2(.5)(.5)(.00217)}$$

$$\sqrt{.00027 + .00118 + .00109} = .05035$$

$$RET_{2,4} = .5(.01667) + .5(.03167) = .02417$$

$$SD_{2,4} = \sqrt{.5^2(.03299)^2 + .5^2(.02970)^2 + 2(.5)(.5)(-.00091)}$$

$$= \sqrt{.00027 + .00022 - .00046} = .00548$$

Because the S&P-Nikkei correlation was negative (-.90), their combination led to a low standard deviation (.00548). On the other hand, the highly positive correlation between the S&P and AMEX (+.96) prevented any meaningful reduction in risk (.05035) when they were combined in a portfolio

8 - 16

# APPENDICES 8A and 8B

# Answers to Problems

## Appendix A

1(a). When $E(\sigma_1) = E(\sigma_2)$, the problem can be solved by substitution,

$$W_1 = \frac{E(\sigma_1)^2 - r_{1,2} \, E(\sigma_1) \, E(\sigma_1)}{E(\sigma_1)^2 + E(\sigma_1)^2 - 2 \, r_{1,2} \, E(\sigma_1) \, E(\sigma_1)}$$

so that

$$W_1 = \frac{E(\sigma_1)^2 \, [1 - r_{1,2}]}{2 \, E(\sigma_1)^2 - 2 \, r_{1,2} \, E(\sigma_1)^2}$$

$$= \frac{E(\sigma_1)^2 \, [1 - r_{1,2}]}{2 \, E(\sigma_1)^2 \, [1 - r_{1,2}]}$$

$$= \tfrac{1}{2} = .5$$

1(b). $$W_1 = \frac{(.06)^2 - (.5) \, (.04) \, (.06)}{(.04)^2 + (.06)^2 - 2(.5) \, (.04) \, (.06)}$$

$$= \frac{.0036 - .0012}{.0016 + .0036 - .0024}$$

$$= \quad \frac{.0024}{.0028} \quad = \quad .8571 \ \ (\text{or } 6/7)$$

## Appendix B

1.  $\quad W_1 \quad = \quad \dfrac{.06}{.04 + .06} \quad = \quad .6$

$\quad\quad W_2 \quad = \quad 1 - .6 \quad = \quad .4$

# CHAPTER 9

## An Introduction To Asset Pricing Models

# Answers to Questions

1. It can be shown that the expected return function is a weighted average of the individual returns. In addition, it is shown that by combining any portfolio with the risk-free asset, the standard deviation of the combination is only a function of the weight for the risky asset portfolio. Therefore, since both the expected return and the variance are simple weighted averages, the combination will lie along a straight line.

2. *Expected Rate of Return*

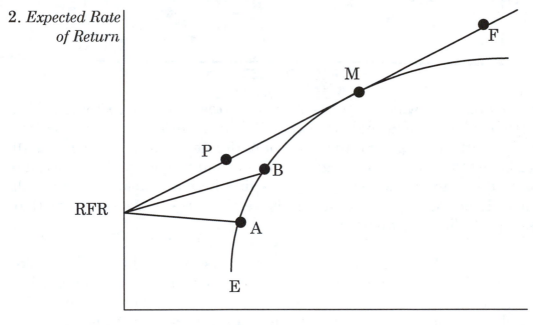

*Expected Risk ($\sigma$ of return)*

The existence of a risk-free asset excludes the E-A segment of the efficient frontier because any point below A is dominated by the RFR. In fact, the entire efficient frontier below M is dominated by points on the RFR-M Line (combinations obtained by investing a part of the portfolio in the risk-free asset and the remainder in M), e.g., the point P dominates the previously efficient B because it has lower risk for the same level of return. As shown,

M is at the point where the ray from RFR is tangent to the efficient frontier. The new efficient frontier thus becomes RFR-M-F.

3.

This figure indicates what happens as a risk-free asset is combined with risky portfolios higher and higher on the efficient frontier. In each case, as you combine with the higher return portfolio, the new line will dominate all portfolios below this line. This program continues until you combine with the portfolio at the point of tangency and this line becomes dominant over all prior lines. It is not possible to do any better because there are no further risky asset portfolios at a higher point.

4.     The "M" or "market" portfolio contains all risky assets available. If a risky asset, be it an obscure bond or a rare stamp, was not included in the market portfolio, then there would be no demand for this asset, and consequently, its price would fall. Notably, the price decline would continue to the point where the return would make the asset desirable such that it would be part of the M portfolio--e.g., if the bonds of ABC Corporation were selling for 100 and had a coupon of 8 percent, the investor's return would be 8 percent; however, if there was no demand for ABC bonds the price would fall, say to 80, at which point the 10 percent (80/800) return might make it a desirable investment. Conversely, if the demand for ABC bonds was greater than supply, prices would be bid up to the point where the return would be in equilibrium. In either case, ABC bonds would be included in the market portfolio.

5.   Leverage indicates the ability to borrow funds and invest these added funds in the market portfolio of risky assets. The idea is to increase the risk of the portfolio (because of the leverage), and also the expected return from the portfolio. It is shown that if you can borrow at the RFR then the set of leveraged portfolios is simply a linear extension of the set of portfolios along the line from the RFR to the market portfolio. Therefore, the full CML becomes a line from the RFR to the M portfolio and continuing upward.

6.   You can measure how well diversified a portfolio is by computing the extent of correlation between the portfolio in question and a completely diversified portfolio--i.e., the market portfolio. The idea is that, if a portfolio is completely diversified and, therefore, only has systematic risk, it should be perfectly correlated with another portfolio that only has systematic risk.

7.   Standard deviation would be expected to decrease with an increase in stocks in the portfolio because an increase in number will increase the probability of having more inversely correlated stocks. There will be a major decline from 4 to 10 stocks, a continued decline from 10 to 20 but at a slower rate. Finally, from 50 to 100 stocks, there is a further decline but at a very slow rate because almost all unsystematic risk is eliminated by about 18 stocks.

8.   Given the existence of the CML, everyone should invest in the same risky asset portfolio, the market portfolio. The only difference among individual investors should be in the financing decision they make, which depends upon their risk preference. Specifically, investors initially make investment decisions to invest in the market portfolio, M. Subsequently, based upon their risk preferences, they make financing decisions as to whether to borrow or lend to attain the preferred point on the CML.

9.   It may be recalled that the relevant risk variable for an individual security in a portfolio is its average covariance with all other risky assets in the portfolio. Given the CML, however, there is only one relevant portfolio and this portfolio is the market portfolio that contains all risky assets. Therefore, the relevant risk measure for an individual risky asset is its covariance with all other assets, namely the market portfolio.

10.  Systematic risk refers to that portion of total variability of returns caused by factors affecting the prices of all securities, e.g., economic, political and sociological changes--factors that are uncontrollable, external, and broad in their effect on all securities.

Unsystematic risk refers to factors that are internal and "unique" to the industry or company, e.g., management capability, consumer preferences, labor strikes, etc. Notably, it is not possible to get rid of the overall systematic risk, but it is possible to eliminate the "unique" risk for an individual asset in a diversified portfolio.

11.    In a capital asset pricing model (CAPM) world the relevant risk variable is the security's systematic risk--its covariance of return with all other risky assets in the market. This risk cannot be eliminated. The unsystematic risk is not relevant because it can be eliminated through diversification--for instance, when you hold a large number of securities, the poor management capability, etc., of some companies will be offset by the above average capability of others.

12.    The CML is an upward-sloping line in total risk-return space along which completely-diversified portfolios plot. The SML is an upward-sloping line in market risk-return space along which fairly-priced assets plot.

13.    Any three of the following are criticisms of beta as used in CAPM.

1. Theory does not measure up to practice. In theory, a security with a zero beta should give a return exactly equal to the risk-free rate. But actual results do not come out that way, implying that the market values something besides a beta measure of risk.

2. Beta is a fickle short-term performer. Some short-term studies have shown risk and return to be negatively related. For example, Black, Jensen and Scholes found that from April 1957 through December 1965, securities with higher risk produced lower returns than less risky securities. This result suggests that (1) in some short periods, investors may be penalized for taking on more risk, (2) in the long run, investors are not rewarded enough for high risk and are overcompensated for buying securities with low risk, and (3) in all periods, some unsystematic risk is being valued by the market.

3.   Estimated betas are unstable. Major changes in a company affecting the character of the stock or some unforeseen event not reflected in past returns may decisively affect the security's future returns.

4. Beta is easily rolled over. Richard Roll has demonstrated that by changing the market index against which betas are measured, one can obtain quite different measures of the risk level of individual stocks and portfolios. As a result, one would make different predictions about the expected returns, and by changing indexes, one could change the risk-adjusted performance ranking of a manager.

14. Under CAPM, the only risk that investors should be compensated for bearing is the risk that cannot be diversified away (systematic risk). Because systematic risk (measured by beta) is equal to one for both portfolios, an investor would expect the same return for Portfolio I and II.

   Since both portfolios are fully diversified, it doesn't matter if the specific risk for each individual security is high or low. The specific risk has been diversified away for both portfolios.

15. Part A

   The concepts are explained as follows:

   The Foundation's portfolio currently holds a number of securities from two asset classes. Each of the individual securities has its own risk (and return) characteristics, described as specific risk. By including a sufficiently large number of holdings, the specific risks of the individual holdings offset each other, diversifying away much of the overall specific risk and leaving mostly nondiversifiable, or market-related, risk.

   Systematic risk is this market-related risk that cannot be diversified away. Because systematic risk cannot be diversified away, investors are rewarded for assuming this risk.

   The variance of an individual security is the sum of the probability-weighted average of the squared differences between the security's expected return and its mean return. The standard deviation is the square root of the variance. Both variance and standard deviation measure total risk, including both systematic and specific risk. Assuming the rates of return are normally distributed, the likelihood for a range of rates may be expressed using standard deviations. For example, 68 percent of returns can be expected to fall within + or -1 standard deviation of the mean, and 95 percent within 2 standard deviations of the mean.

Covariance measures the extent to which two securities tend to move, or not move, together. The level of covariance is heavily influenced by the degree of correlation between the securities (the correlation coefficient) as well as by each security's standard deviation. As long as the correlation coefficient is less than 1, the portfolio standard deviation is less than the weighted average of the individual securities' standard deviations. The lower the correlation, the lower the covariance and the greater the diversification benefits (negative correlations provide more diversification benefits than positive correlations).

The capital asset pricing model (CAPM) asserts that investors will hold only fully diversified portfolios. Hence, total risk as measured by the standard deviation is not relevant because it includes specific risk (which can be diversified away).

Under the CAPM, beta measures the systematic risk of an individual security or portfolio. Beta is the slope of the characteristic line that relates a security's returns to the returns of the market portfolio. By definition, the market itself has a beta of 1.0. The beta of a portfolio is the weighted average of the betas of each security contained in the portfolio. Portfolios with betas greater than 1.0 have systematic risk higher than that of the market; portfolios with betas less than 1.0 have lower systematic risk. By adding securities with betas that are higher (lower), the systematic risk (beta) of the portfolio can be increased (decreased) as desired.

Part B

Without performing the calculations, one can see that the portfolio return would increase because: (1) Real estate has an expected return equal to that of stocks. (2) Its expected return is higher than the return on bonds.

The addition of real estate would result in a reduction of risk because: (1) The standard deviation of real estate is less than that of both stocks and bonds. (2) The covariance of real estate with both stocks and bonds is negative.

9 - 8

The addition of an asset class that is not perfectly correlated with existing assets will reduce variance. The fact that real estate has a negative covariance with the existing asset classes will reduce risk even more.

Part C

Capital market theory holds that efficient markets prevent mispricing of assets and that expected return is proportionate to the level of risk taken. In this instance, real estate is expected to provide the same return as stocks and a higher return than bonds. Yet, it is expected to provide this return at a lower level of risk than both bonds and stocks. If these expectations were realistic, investors would sell the other asset classes and buy real estate, pushing down its return until it was proportionate to the level of risk.

Appraised values differ from transaction prices, reducing the accuracy of return and volatility measures for real estate. Capital market theory was developed and applied to the stock market, which is a very liquid market with relatively small transaction costs. In contrast to the stock market, real estate markets are very thin and lack liquidity.

# Answers to Problems

1.

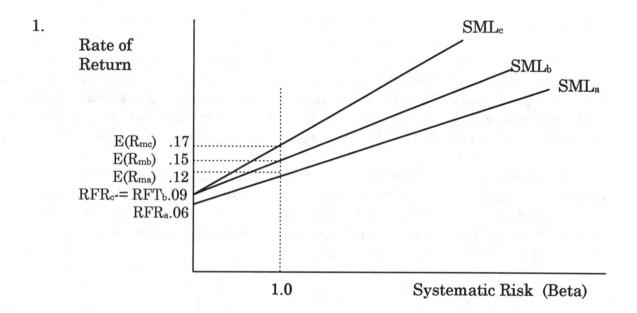

In (b), a change in risk-free rate, with other things being equal, would result in a new SML$_b$, which would intercept with the vertical axis at the new risk-free rate (.09) and would be parallel in the original SML$_a$.

In (c), this indicates that not only did the risk-free rate change from .06 to .09, but the market risk premium per unit of risk [E(Rm) - Rf] also changed from .06 (.12 - .06) to .08 (.17 - .09). Therefore, the new SMLc will have an intercept at .09 and a different slope so it will no longer be parallel to SMLa.

2.     E(Ri)  = RFR + Bi(RM - RFR)

          = .10 + Bi(.14 - .10)

          = .10 + .04Bi

| Stock | Beta | (Required Return) E(Ri) = .10 + .04Bi |
|-------|------|----------------------------------------|
| U | .85 | .10 + .04(.85) = .10 + .034 = .134 |
| N | 1.25 | .10 + .04(1.25) = .10 + .05 = .150 |
| D | -.20 | .10 + .04(-.20) = .10 - .008 = .092 |

3.

| Stock | Current Price | Expected Price | Expected Dividend | Estimated Return | |
|-------|---------------|----------------|-------------------|------------------|-----|
| U | 22 | 24 | 0.75 | $\dfrac{24 - 22 + 0.75}{22}$ | = .1250 |
| N | 48 | 51 | 2.00 | $\dfrac{51 - 48 + 2.00}{48}$ | = .1042 |
| D | 37 | 40 | 1.25 | $\dfrac{40 - 37 + 1.25}{37}$ | = .1149 |

| Stock | Beta | Required | Estimated | Evaluation |
|-------|------|----------|-----------|------------|
| U | .85 | .134 | .1250 | Overvalued |
| N | 1.25 | .150 | .1042 | Overvalued |
| D | -.20 | .092 | .1149 | Undervalued |

If you believe the appropriateness of these estimated returns, you would buy stocks D and sell stocks U and N.

Graph applies to both problem 2 and problem 3.

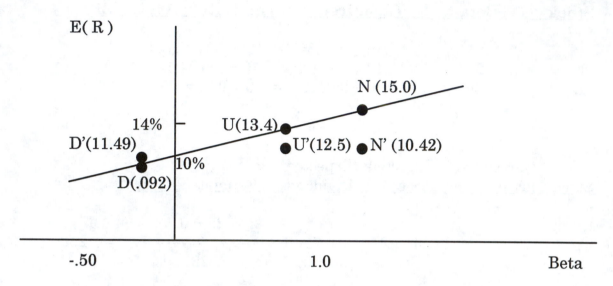

U, N, D : Required returns
U', N', D' : Estimated returns

4.    Student Exercise

5.    Student Exercise

6.    Student Exercise

7.    Student Exercise

8.    Student Exercise

9.    Student Exercise

10.   Student Exercise

11(a). $B_i = \dfrac{COV_{i,m}}{\sigma_m^2}$   and   $r_{i,m} = \dfrac{COV_{i,m}}{(\sigma_i)(\sigma_m)}$

then  COVi,m      =        (ri,m)(åi)(åm)

**For Apple:**

COVi,m      =        (.72)(.1210)(.0550) = .00479

Beta  =        $\dfrac{.00479}{.0030}$      = 1.597

**For Chrysler:**

COVi,m      =        (.33)(.1460)(.0550) = .00265

Beta  =        $\dfrac{.00265}{.0030}$      = .883

**For Anheuser Busch:**

COVi,m      =        (.55)(.0760)(.0550) = .00230

Beta  =        $\dfrac{.00230}{.0030}$      = .767

**For Monsanto:**

COVi,m      =        (.60)(.1020)(.0550) = .00337

Beta  =        $\dfrac{.00337}{.0030}$      = 1.123

9 - 13

11(b).  $E(R_i) = RFR + B_i(R_M - RFR)$

   $= .08 + B_i(.15 - .08)$

   $= .08 + .07B_i$

| Stock | Beta | $E(R_i) = .08 + .07B_i$ |
|---|---|---|
| Apple | 1.597 | .08 + .1118 = .1918 |
| Chrysler | .883 | .08 + .0618 = .1418 |
| Anheuser Busch | .767 | .08 + .0537 = .1337 |
| Monsanto | 1.123 | .08 + .0786 = .1586 |

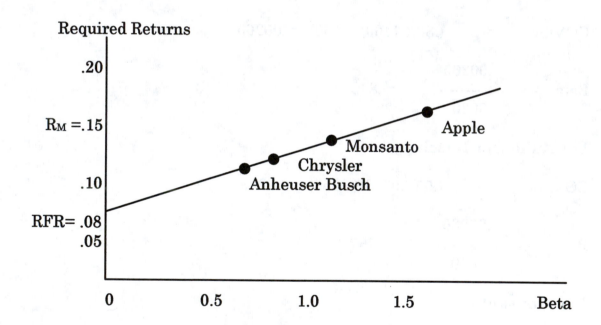

9 - 14

11(c). **Estimated Returns**

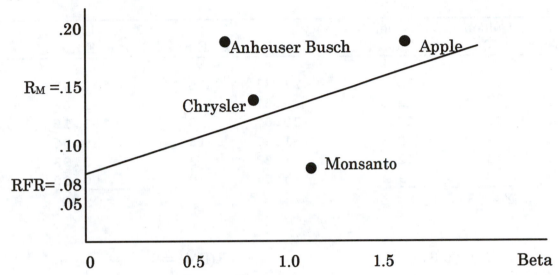

Undervalued stocks: Anheuser Busch, Chrysler, Apple
Overvalued stocks: Monsanto

12.    E(Ri) = RFR + Bi (RM - RFR)

        = .08 + Bi (.15 - .08)

        = .08 + .07Bi

12(a).    E(RA) = .08 + .07(1.72) = .08 + .1204 = .2004 = 20.04%

12(b).    E(RB) = .08 + .07(1.14) = .08 + .0798 = .1598 = 15.98%

12(c).    E(RC) = .08 + .07(0.76) = .08 + .0532 = .1332 = 13.32%

12(d).    E(RD) = .08 + .07(0.44) = .08 + .0308 = .1108 = 11.08%

12(e).    E(RE) = .08 + .07(0.03) = .08 + .0021 = .0821 = 8.21%

12(f).    E(RF) = .08 + .07(-0.79) = .08 + -.0553 = .0247 = 2.47%

**13.**

| Year | Golden $(R_1)$ | General Index $(R_M)$ | $R_1 - E(R_1)$ | $R_M - E(R_M)$ | $(R_1 - E(R_1))$ X $R_M - E(R_M)$ |
|------|------|------|------|------|------|
| 1 | 37 | 15 | 27.33 | 6 | 163.98 |
| 2 | 9 | 13 | -.67 | 4 | -2.68 |
| 3 | -11 | 14 | -20.67 | 5 | -103.35 |
| 4 | 8 | -9 | -1.67 | -18 | 30.06 |
| 5 | 11 | 12 | 1.33 | 3 | 3.99 |
| 6 | 4 | 9 | -5.67 | 0 | 0.00 |
| | $\Sigma = 58$ | $\Sigma = 54$ | | | $\Sigma = 92.00$ |

$$E(R1) = 9.67 \qquad\qquad E(RM) = 9$$

$$\text{Var}_1 = \frac{1211.33}{6} = 201.89 \qquad\qquad \text{Var}_M = \frac{410}{6} = 68.33$$

$$\sigma_1 = \sqrt{201.89} = 14.21 \qquad\qquad \sigma_M = \sqrt{68.33} = 8.27$$

$$\text{COV}_{1,M} = \frac{92.00}{6} = 15.33$$

**13(a).** The correlation coefficient can be computed as follows:

$$r_{1,M} = \frac{\text{COV}_{1,M}}{\sigma_1 \, \sigma_M} = \frac{15.33}{(14.21)(8.27)} = \frac{15.33}{117.52} = .13$$

**13(b).** $\sigma_1 = 14.21\%$

$\sigma_M = 8.27\%$

13(c). Beta for Golden Computer is computed as follows:

$$B_1 \; = \; \frac{COV_{1,M}}{Var_M} \; = \; \frac{15.33}{68.33} \; = .2244$$

14(a). Security market line

The security market line (SML) shows the required return for a given level of systematic risk. The SML is described by a line drawn from the risk-free rate: expected return is 5 percent, where beta equals O through the market return; expected return is 10 percent, where beta equals 1.0.

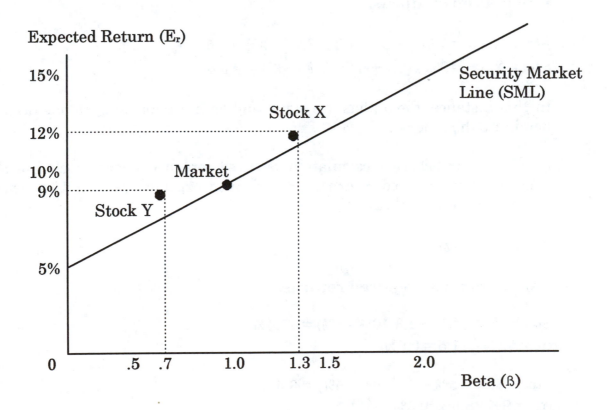

9 - 17

14(b). The expected risk-return relationship of individual securities may deviate from that suggested by the SML, and that difference is the asset's alpha. Alpha is the difference between the expected (estimated) rate of return for a stock and its required rate of return based on its systematic risk. Alpha is computed as

$$\text{ALPHA or } \alpha = E(r_i) - [r_f + \beta_i(E(r_M) - r_f)],$$

where

$E(r_i)$ = expected return on Security I
$r_f$ = risk-free rate
$\beta_i$ = beta for Security I
$E(r_M)$ = expected return on the market

**Calculation of alphas:**

Stock X: $\alpha_x = 12\% - [5\% + 1.3 (10\% - 5\%)] = 0.5\%$
Stock Y: $\alpha_r = 9\% - [5\% + 0.7(10\% - 5\%)] = 0.5\%$

In this instance, the alphas are equal and both are positive, so one does not dominate the other.

Another approach is to calculate a required return for each stock and then subtract that required return from the given expected return. The formula for required return (k) is

$$k = r_f + \beta_i (r_M - r_f).$$

**Calculations of required returns:**

Stock X: k = 5% + 1.3(10% - 5%) = 11.5%
$\alpha_x$ = 12% - 11.5 = 0.5%

Stock Y: k = 5% + 0.7(10% - 5%) = 8.5%
$\alpha_x$ = 9% - 8.5%=0.5%

14(c). By increasing the risk-free rate from 5 percent to 7 percent and leaving all other factors unchanged, the slope of the SML flattens and the expected return per unit of incremental risk becomes less. Using the formula for alpha, the alpha of Stock X increases to 1.1 percent and the alpha of Stock Y falls to -0.1 percent. In this situation, the expected return (12.0 percent) of Stock X exceeds its required return (10.9 percent) based on the CAPM. Therefore, Stock X's alpha (1.1 percent) is positive. For Stock Y, its expected return (9.0 percent) is below its required return (9.1 percent) based on the CAPM. Therefore, Stock Y's alpha (-0.1 percent) is negative. Stock X is preferable to Stock Y under these circumstances.

**Calculations of revised alphas:**

Stock X: $\alpha_x = 12\% - [7\% + 1.3 (10\% - 7\%)]$

$= 12\% - 10.95\% = 1.1\%$

Stock Y: $\alpha_y = 9\% - [7\% + 0.7(10\% - 7\%)]$

$= 9\% - 9.1\% = -0.1\%$

# CHAPTER 10

# Extensions And Testing Of Asset Pricing Theories

# Answers to Questions

1. First, the stability of beta: It is important to know whether it is possible to use past betas as estimates of future betas. Second, is there a relationship between beta and rates of return? This would indicate whether the CAPM is a relevant pricing model that can explain rates of return on risky assets.

2. Given that beta is the principal risk measure, stable betas make it easier to forecast future beta measures of systematic risk – i.e., can betas measured from past data be used in making investment decisions?

3. The results of the stability of beta studies indicate that betas for individual stocks are generally **not** stable, but **portfolios** of stocks have **stable** betas.

4. Is there a positive linear relationship between the systematic risk of risky assets and the rates of return on these assets? Are the coefficients positive and significant? Is the intercept close to the risk-free rate of return?

5. 

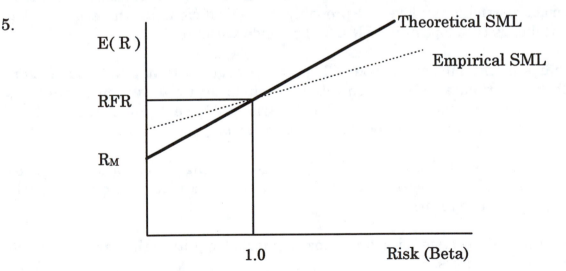

In the empirical line, low risk securities did better than expected, while high risk securities did not do as well as predicted.

6.  The "market" portfolio contains all risky assets available. If a risky asset, be it an obscure bond or rare stamp, was not included in the market portfolio, then there would be no demand for this asset and, consequently, its price would fall. Notably, the price decline would continue to the point where the return would make the asset desirable such that it would be part of the "market" portfolio. The weights for all risky assets are equal to their relative market value.

    While the concept of a market portfolio is reasonable in theory, it is difficult, if not impossible, to implement when testing or using the CAPM. As a result, the majority of studies have used the S & P 500 Index as a proxy for the market portfolio.

7.  According to Roll, a mistakenly specified proxy for the market portfolio can have two effects. First, the beta computed for alternative portfolios would be wrong because the market portfolio is inappropriate. Second, the SML derived would be wrong because it goes from the RFR through the improperly specified market portfolio. In general, when comparing the performance of a portfolio manager to the "benchmark" portfolio, these errors will tend to **overestimate** the performance of portfolio managers because the proxy market portfolio employed is probably not as efficient as the true market portfolio, so the slope of the SML will be underestimated.

8.  Studies of the efficient markets hypothesis suggest that additional factors affecting estimates of expected returns include firm size, the price-earnings ratio, and financial leverage. These variables have been shown to have predictive ability with respect to security returns.

9.  Fama and French found that size, leverage, earnings-price ratios, and book value to market value of equity all have a significant impact on univariate tests on average return.

    In multivariate tests, size and book to market equity value are the major explanatory factors.

10. Three major assumptions of APT:

    A.  Capital markets are perfectly competitive.

B.      Investors always prefer more wealth to less wealth with certainty.

C.      The stochastic process generating asset returns can be represented as a k factor model.

This theory does not require that investors have a quadratic utility function, that security returns be normally distributed, nor that there be a market portfolio which contains all risky assets that are mean-variance efficient.

11.     Various studies have been performed to test specific hypotheses implicit in the theory. One such hypothesis was that the APT theory would be able to account for the differences in average returns between small firms and large firms. A study by Reinganum concluded that the APT does not explain these returns. Even after taking account of all risk as specified by the APT, the small firms have superior risk-adjusted returns. A subsequent study by Chen provided evidence related to the small firm effect contrary to Reinganum. After adjusting for risk by APT factor loadings, Chen concluded that firm size had no explanatory power.

12.     Shanken contends that because the APT is unable to identify the relevant factor structure that affects the asset returns of various securities, the theory is rendered incapable of explaining differential returns between securities. He feels that the APT is not testable because the relevant factor structure must be identified before you can test the APT.

13.     CFA Exam III (June 1986)

13(a).  The basic Capital Asset Pricing Model (CAPM) assumes that investors care only about portfolio risk and expected return; i.e., they are risk averse. From this assumption comes the conclusion that a portfolio's expected return will be related to only one attribute – its beta (sensitivity) relative to the broadly-based market portfolio.

Arbitrage Price Theory (APT) takes a different approach: it is not much concerned about investor preferences, and it assumes that returns are generated by a multi-factor model. APT reflects the fact that several major (systematic) economic factors may effect a given asset in varying degrees. Further, unlike the CAPM, whose single factor is unchanging, APT recognizes that these key factors can change over time (as can investor preferences).

Summarizing, APT 1) identifies several key systematic macroeconomic factors as part of the process that generates security returns vs. only one factor recognized by the CAPM, 2) recognizes that these key factors can change over time, whereas the CAPM's single factor is unchanging, 3) makes fewer assumptions about investor preferences than the CAPM, and 4) recognizes that these preferences can change over time.

13(b). The four systematic factors identified by Roll and Ross are unanticipated changes in: 1) inflation, 2) industrial production, 3) risk premiums, and 4) the slope of the term structure of interest rates.

The APT asserts that an asset's riskiness and, hence, the average long-term return, is directly related to its sensitivities in unanticipated changes in these four economic variables. This relationship may be expressed in equation form as follows:

$$R_i = R_0 + b_{i1} F_1 + b_{i2} F_2 + \ldots + b_{in} F_n$$

This means the return ($R_i$) that a certain asset (i) will produce is a combination of some "base" return ($R_0$) plus returns occasioned by the influences or sensitivities ($b_n$) of some systematic external factors ($F_n$).

# Answers to Problems

1.  The results indicate that the betas for Stock E will be smaller relative to the market proxy (1.25) than when compared to the true market (1.72). The reason for the differences in the measured beta stems from the fact that the market proxy does not contain all possible risky assets represented by the true market portfolio. This is a very reasonable relationship because it illustrates the smaller variances in return experienced by the true market portfolio as a result of greater diversification.

2.  Use Graph for both problem 2 and problem 3.

Condition B, with the SML line estimated with the true market portfolio, will present a more difficult scenario for the portfolio manager. The SML for the true market portfolio requires higher returns associated with a given amount of risk in order to outperform the market.

3. The student should superimpose the given portfolios on the graph used for problem 2. The graph indicates that no matter which SML line is used, portfolios A, C and D will achieve superior results, while portfolio B will tend to be overvalued.

4(a). The student should draw SML graphs based on the stated conditions and the following calculations:

| Period | Return of Radius | Proxy Index Return | True Index Return | Rradius-Rradius x (Rproxy-Rproxy) | (Rradius-Rradius) x (Rtrue-Rtrue) |
|--------|------------------|--------------------|--------------------|-----------------------------------|-----------------------------------|
| 1 | 29 | 12 | 15 | 94.0 | 75.2 |
| 2 | 12 | 10 | 13 | 5.4 | 3.6 |
| 3 | -12 | -9 | -8 | 355.2 | 421.8 |
| 4 | 17 | 14 | 18 | 47.6 | 47.6 |
| 5 | 20 | 25 | 28 | 176.4 | 166.6 |
| 6 | -5 | -10 | 0 | 258.4 | 167.2 |
| | R=10.2 | 7 | 11 | 937 | 882 |

4(b).

$$COV_{radius,\ proxy} = \frac{937}{6} = 156.2$$

$$COV_{radius,\ true} = \frac{882}{6} = 147.0$$

$$\text{Variance of Proxy Index} = \frac{952}{6} = 158.667$$

$$\text{Variance of True Index} = \frac{840}{6} = 140$$

10 - 8

$$\beta \text{ (using proxy index)} = \frac{156.2}{158.667} = .984$$

$$\beta \text{ (using true index)} = \frac{147.0}{140} = 1.050$$

4(c). $E(R_i) = RFR + \beta_i (R_m - RFR)$

$= .08 + .984 (.12 - .08)$

$= .08 + .039$

$= .119$

$E(R_i) = RFR + \beta_i (R_{m(true)} - RFR)$

$= .06 + 1.050(.15 - .06)$

$= .06 + .095$

$= .155$

Since the 11 percent actually earned is less than the expected 11.9 percent using the market proxy, the manager has not done a superior job.

5. $E(J) = .05 + .02(.80) + .04(1.4)$

$= .122$

$E(L) = .05 + .02(1.6) + .04 (2.25)$

$= .172$

# CHAPTER 11

## An Introduction To Derivative Markets And Securities

# Answers to Questions

1.  Since call values are positively related to stock prices while put values are negatively related, any action that causes a decline in stock price (e.g., a dividend) will have a differential impact on calls and puts. Specifically, an impending dividend will boost put values and depress call values.

    Another way to consider the situation is to represent the difference between the theoretical price of a call option (C) and the theoretical price of a put option (P) as C-P. This is the same as a portfolio that is long a call option and short a put option. For a firm that pays dividends, we expect that the price of its stock will decline by the amount of the dividend on the last day before the stock goes ex-dividend. A decline in stock price makes a call less valuable and a put more valuable, so C-P will decrease.

    This portfolio has the same payoff as being long a forward contract with a contract price equal to the strike price. Since there is no guarantee that the strike price is the forward price, this forward contract will typically have a non-zero value (i.e. the call and put will have different prices). A dividend will decrease the up-front premium for a long position in a forward contract because the expected stock price at expiration decreases. Consequently, C-P is decreased by dividends.

2.  It is generally true that futures contracts are traded on exchanges whereas forward contracts are done directly with a financial institution. Consequently, there is a liquid market for most exchange traded futures whereas there is no guarantee of closing-out a forward position quickly or cheaply. The liquidity of futures comes at a price, though. Because the futures contracts are exchange traded, they are standardized with set delivery dates and contract sizes.

    If having a delivery date or contract size that is not easily accommodated by exchange traded contracts is important to a future/forward end user then the forward may be more appealing. If liquidity is an important factor then the user may prefer the futures contract.

Another consideration is the mark-to-market property of futures. If a firm is hedging an exposure that is not marked-to-market, it may prefer to not have any intervening cash flows, hence it will prefer forwards.

3.  For forwards, calls and puts, what the long position gains, the short position loses, and vice versa. However, while payoffs to forward positions are *symmetric*, payoffs to call and put positions are *asymmetric*. That is to say, long and short forwards can gain as much as they can lose, whereas long calls and puts have a gain potential dramatically greater than their loss potential. Conversely, short calls and puts have gains limited to the option premium but fact unlimited liability.

For example, if the price of wheat declines by 10%, the losses to a long position in a futures contract on wheat would be the same as the gains if the price were to increase by 10%. For an at-the-money call option, there would be an asymmetric change in value. A long position in an at-the-money call option on wheat would decline in value less for a 10% fall in wheat prices than it would increase from a 10% rise in wheat prices.

|  | Loss Potential | Gain Potential | Symmetry |
|---|---|---|---|
| 1. Long Forward | -K | unlimited | symmetric |
| 2. Short Forward | unlimited | K | symmetric |
| 3. Long Call | Call premium | unlimited | asymmetric |
| 4. Short Call | unlimited | Call premium | asymmetric |
| 5. Long Put | Put premium | K | asymmetric |
| 6. Short Put | K | Put Premium | asymmetric |

4(a).  Derivatives can be used in an attempt to bridge the 90-day time gap in the following three ways:

(1)  The foundation could buy (long) calls on an equity index such as the S&P 500 Index and on Treasury bonds, notes, or bills. This strategy would require the foundation to make an immediate cash outlay for the "premiums" on the calls. If the foundation were to buy calls on the entire $45 million, the cost of these calls could be substantial, particularly if their strike prices were close to current stock and bond prices (i.e., the calls were close to being "in the money").

(2).    The foundation could write or sell (short) puts on an equity index and on Treasury bonds, notes, or bills. By writing puts, the foundation would receive an immediate cash inflow equal to the "premiums" on the puts (less brokerage commissions). If stock and bond prices rise as the committee expects, the puts would expire worthless, and the foundation would keep the premiums, thus hedging part or all of the market increase. If the prices fall, however, the foundation loses the difference between the strike price and the current market price, less the value of the premiums.

(3).    The foundation could buy (long) equity and fixed-income futures. This is probably the most practical way for the foundation to hedge its expected gift. Futures are available on the S&P 500 Index and on Treasury bonds, notes, and bills. No cash outlay would be required. Instead, the foundation could use some of its current portfolio as a good faith deposit or "margin" to take the long positions. The market value of the futures contracts will, in general, mirror changes in the underlying market values of the S&P 500 Index and Treasuries. Although no immediate cash outlay is required, any gains (losses) in the value of the contracts will be added (subtracted) from the margin deposit daily. Hence, if markets advance as the committee expects, the balances in the foundation's futures account should reflect the market increase.

4(b).    There are both positive and negative factors to be considered in hedging the 90 day gap before the expected receipt of the Franklin gift.

*Positive factors.*

(1).    The foundation could establish its position in stock and bond markets using derivatives today, and benefit in any subsequent increases in market values in the S&P Index and Treasury instruments in the 90-day period. In effect, the foundation would have a synthetic position in those markets beginning today.

(2).    The cost of establishing the synthetic position is relatively low, depending on the derivative strategy used. If calls are used, the cost is limited to the premiums paid. If futures are used, the losses on the

11 - 5

futures contracts would be similar to the amounts that would be lost if the foundation invested the gift today. Writing the puts is the riskiest strategy because there is an open ended loss if the market declines, but here again the losses would be similar if the foundation invested today and stock and bond markets declined.

(3).   Derivative markets (for the types of contracts under consideration here) are liquid.

*Negative factors.*

(1).   The Franklin gift could be delayed or not received at all. This would create a situation in which the foundation would have to unwind its position and could experience losses, depending on market movements in the underlying assets.

(2).   The committee might be wrong in its expectation that stock and bond prices will rise in the 90 day period. If prices decline on stocks and bonds, the foundation would lose part or all of the premium on the calls and have losses on the futures contracts and the puts written. The risk of loss of capital is a serious concern. (Given that the current investment is primarily bonds and cash, the foundation may not be knowledgeable enough to forecast stock prices over the next 90 days.)

(3).   Because there is a limited choice of option and futures derivative contract compared to the universe that the committee might wish to invest in, there could be a mismatch between the specific equities and bonds the foundation wishes to invest in and the contracts available in size for $45 million. Unless the 90 day period exactly matches the 90 day period before expiration  dates on the contracts, there may be a timing mismatch.

(4).   The cost of the derivatives is (potentially) high. For example, if the market in general shares the committee's optimistic outlook, the premiums paid for calls would be expensive and the premiums received on puts would be lean. The opportunity cost on all derivative strategies discussed would be large if the committee is wrong on the outlook for one or both markets.

(5). There may exist regulatory restrictions on the use of derivatives by endowment funds.

*Evaluation.*

The negative factors appear to outweigh the positive factors if the outlook for the market is neutral; therefore, the committee's decision on using derivatives to bridge the gap for 90 days will have to be related to the strength of its conviction that stock and bond prices will rise in that period. The certainty of receiving the gift in 90 days is also a factor. The committee should certainly beware that there is a cost to establish the derivative positions, especially if its expectations do not work out. The committee might want to consider a partial hedge of the $45 million.

5. Because Chen is considering adding either short index futures or long index options (a form of protective put) to an existing well-diversified equity portfolio, he evidently intends to create a hedged position for the existing portfolio. Both the short futures and the long options positions will reduce the risk of the resulting combined portfolios, but in different ways.

Assuming that the short futures contract is perfectly negatively correlated with the existing equity portfolio, and that the size of the futures position is sufficient to hedge the risk of the entire equity portfolio, any movement up or down in the level of stock market prices will result in offsetting gains and losses in the combined portfolio's two segments (the equity portfolio itself and the short futures position). Thus, Chen is effectively removing the portfolio from exposure to market movements by eliminating all systematic (market) risk (unsystematic (specific) risk has already been minimized because the equity portfolio is a well-diversified one). Once the equity portfolio has been perfectly hedged, no risk remains, and Chen can expect to receive the risk-free rate of return on the combined portfolio. If the hedge is less than perfect, some risk and some potential for return beyond the risk-free rate are present, but only in proportion to the completeness of the hedge.

If, on the other hand, Chen hedges the portfolio by purchasing stock index puts, he will be placing a floor price on the equity portfolio. If the market declines and the index value drops below the strike price of the puts, the value of the puts increases, offsetting the loss in the equity portfolio. Conversely, if the stock market rises, the value of the put options will decline, and they may expire worthless; however, the potential return to the combined portfolio is unlimited and reduced only by the cot of the puts. As with the short futures, if the long options hedge is less than perfect, down-side risk remains in the combined portfolio in proportion to the amount not covered by the puts.

In summary, either short futures or long options (puts) can be used to reduce or eliminate risk in the equity portfolio. Use of the options (put) strategy, however, permits unlimited potential returns to be realized (less the cost of the options) while use of the short futures strategy effectively guarantees the risk-free rate but reduces or eliminates potential returns above that level. Neither strategy dominates the other; each offers a different risk/return profile and involves different costs. Arbitrage ensures that, on a risk-adjusted basis, neither approach is superior.

6(a).   The important distinction between a futures contract and an options contract is that the futures contract is an obligation. When an investor purchases or sells a futures contract, the investor has an obligation to accept or deliver, respectively, the underlying commodity on the expiration date. In contrast, the buyer of an option contract is not obligated to accept or deliver the underlying commodity but instead has the right, or choice, to accept or deliver the underlying commodity anytime during the life of the contract.

Futures and options modify a portfolio's risk in different ways. Buying or selling a futures contract impacts on a portfolio's upside risk (volatility) and downside risk by a similar magnitude. This is referred to as symmetrical impact. Thus, the price of a futures contract varies directly with the price of the underlying obligation. On the other hand, the addition of a call or put option to a portfolio does not impact or portfolio's upside risk and downside risk to a similar magnitude. Unlike futures contracts, the impact of options on the risk profile of a portfolio is not asymmetrical.

6(b).   Although both options strategies reduce risk, they do so in very different ways and to different extents.

Under the covered call writing strategy, the owner of an asset writes (sells) a call option against the asset with the objective of retaining the option premium received. The receipt of this premium cushions against losses in the value of the asset (but only to the extent of the amount of the premium). However, the asset owner forfeits any gains in the asset's price beyond the strike (exercise) price of the call option.

The purchaser of a (protective) put option on an asset already owned limits possible losses to the price of the asset when the put is purchased less the put's striking price plus the premium paid. On the other hand, asset gains are unlimited after reduction by the amount of the put's cost.

Therefore, the asset owner pays a premium to purchase downside price protection with the protective put strategy, whereas a covered call writer receives a premium but in exchange foregoes much of the underlying asset's upside potential. The put strategy enables the investor to retain most of the upside potential of the underlying asset.

7.   The important distinction is whether the option is a covered or uncovered position.  If the option is added to a portfolio that already contains the underlying asset (or something highly correlated), then the option will frequently be a covered position and, consequently, lower overall risk.  For example, selling a call without owning the underlying asset leaves the seller open to unlimited liability and (probably) increases portfolio price fluctuation (risk).  But if the seller of the call owns the underlying asset, then selling the call neutralizes the portfolio from price changes above the strike price and (probably) decreases risk.

Because options are bets that an asset's price will be above or below some level (the strike price), they represent a way of leveraging one's subjective view on the asset's future price.  Options always cost less than the underlying asset and consequently can change in price more (on a percentage basis) than the underlying asset does.  This provides the same effect as borrowing money to buy the asset or selling the asset short and investing the proceeds in bonds.  (In fact, this is how option pricing theory values options, by replicating the price of an option using the underlying asset and bonds.)

8.   Call options differ from forward contracts in that calls have unlimited upside potential and limited downside potential, whereas the gains and losses from a forward contract are both unlimited.  Therefore, since call options do not

have the downside potential of forwards, they represent only the "good half" (the upside potential) of the forward contract. The "bad half" of the long forward position is the unlimited downside potential that is equivalent to being short a put. This is consistent with put-call parity where being long a call and short a put yields the same payoff as a forward contract.

9.  Since options have nonlinear (kinked) payoffs, broad market movements may have different relative effects on the value of a portfolio with options depending on whether the market moves up or down. For example, a portfolio that is put-protected may not move down much if the market declines 10% but may move up nearly 10% if the market rises 10%. Consequently, the returns are asymmetric or skewed. This makes standard deviation a less informative statistic because it reveals information only about the degree of variation and not the "direction" of the variation. Since investors usually care about downside risk (standard deviation), investors probably will not care as much if all of the variation is in the upside return. The standard deviation statistic could be modified to only measure the variation in negative returns (the so-called semi-variance) so that it was a measure of downside risk only.

10. A synthetic off-market forward contract with a forward price of $25 could be created using put-call parity. Buying a call struck at $25 and selling a put struck at $25 assures the investor of buying the stock at the expiration date for $25. This portfolio then has the same requirements as the off-market forward at $25. C-P is one-half of the put-call parity relationship, and we know it has to equal S-PV(K). Since S = $32 and the risk free-rate can be calculated as (35-32)/32 = 9.375%, we can calculate that the off-market forward is worth S-P($25) = $32-$25 / (1 + .09375) = $9.14.

# Answers to Problems

1(a).

(i) A long position in a forward with a contract price of $50.

| Expiration Date Tando Stock Price (S) | Long Forward (K=$50) Payoff = S-50 | Initial Long Forward Premium | Net Profit |
|---|---|---|---|
| 25 | ($25.00) | $0.00 | ($25.00) |
| 30 | ($20.00) | $0.00 | ($20.00) |
| 35 | ($15.00) | $0.00 | ($15.00) |
| 40 | ($10.00) | $0.00 | ($10.00) |
| 45 | ($5.00) | $0.00 | ($5.00) |
| 50 | $0.00 | $0.00 | $0.00 |
| 55 | $5.00 | $0.00 | $5.00 |
| 60 | $10.00 | $0.00 | $10.00 |
| 65 | $15.00 | $0.00 | $15.00 |
| 70 | $20.00 | $0.00 | $20.00 |
| 75 | $25.00 | $0.00 | $25.00 |

(ii) A long position in a call option with a exercise price of $50 and a front-end premium expense of $5.20.

| Expiration Date Tando Stock Price (S) | Long Call (K=$50) Payoff = max (0,S-50) | Initial Long Call Premium | Net Profit |
|---|---|---|---|
| 25 | $0.00 | ($5.20) | ($5.20) |
| 30 | $0.00 | ($5.20) | ($5.20) |
| 35 | $0.00 | ($5.20) | ($5.20) |
| 40 | $0.00 | ($5.20) | ($5.20) |
| 45 | $0.00 | ($5.20) | ($5.20) |
| 50 | $0.00 | ($5.20) | ($5.20) |
| 55 | $5.00 | ($5.20) | ($0.20) |
| 60 | $10.00 | ($5.20) | $4.80 |
| 65 | $15.00 | ($5.20) | $9.80 |
| 70 | $20.00 | ($5.20) | $14.80 |
| 75 | $25.00 | ($5.20) | $19.80 |

(iii.) A short position in a call option with an exercise price of $50 and a front-end premium receipt of $5.20.

| Expiration Date Tando Stock Price (S) | Short Call (K=$50) Payoff = -max (0,S-50) | Initial Short Call Premium | Net Profit |
|---|---|---|---|
| 25 | $0.00 | $5.20 | $5.20 |
| 30 | $0.00 | $5.20 | $5.20 |
| 35 | $0.00 | $5.20 | $5.20 |
| 40 | $0.00 | $5.20 | $5.20 |
| 45 | $0.00 | $5.20 | $5.20 |
| 50 | $0.00 | $5.20 | $5.20 |
| 55 | ($5.00) | $5.20 | $0.20 |
| 60 | ($10.00) | $5.20 | ($4.80) |
| 65 | ($15.00) | $5.20 | ($9.80) |
| 70 | ($20.00) | $5.20 | ($14.80) |
| 75 | ($25.00) | $5.20 | ($19.80) |

1(b). (i.) A long position in a forward with a contract price of $50.

**Long Forward**

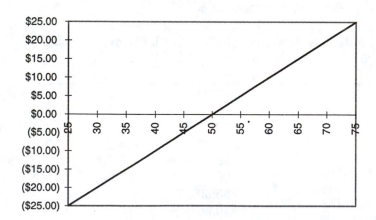

(ii.) A long position in a call option with an exercise price of $50 and a front-end premium expense of $5.20:

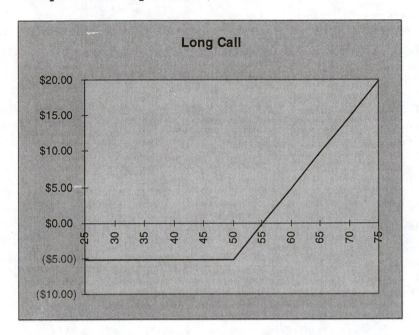

(iii.) A short position in a call option with an exercise price of $50 and a front-end premium receipt of $5.20

THE BREAKEVEN POINT FOR THE CALL OPTIONS IS $55.20.

1(c). The long position in a forward with a contract price of $50: The purchaser believes that the price of Tando stock will be <u>above $50</u>.

The long position in a call option with an exercise price of $50 and a front-end premium expense of $5.20: The purchaser believes the price will be <u>above $55.20</u>.

The short position in a call option with an exercise price of $50 and a front-end premium receipt of $5.20: The seller believes the price of Tando stock will be <u>below $55.20</u>.

2(a).

(i.) A short position in a forward with a contract price of $50.

| Expiration Date Tando Stock Price (S) | Short Forward (K=$50) Payoff = S-50 | Initial Short Forward Premium | Net Profit |
|---|---|---|---|
| 25 | $25.00 | $0.00 | $25.00 |
| 30 | $20.00 | $0.00 | $20.00 |
| 35 | $15.00 | $0.00 | $15.00 |
| 40 | $10.00 | $0.00 | $10.00 |
| 45 | $5.00 | $0.00 | $5.00 |
| 50 | $0.00 | $0.00 | $0.00 |
| 55 | ($5.00) | $0.00 | ($5.00) |
| 60 | ($10.00) | $0.00 | ($10.00) |
| 65 | ($15.00) | $0.00 | ($15.00) |
| 70 | ($20.00) | $0.00 | ($20.00) |
| 75 | ($25.00) | $0.00 | ($25.00) |

(ii.) A long position in a put option with a exercise price of $50 and a front-end premium expense of $3.23.

| Expiration Date Tando Stock Price (S) | Long Put (K=$50) Payoff = max (0,50-S) | Initial Long Put Premium | Net Profit |
|---|---|---|---|
| 25 | $25.00 | ($3.23) | $21.77 |
| 30 | $20.00 | ($3.23) | $16.77 |
| 35 | $15.00 | ($3.23) | $11.77 |
| 40 | $10.00 | ($3.23) | $6.77 |
| 45 | $5.00 | ($3.23) | $1.77 |
| 50 | $0.00 | ($3.23) | ($3.23) |
| 55 | $0.00 | ($3.23) | ($3.23) |
| 60 | $0.00 | ($3.23) | ($3.23) |
| 65 | $0.00 | ($3.23) | ($3.23) |
| 70 | $0.00 | ($3.23) | ($3.23) |
| 75 | $0.00 | ($3.23) | ($3.23) |

(iii.) A short position in a put option with an exercise price of $50 and a front-end premium receipt of $3.23.

| Expiration Date Tando Stock Price (S) | Short Put (K=$50) Payoff = -max (0,50-S) | Initial Short Put Premium | Net Profit |
|---|---|---|---|
| 25 | ($25.00) | $3.23 | ($21.77) |
| 30 | ($20.00) | $3.23 | ($16.77) |
| 35 | ($15.00) | $3.23 | ($11.77) |
| 40 | ($10.00) | $3.23 | ($6.77) |
| 45 | ($5.00) | $3.23 | ($1.77) |
| 50 | $0.00 | $3.23 | $3.23 |
| 55 | $0.00 | $3.23 | $3.23 |
| 60 | $0.00 | $3.23 | $3.23 |
| 65 | $0.00 | $3.23 | $3.23 |
| 70 | $0.00 | $3.23 | $3.23 |
| 75 | $0.00 | $3.23 | $3.23 |

2(b).

(i.) A short position in a forward with a contract price of $50:

(ii.) A long position in a put option with an exercise price of $50 and front-end premium expense of $3.23:

(iii.) A short position in a put option with an exercise price of $50 and a front-end premium receipt of $3.23:

THE BREAKEVEN POINT FOR BOTH PUT OPTIONS IS $46.77.

2(c). A short position in a forward with a contract price of $50: The seller believes the price of Tando will be <u>below $50.</u>

A long position in a put option with an exercise price of $50 and front-end premium expense of $3.23: The buyer of the put believes the price will be <u>below $46.77.</u>

A short position in a put option with an exercise price of $50 and a front-end premium receipt of $3.23: The seller of the put believes the price will be <u>above $46.77.</u>

3(a).

(i.) A short position in a forward option with a exercise price of $50

| Expiration Date Tando Stock Price (S) | Short Forward (K=$50) Payoff =max (0, S-50) | Initial Short Forward Premium | Net Profit |
|---|---|---|---|
| 25 | $25.00 | $0.00 | $50.00 |
| 30 | $20.00 | $0.00 | $50.00 |
| 35 | $15.00 | $0.00 | $50.00 |
| 40 | $10.00 | $0.00 | $50.00 |
| 45 | $5.00 | $0.00 | $50.00 |
| 50 | $0.00 | $0.00 | $50.00 |
| 55 | ($5.00) | $0.00 | $50.00 |
| 60 | ($10.00) | $0.00 | $50.00 |
| 65 | ($15.00) | $0.00 | $50.00 |
| 70 | ($20.00) | $0.00 | $50.00 |
| 75 | ($25.00) | $0.00 | $50.00 |

(ii.) A long position in a put option with a exercise price of $50 and a front-end premium expense of $3.23.

| Expiration Date Tando Stock Price (S) | Long Put (K=$50) Payoff = max (0,50-S) | Initial Long Put Premium | Net Profit |
|---|---|---|---|
| 25 | $25.00 | ($3.23) | $46.77 |
| 30 | $20.00 | ($3.23) | $46.77 |
| 35 | $15.00 | ($3.23) | $46.77 |
| 40 | $10.00 | ($3.23) | $46.77 |
| 45 | $5.00 | ($3.23) | $46.77 |
| 50 | $0.00 | ($3.23) | $46.77 |
| 55 | $0.00 | ($3.23) | $51.77 |
| 60 | $0.00 | ($3.23) | $56.77 |
| 65 | $0.00 | ($3.23) | $61.77 |
| 70 | $0.00 | ($3.23) | $66.77 |
| 75 | $0.00 | ($3.23) | $71.77 |

(iii.)    A short position in a call option with an exercise price of $50 and a front-end premium receipt of $5.20.

| Expiration Date Tando Stock Price (S) | Short Call (K=$50) Payoff = -max (0,S-50) | Initial Short Call Premium | Net Profit |
|---|---|---|---|
| 25 | $0.00 | $5.20 | $30.20 |
| 30 | $0.00 | $5.20 | $35.20 |
| 35 | $0.00 | $5.20 | $40.20 |
| 40 | $0.00 | $5.20 | $45.20 |
| 45 | $0.00 | $5.20 | $50.20 |
| 50 | $0.00 | $5.20 | $55.20 |
| 55 | ($5.00) | $5.20 | $55.20 |
| 60 | ($10.00) | $5.20 | $55.20 |
| 65 | ($15.00) | $5.20 | $55.20 |
| 70 | ($20.00) | $5.20 | $55.20 |
| 75 | ($25.00) | $5.20 | $55.20 |

3(b).

(i.) A short position in a forward with a contract price of $50:

11 - 19

(ii.) A long position in a put option with an exercise price of $50 and a front-end premium expense of $3.23:

(iii.) A short position in a call option with an exercise price of $50 and a front-end premium expense of $5.20:

11 - 20

3(c).  $F_{0,T}$  = Call - Put + PV(Strike)
$50.00   = 5.20 - 3.23 + PV($50)
$48.03   = PV ($50)

PV factor   = 1.041

S   = F/(PV Factor)
$50   = F / 1.041
$50 x 1.041  = F
$52.05   = F

The zero value contract price, $52.05, differs from the $50 contract price because the put and the call prices are not the same. If they were, the combination of the two would yield a zero-value forward price.

4(a).  *Writing covered calls*--This strategy involves the purchase of common shares and the simultaneous writing (selling) of call options on that stock with the intent of earning the time value premium on the call options. A call option allows the call holder to purchase the stock at a guaranteed price, the strike price, over a limited period of time.

*Purchasing protective puts* (long stock, long put)--This strategy entails the purchase of a put option(s) on a stock(s) held in the portfolio in order to protect against a significant decline in the price of the respective stock(s). A put option allows the put holder the right to sell the stock to the put writer at a guaranteed price for a limited period of time.

*Selling stock market index futures*--This strategy involves the selling of some stock market index futures (forward) contract (such as the S&P 500, NYSE Composite, Value Line Average, or S&P 100) while at the same time owning a diversified portfolio of common stocks in order to hedge against a decline in the general market or as a speculation that the market or common stocks will decline.

4(b).  *Writing covered calls* can be used to modify a portfolio's risk/return relationship as follows:

(1)   *Covered calls at-the-money* limit the upside gain potential on a stock, but provide more downside protection than the uncovered ownership of the stock. The following figure graphically displays this relationship:

**COVERED CALL AT-THE-MONEY**

(NOTE: For each graph, the 45° diagonal (broken) line represents the return before risk modification via the option/hedging strategy. The heavy line is the return from the option/hedging strategy.)

*Writing covered calls in-the-money* limits upside gains even more than the at-the-money strategy but provides greater downside protection as shown by the following graph:

GAIN OR LOSS

STOCK

Long Stock-Write Call

STOCK PRICE

Strike Price

Purchase Price

TOTAL PREMIUM

## COVERED CALL IN-THE-MONEY

In all instances, covered writing serves to lower a given stock's risk/return characteristics versus the outright ownership of the stock. The greater that the call is in-the-money, the greater the reduction in both the expected return and risk.

(2)    *Buying protective puts* provides an opportunity to make substantial positive returns when the underlying stock appreciates, and provides a fixed maximum loss no matter how much the stock may decline. This appreciation potential is, however, always less than the return from the underlying stock. The difference in return is the cost of the put option. The cost for an at-the-money put purchase is analogous to the purchase of insurance protection against any large loss. Out-of-the-money protective put purchases are akin to the purchase of insurance with a deductible clause.

*11 - 23*

Graphically the at-the money strategy appears as follows:

## LONG STOCK LONG PUT AT-THE-MONEY

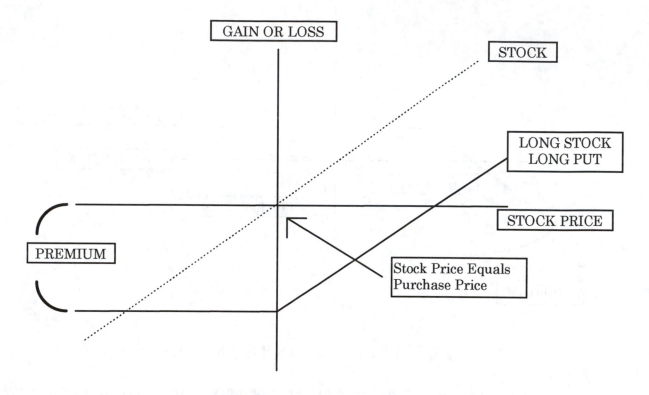

(3) *Selling stock market index futures* against a diversified portfolio hedges against general market movements, as the general market fluctuates, the gain or loss in your portfolio is largely offset by a loss or gain due to change in value of the futures contract.

Therefore, selling stock market index futures against a diversified portfolio substantially reduces expected return (to the risk-free return) and risk, and is graphically shown as follows:

# HEDGED LONG STOCK PORTFOLIO/MARKET INDEX –
## SHORT INDEX FUTURES

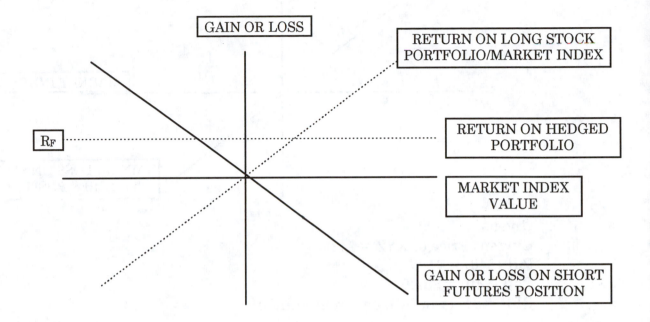

An alternate speculative strategy would be to short the stock market index futures in anticipation of a decline in the market in the near future. This is a highly leveraged strategy because only a margin payment need be deposited and maintained and, as a result, it involves a high return risk tradeoff. The graph for this strategy is as follows:

# SPECULATIVE SHORT STOCK MARKET INDEX FUTURES

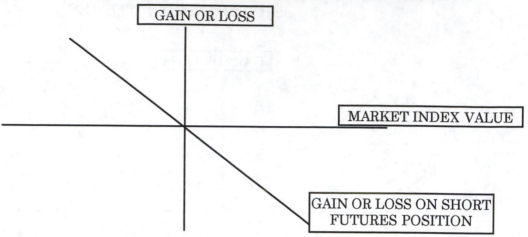

5(a). Givens:
Current Price of XYZ = $42
Put ($40) = $1.45
Call ($40) = $3.90
RFR = 8% (annual); 4% (semi-annual)

(i.) Buy one call option

| Expiration Date XYZ Stock Price (S) | Long Call (K=$40) Payoff = max (0,S-40) | Initial Long Call Premium | Net Profit |
|---|---|---|---|
| 20 | $0.00 | ($3.90) | ($3.90) |
| 25 | $0.00 | ($3.90) | ($3.90) |
| 30 | $0.00 | ($3.90) | ($3.90) |
| 35 | $0.00 | ($3.90) | ($3.90) |
| 40 | $0.00 | ($3.90) | ($3.90) |
| 45 | $5.00 | ($3.90) | $1.10 |
| 50 | $10.00 | ($3.90) | $6.10 |
| 55 | $15.00 | ($3.90) | $11.10 |
| 60 | $20.00 | ($3.90) | $16.10 |

*11 - 26*

Long Call

## (ii.) Short one call option

| Expiration Date XYZ Stock Price (S) | Short Call (K=$40) Payoff =-max (0,S-40) | Initial Short Call Premium | Net Profit |
|---|---|---|---|
| 20 | $0.00 | $3.90 | $3.90 |
| 25 | $0.00 | $3.90 | $3.90 |
| 30 | $0.00 | $3.90 | $3.90 |
| 35 | $0.00 | $3.90 | $3.90 |
| 40 | $0.00 | $3.90 | $3.90 |
| 45 | ($5.00) | $3.90 | ($1.10) |
| 50 | ($10.00) | $3.90 | ($6.10) |
| 55 | ($15.00) | $3.90 | ($11.10) |
| 60 | ($20.00) | $3.90 | ($16.10) |

Short Call

*11 - 27*

Both call positions will break even at a stock price of $43.90.

5(b).

(i.) Buy one put option

| Expiration Date XYZ Stock Price (S) | Long Put (K=$40) Payoff = max (0,40-S) | Initial Long Put Premium | Net Profit |
|---|---|---|---|
| 20 | $20.00 | ($1.45) | $18.55 |
| 25 | $15.00 | ($1.45) | $13.55 |
| 30 | $10.00 | ($1.45) | $8.55 |
| 35 | $5.00 | ($1.45) | $3.55 |
| 40 | $0.00 | ($1.45) | ($1.45) |
| 45 | $0.00 | ($1.45) | ($1.45) |
| 50 | $0.00 | ($1.45) | ($1.45) |
| 55 | $0.00 | ($1.45) | ($1.45) |
| 60 | $0.00 | ($1.45) | ($1.45) |

(ii) Short one put option

| Expiration Date XYZ Stock Price (S) | Short Put (K=$40) Payoff =-max (0,40-S) | Initial Short Put Premium | Net Profit |
|---|---|---|---|
| 20 | ($20.00) | $1.45 | ($18.55) |
| 25 | ($15.00) | $1.45 | ($13.55) |
| 30 | ($10.00) | $1.45 | ($8.55) |
| 35 | ($5.00) | $1.45 | ($3.55) |
| 40 | $0.00 | $1.45 | $1.45 |
| 45 | $0.00 | $1.45 | $1.45 |
| 50 | $0.00 | $1.45 | $1.45 |
| 55 | $0.00 | $1.45 | $1.45 |
| 60 | $0.00 | $1.45 | $1.45 |

Both put positions will break even at a stock price of $38.55.

5(c).   Does Call - Put = S - PV(K) ???????

$3.90 - $1.45 = $42 - 40/(1.04)   ???????

$2.45 = $3.53  ???????

NO!  Put-call parity does not hold for this European-style contract.


6(a).   The manager wishes to be protected from any decline in the government bonds' price (any rise in rates) while maintaining a participation in a price advance, should it occur. The manager also wishes to hold the existing bond position over the next six months. The option strategy best suited for this goal is a protected put strategy.

The manager should purchase the put options in size sufficient to protect the $1.0 million portfolio. The manager should purchase 10 put contracts. In this strategy, the bond portfolio will be protected against any price decline below 98, (the put strike price - the put premium) yet will participate with any price advance on the bond less 2.00 (the put premium).

6(b).  The manager is now willing to sell the existing bonds in order to create a portfolio structure that achieves the goal. Two strategic options structures equivalent to the structure in Part A above can be designed as follows:

Alternative 1

- Sell the government 8% bonds
- Invest the proceeds in the T-bills and buy the appropriate amount of 8% bond futures
- Buy the put options to protect against price declines while participating in price advances.

Buying T-bills and futures is equivalent to holding the bonds. The manager could purchase $1.0 million in T-bills and 10 futures contracts.

The manager would complete the option strategy alternative 1 by buying 10 put options.

Alternative 2

- Sell the government 8% bonds
- Invest the proceeds in the T-bills
- Buy the appropriate amount of call options

A T-bill plus call option position is equivalent in structure to a bond plus put option position. The bill plus call options provides protection against bond price declines since the investor can only lose the premium on the call option. Participation in any bond price advance is achieved since the call option premium will increase.

Specifically, the manager could purchase $1.0 million in T-bills and 10 call options.

6(c).  Given the put-call parity pricing relationship, the put options and call options appear misvalued versus each other.

If the call is correctly priced at 4.00, the put should be priced at:

put      = 4.00 - bond price + present value of strike
         = 4.00 - 100 + 100/1.03
         = 4.00 - 100 + 97.09
         = 1.09

If the put is correctly priced at 2.00, the call should be priced at:

call     = 2.00 + 100 - 100/1.03
         = 2.00 + 100 - 97.09
         = 4.91

The put is <u>overpriced</u> versus the call. Therefore:

(1) in the put buying strategies the put premium appears very fully priced.
(2) in the future buying- put buying strategy, similar comments hold. Also the future appears overvalued.
(3) In the buy bills/buy calls strategy, the call option price appears attractive.

In addition, the price of the future at 101 appears high; however, a fair price for the future would be:

price future  = price bond + (bill income - bond income) price
              = 100 + (-1)
              = 99

The option strategy involving buying T-bills and the call options is recommended.

7(a).   To solve this problem, express put call parity in the following form:

$C(K) - P(K) - S + PV(K) = 0$

Now we can equate put-call parity for two different options:

$C(40) - P(40) - S + PV(40) = C(50) - P(50) - S + PV(50)$

Note that the S on each side cancels.

Then the only unknown is P(50).  Solving for P(50) yields

P(50)  = C(50) + PV(50) - C(40) + P(40) - PV(40)
P(50)  = 2.47 + 50/1.03 - 8.73 + .59 - 40/1.03
P(50)  = $4.03

The same can be done to find the value of C(45)
C(40) - P(40) - S + PV(40) = C(45) - P(45) - S P PV(45)
C(45)  = C(40) - P(40) + PV(40) +P(45) - PV(45)
C(45)  = 8.73 - .59 +40/1.03 + 1.93 - 45/1.03
C(45)  = $5.21

7(b).  If the future price of Commodity Z is $48, then the spot price (S) should be S = PV($48) = 48/1.03 = $46.60.

Then solving for the theoretical price differential between calls and puts (K=$40) gives
C(40) - P(40) = S - PV(40)
C(40) - P(40) = $46.60 - 4/1.03
C(40) - P(40) = $7.77 which is less than the $8.14 difference observed in the market.

By selling the "overpriced" portfolio C(40) - P(40) = $8.14 and buying the "underpriced" portfolio S - PV(40) = $7.77, we can obtain an arbitrage profit of $8.14 - $7.77 = $.37 since we know by put-call parity that these two portfolios must have the same payoff at expiration.

This total portfolio position is:

- short the call
- Long the put
- long the stock
- borrow PV(40)

8(a).  Distribution of returns:
Portfolio 1 holds stock index put options on $1 million of /stocks, which is a protective put strategy. The protective put strategy has an asymmetric

11 - 32

impact on return distributions, by reducing downside risk while allowing upside returns.

Portfolio 2 has sold $2 million of stock index futures, which hedges both downside and upside returns and has a symmetrical impact on return distributions.

Systematic and specific risk:
Both stock index put options and stock index futures modify systematic risk, but not specific risk. Since the stock portfolio is broadly diversified, but not an index fund, neither hedge is riskless, but are cross hedges. Both Portfolios 1 and 2 continue to have specific risk on the entire $9 million stock portfolio.

8(b).    Mispricing of futures and options:
Portfolio 1 is subject to mispricing of options when the puts are initially purchased or when they expire and must be rolled over. Mispricing represents a cost or risk when the puts are purchased at a price different from a theoretical value determined by a model, such as Black-Scholes.

Portfolio 3, which uses a dynamic hedging process, may require frequent trading of futures to maintain the appropriate hedge ratio. Frequent trading subjects the portfolio to the risk that the futures must be purchased or sold at prices different from fair value.

Unexpected change in stock volatility:
For put options already owned, unexpected changes in volatility do not affect the put's cost or ability to hedge downside risk. Changes in volatility will impact the prices of subsequent option transactions. Thus, Portfolio 1 is not subject to the risk of unexpected changes in stock volatility until the puts expire and are rolled over at then prevailing prices.

Unexpected increases in stock volatility results in more frequent trading of futures and a higher hedging cost in Portfolio 3. Increases in stock volatility together with futures mispricing may produce significantly higher costs in a dynamic asset allocation process.

8(c).    Constructing Portfolio 1 requires buying $1 million of at-the-money index puts, which are normally fairly liquid, but their cost may be somewhat unpredictable due to the impact of stock volatility on option prices. Portfolio 1 requires revision when the puts expire, at which time they must be rolled over, again at somewhat unpredictable prices. The $950,000 of cash plus the puts on $1 million of the stock portfolio eliminates the downside risk on about $2 million of Portfolio 1. A withdrawal of $3 million would risk realizing a loss on $1 million of the stock portfolio. Since Portfolio 1 requires revision only at the expiration of the puts, it is as practical for Mr. Selbst as Portfolio 2 and more practical than Portfolio 3.

Constructing Portfolio 2 requires selling $2 million of stock index futures, which are normally fairly liquid and normally priced close to fair value. Portfolio 2 requires revision when the futures expire, at which time they must be rolled over. The $1 million of cash plus the $2 million futures hedge on the stock portfolio eliminates the systematic risk on $3 million of Portfolio 2, making it possible to withdraw $3 million without the risk of loss. Since Portfolio 2 requires revision only at the expiration of the futures, it is as practical for Mr. Selbst as Portfolio 1 and more practical than Portfolio 3.

Portfolio 3 requires the use of some type of option model (binomial, Black-Scholes, etc.) to determine the appropriate hedge ratio. Constructing and revising Portfolio 3 requires nearly constant monitoring and sometimes frequent trading of futures to maintain the hedge ratio. The $1 million of cash plus the dynamic hedge on $1 million of the stock portfolio eliminates the downside risk on about $2 million of Portfolio 3. A withdrawal of $3 million would risk realizing a loss on $1 million of the stock portfolio. Since Portfolio 3 may require frequent revision, it is not as practical for Mr. Selbst as Portfolios 1 or 2. Among the three alternative portfolios, Portfolio 2 is recommended for Mr. Selbst. Portfolio 2 is easy to construct and revise, has no risk of loss on the withdrawal of $3 million, and is practical for Mr. Selbst.

8(d). For Approaches 1 and 2 the protection against loss due to a decline in stock price is identical. At any stock price for X or Y below their current levels, the minimum value of the put, either on the stock or on the index, exactly matches the decline in value of the stocks. For example:

|  | New Stock Price | New Stock Value | Option Price | Option Value |
|---|---|---|---|---|
| X | 50 | 5000 | 10 | 1000 |
| Y | 30 | 3000 | 10 | 1000 |
|  |  | 8000 |  | 2000 |
|  | Portfolio Value | $10,000 |  |  |

| New Index Price | New Index Value | Index Option Price | Index Option Value |
|---|---|---|---|
| 40 | 4000 | 10 | 2000 |

Portfolio Value     $10,000

The second approach costs less than the first because the volatility (variance) of the index is less. The variance of the index is less because the variance of the index portfolio (50% X and 50%Y) is not the sum of the variances of X and Y. Instead, portfolio variance recognizes the covariance (or correlation) of the stocks in the portfolio. In almost every case, the variance of a portfolio is less than the sum of the variances of the stocks.

A portfolio of puts insures against the risks of each stock. This strategy is unnecessarily expensive because the investor wants a put on the portfolio as a whole to protect against the risk of that portfolio.

9(a).  Alternative 1 (Buy Puts)

•   Buy S&P 500 put options with market exposure equal to equity holdings to protect these holdings.
•   Buy Government bond put options with market exposure equal to the bond holdings to protect these holdings.

This could be done by (1) buying $150 million of S&P 500 put options.  Since each option is equivalent to $35,000 market exposure, this could be done by buying:

$$\frac{\$150,000,000}{\$35,000/option} = 4,286 \text{ S\&P 500 put options}$$

and (2) buying $150 million of Government bond put options.  Since each option is equivalent to $100,000 market exposure, this could be done by buying:

$$\frac{\$150,000,000}{\$100,000/option} = 1,500 \text{ Government bond put options}$$

By buying 4,286 S&P 500 put options and 1,500 Government bond put options, the portfolio is protected and upside participation is achieved.

Alternative 2 (Sell Futures/Buy Calls)

• Sell S&P stock index futures equal to the equity exposure in the portfolio and buy S&P 500 call options equal to the exposure.
• Sell Government bond futures equal to the bond exposure in the portfolio and buy bond call options equal to the exposure.

This could be done by:

(1) Selling $150 million of S&P futures. Since each future is equivalent to $175,000 of equity exposure, this could be done by selling:

$$\frac{\$150,000,000}{\$175,000/future} = 857 \text{ S\&P futures}$$

Buying $150 million of S&P 500 call options or 4,286 call options (see above calculation).

(2) Selling $150 million of Government bond futures contracts. Since each bond future is equivalent to $100,000 of bond exposure, this could be done by selling:

$$\frac{\$150,000,000}{\$100,000/future} = 1,500 \text{ bond futures}$$

Buying $150 million of Government bond call options or 1,500 call options (see above calculation).

By selling 857 S&P futures and 1,500 bond futures, and buying 4,286 S&P call options and 1,500 bond options, the portfolio is protected from loss and upside participation is achieved.

9 (b).  Given the put-call parity relationship, the put options appear misvalued compared to the call options.

Given the S&P 500 call price, the put should be priced at:

put  =      8.00 - index price + present value of (strike + income)
     =      8.00 - 350 + (.01) x (350)
     =      8.00 - 350 + 1.015
     =      6.28

Given the bond call price, the bond put option should be priced at:
put  =      2.50 - bond price + present value of (strike + income)
     =      2.50 - 100 + (.02) x (100)
     =      2.50 - 100 + 1.015
     =      2.99

For both the S&P 500 options and the Government bond options, the put options appear <u>overvalued</u> compared to the prices of the calls.

The prices of the futures also appear high.  A fair price for the S&P 500 future would be:

S& P 500 future    = index price + (bill income - dividend income)
          = 350 + (.015 - .01) x (350)
          = 351.75

A fair price for the bond future would be:

Bond future price  = bond price + (bill income - bond income)
          = 100 + (.015 - .02) x (100)
          = 99.5

From this analysis the futures are somewhat overvalued and the put options are relatively overpriced compared o the call options.

<u>Alternative 1</u> involves buying relatively expensive assets (the put options). <u>Alternative 2</u> involves selling expensive assets (the futures contracts) and buying relatively inexpensive assets (the call options).

<u>Alternative 2, where protection is gained by selling futures and buying call options, is recommended.</u>

10(a.) A synthetic put can be created by shorting the stock, buying a call, and lending PV(x) - S.

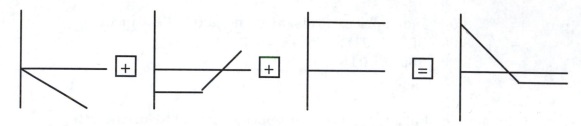

Since the synthetic put and an actual put have the same payoff at maturity, they must have the same price today or there would be an arbitrage opportunity. The arbitrage would be to sell the more expensive "put" and buy the less expensive "put" netting the difference in price.

10(b). Buying a call and selling a put gives the same payoff as a long forward:

11(a).

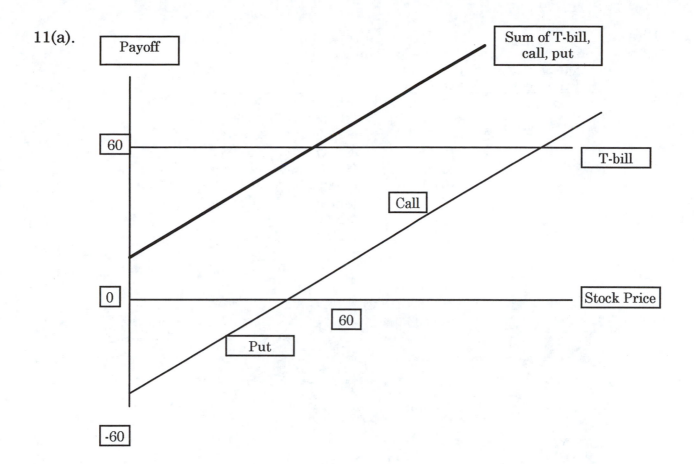

11(b). Using put-call parity the "no arbitrage price" is
S= PV(K)+C-P
S = 0.6*97 + 3.18 - 3.38
S = $58.00

11(c). Since put-call parity indicates the "no arbitrage" price of the stock is $58 and the stock selling at $60, the arbitrage would be to sell the over-valued portfolio (the stock) and use the proceeds ($60) to buy the undervalued portfolio (.6 t-bills, long 1 call, short 1 put). This set of trades yields $2 in arbitrage profits. Since by put-call parity we know that the two portfolios will have exactly offsetting terminal payoffs, the trade is riskless.

12(a).

| Expiration Date Stock Price (S) | Long Put (K=$55) Payoff = max (0,55-S) | Initial Long Put Premium | Net Profit |
|---|---|---|---|
| 35 | $20.00 | ($1.32) | $53.68 |
| 40 | $15.00 | ($1.32) | $53.68 |
| 45 | $10.00 | ($1.32) | $53.68 |
| 50 | $5.00 | ($1.32) | $53.68 |
| 55 | $0.00 | ($1.32) | $53.68 |
| 60 | $0.00 | ($1.32) | $58.68 |
| 65 | $0.00 | ($1.32) | $63.68 |
| 70 | $0.00 | ($1.32) | $68.68 |
| 75 | $0.00 | ($1.32) | $73.68 |

12(b).

Using put-call parity, the position could have been replicated by selling the portfolio, buying the call option at the ask price, and investing the balance in T-bills yielding 7%.

12(c).

| Expiration Date Stock Price (S) | Short Call (K=$55) Payoff = - max (0,S-55) | Initial Short Call Premium | Net Profit |
|---|---|---|---|
| 35 | $0.00 | $2.55 | $37.55 |
| 40 | $0.00 | $2.55 | $42.55 |
| 45 | $0.00 | $2.55 | $47.55 |

| Expiration Date Stock Price (S) | Short Call (K=$55) Payoff = - max (0,S-55) | Initial Short Call Premium | Net Profit |
|---|---|---|---|
| 50 | $0.00 | $2.55 | $52.55 |
| 55 | $0.00 | $2.55 | $57.55 |
| 60 | ($5.00) | $2.55 | $57.55 |
| 65 | ($10.00) | $2.55 | $57.55 |
| 70 | ($15.00) | $2.55 | $57.55 |
| 75 | ($20.00) | $2.55 | $57.55 |

12(d).

Using put-call parity, the position could have replicated by selling the portfolio, selling the put option at the bid price, and then investing the balance in T-bills yielding 7%.

13(a). Since the forward price is the same as the strike price, going long a call and short a put is the same as a zero-value forward contract. Hence, the call price must equal the put price, so C =3.22 for the "no arbitrage" price. Rounding to the nearest eighth yields,

|  | bid | ask |
|---|---|---|
| Call | $ 3.125 | $ 3.250 |

13(b). Using put-call parity $S = C - P + PV(K)$
from part a) C-P=0, so
$S = 45/(1.065^{.75})$
$S = 42.92$

13(c). To make an arbitrage profit you want to sell the overvalued portfolio (short 0.45 t-bills, short call, long put) and use the proceeds to buy the undervalued portfolio (the stock).
The arbitrage profit would be,
Profit = $45/(1.065^{.75}) + 3.125 - 3.25 - 41$
Profit = $1.80

13(d). The present value of the dividend would have to be equal to the difference in theoretical and actual prices, so PV(div) = 42.92 - 41.00
div = $(1.065^{.75})*1.92$
div = $2.01

# CHAPTER 12

# Analysis of Financial Statements

# Answers to Questions

1.  The kind of decisions that require the analysis of financial statements include whether to lend money to a firm, whether to invest in the preferred or the common stock of a firm, and whether to acquire a firm. To properly make such decisions, it is necessary to understand what financial statements are available, what information is included in the different types of statements, and how to analyze this financial information to arrive at a rational decision.

2.  Analysts employ financial ratios simply because numbers in isolation are typically of little value. For example, a net income of $100,000 has little meaning unless analysts know the sales figure that generated the income and the assets or capital employed in generating these sales or this income. Therefore, ratios are used to provide meaningful relationships between individual values in the financial statements.

3.  A return on equity of 12% indicates that the manager is earning 12 cents on one dollar of the capital provided by the owner after taking into account payments to all other capital suppliers. However, in examining a firm's return of equity (ROE), it is necessary to break it down into components:

$$ROE = \frac{Net\ Income}{Equity}$$

$$= \frac{Sales}{Equity} \times \frac{Net\ Income}{Sales}$$

$$= (Equity\ Turnover) \times (Net\ Profit\ Margin)$$

$$= \frac{\text{Sales}}{\text{Total Assets}} \text{ x } \frac{\text{Total Assets}}{\text{Equity}} \text{ x } \frac{\text{Net Income}}{\text{Sales}}$$

= (Total Assets Turnover)  x  (Financial Leverage)  x (Net Profit Margin)

This means that while an increase in ROE can be due to greater asset efficiency and increasing profitability, it can also be due to increasing financial leverage which would ultimately cause an increase in equity holder's required rate of return on the stock. Therefore, in addition to Kelly's ROE of 12%, we would need to know what factors contributed to it and the trend of each of these components.

4.    A major problem with comparing a firm to its industry is that you may not feel comfortable with the measure of central tendency for the industry. Specifically, you may feel that the average value is not a very useful measure because of the wide dispersion of values for the individual firms within the industry. Alternatively, you might feel that the firm being analyzed is not "typical," that it has a strong "unique" component. In either case, it might be preferable to compare the firm to one or several other individual firms within the industry that are considered comparable to the firm being analyzed in terms of size or clientele. For example, within the computer industry it might be optimal to compare IBM to Compaq rather than to some total industry data that might include numerous small firms.

5.    In general, jewelry stores have very high profit margins but low asset turnover. It could take them months to sell a 1-carat diamond ring, but once it is sold, the profit could be tremendous. On the other hand, grocery stores usually have very low profit margins but very high asset turnover. Since ROE = TAT x NPM, it's conceivable that both businesses could have the same return-on-assets ratio.

6.    Business risk is measured by the relative variability (i.e., the coefficient of variation) of operating earnings for a firm over time. In turn, the variability of operating earnings is caused by sales volatility and the amount of operating leverage employed by the firm. Sales variability is the prime determinant of earnings volatility because operating earnings variability cannot be lower than sales variability. In addition, the greater the firm's

operating leverage, the more variable the operating earnings series will be relative to the sales variability.

7.    The steel company would be expected to have greater business risk.    As discussed in question #6, sales variability and operating leverage are the two components of business risk.  While both the steel and the retail food chain will have high operating leverage, the steel firm is more sensitive to the business cycle than the retail food chain.  That is, the steel firm will have a very volatile sales pattern over the business cycle.  Therefore, the steel firm should have higher business risk than the retail food chain.

8.    When examining a firm's financial structure, we would also be concerned with its business risk.  Since financial risk is the additional uncertainty of returns faced by equity holders because the firm uses fixed-obligation debt securities, the acceptable level of financial risk usually depends on the firm's business risk.  For a firm with low business risk, investors are willing to accept higher financial risk.  On the other hand, if the firm has very high business risk, investors probably would not feel comfortable with high financial risk also.

9.    The total debt/total assets ratio is a balance sheet ratio that indicates the stock of debt as compared to the stock of equity.  While the total debt/total assets ratio is a common measure of financial risk, many analysts prefer to employ the fixed charge coverage ratio, which reflects the flow of funds from earnings that are available to meet fixed-payment debt obligations.

10.    A cash flow ratio represents the cash available to service the debt issue, whereas a proportion of debt ratio simply indicates the amount of debt outstanding.  For example, a large amount of debt (i.e. high proportion of debt indicating greater financial risk) could be issued with a low coupon rate, thereby requiring only a small amount of cash to service the debt.  Generally, when these two types of debt ratios diverge, one should concentrate on the cash flow ratios since they represent the firm's ability to make its debt obligations.

11.    Growth analysis is important to common stockholders because the future value of the firm is heavily dependent on future growth in earnings and dividends.  As discussed in Chapter 10, the present value of a firm with perpetual dividends payment is:

$$V = \frac{\text{Dividend Next Period}}{\text{Required Rate of Return - Growth Rate}}$$

Therefore, an estimation of expected growth of earnings and dividends on the basis of the variables that influence growth is obviously crucial. Growth analysis is also important to debt-investors because the major determinant of the firm's ability to pay an obligation is the firm's future success which, in turn, is influenced by its growth.

12. The rate of growth of any economic unit depends on (1) the amount of resources retained and reinvested in the entity and (2) the rate of return that is earned on the resources retained. Obviously, the more a firm reinvests, the faster it will grow. Alternatively, for a given level of reinvestment, a firm will grow faster if it is able to earn a higher rate of return on the resources reinvested.

13. Assuming the risk of the firm is not abnormally high, a 24% ROE is quite high and probably exceeds the return that the equity investor could earn on the funds. Therefore, the firm should retain their earnings and invest them at this rate.

14. This does not mean that Orange Company is better than Blue Company. In order to make this judgment, we have to know what factors (components) caused the extra four points of ROE. If it comes from either the profit margin or the total asset turnover component of the ROE, we can comfortably claim that equity holders of Orange Company are better off than equity holders of Blue Company. On the other hand, it would not be so if the extra four points is because the Orange Company has higher financial leverage, since this extra return is simply a compensation to its equity holders for the higher financial risk they bear. Finally, we are not told anything about the business risks of the two firms.

15. External market liquidity is the ability to buy or sell an asset quickly with little change in price (from prior transaction), assuming no new information has been obtained. The two components of external market liquidity are: (1) the time it takes to sell (or buy) the asset, (2) the selling (or buying) price as compared to recent selling (buying) prices.

Real estate is considered an illiquid asset because it can take months to find a buyer (or seller), and the price can vary substantially from the last transaction or comparable transactions.

16. Some internal corporate variables such as the total market value of outstanding securities and the number of security owners are good indicators of market liquidity. If the firm has a fairly large number of stockholders, it would be very likely that, at any point in time, some of these investors will be buying or selling for a variety of purposes. Therefore, the firm's security would enjoy a liquid secondary market. On the other hand, a small number of security holders would probably indicate an illiquid secondary market. The ultimate indicator is the volume of trading in the security either in absolute terms or relative turnover (shares traded as a percent of outstanding shares).

17. Student Exercise

# Answers to Problems

1(a). Return on Total Equity $= \dfrac{\text{Net income}}{\text{Equity}} = \dfrac{400{,}000}{1{,}160{,}000} = 34.5\%$

based on the 3 components:

$$\text{ROE} = \dfrac{\text{Sales}}{\text{Total Assets}} \times \dfrac{\text{Total Assets}}{\text{Equity}} \times \dfrac{\text{Net Income}}{\text{Sales}}$$

$$= \dfrac{6{,}000{,}000}{4{,}000{,}000} \times \dfrac{4{,}000{,}000}{1{,}160{,}000} \times \dfrac{400{,}000}{6{,}000{,}000}$$

$$= 1.5 \quad \times \quad 3.45 \quad \times \quad .067$$

$$= 34.7\% \text{ (slight difference is due to rounding)}$$

1(b). Growth Rate
$= $ (retention rate) x (return on equity)
$= $ (1 - 160,000/400,000) x .345
$= $ (1 - .40) x .345
$= $ .60 x .345
$= $ 20.7%

1(c). ROE $= \dfrac{240{,}000}{1{,}160{,}000} = 20.7\%$

ROE $=$ 1.5 x 3.45 x .04 = 20.7%

1(d). Growth Rate $=$ .60 x .207 $=$ 12.42%

If dividends were $40,000, then RR $=$ (1 - $40,000/400,000)
$=$ 1 - .10 = .90

Then growth rate = .90 x .207 = 18.63%

2(a). ROE $=$ Total asset turnover x Total assets/equity x Net profit margin

Company A: ROE = 2.2 x 2.4 x .04 = .21

Company B: ROE = 2.0 x 2.2 x .06 = .26

Company C: ROE = 1.4 x 1.5 x .10 = .21

2(b). Growth Rate= Retention Rate x ROE
= (1 - Payout Rate) x ROE

Company A: Growth Rate = (1 - 1.25/2.75) x .21
= .55 x .21 = .1155

Company B: Growth Rate = (1 - 1.00/3.00) x .26
= .67 x .26 = .1742

Company C: Growth Rate = (1 - 1.00/4.50) x .21
= .78 x .21 = .1638

3. Current ratio $=$ 650 / 350 $=$ 1.857

Quick ratio $=$ 320 / 350 $=$ 0.914

Receivables turnover $=$ 3500.7 / 195 = 17.952 X

| | | | | |
|---|---|---|---|---|
| Average coll. period | = | 365 / 17.952 = | 20.332 days | |
| Total asset turnover | = | 3500.7 / 2182.5 | = | 1.604 X |
| Inventory turnover | = | 2135.2 / 280 = | 7.626 X | |
| Fixed asset turnover | = | 3500.7 / 1462.5 | = | 2.394 X |
| Equity turnover | = | 3500.7 / 1035 | = | 3.382 X |
| Gross profit margin | = | (3500.7 - 2135.2) / 3500.7 = | .390 | |
| Operating profit margin | = | 258.2 / 3500.7 | = | .074 |
| Return on capital | = | (129.2 + 62.5) / 2182.5 | = | .088 |
| Return on equity | = | 129.2 / 1185 = | .109 | |
| Return on common equity | = | 114.2 / 1035 = | .110 | |
| Debt/equity ratio | = | 625 / 1225 | = | 0.51 |
| Debt/total capital ratio | = | 625 / 1850 | = | .338 |
| Interest coverage | = | 258.2 / 62.5 | = | 4.131 X |
| Fixed charge coverage | = | 258.2 / [62.5 + (15/.66)] | = | 3.030 X |
| Cash flow/long-term debt | = | (129.2 + 125 + 20) / 625= | .439 | |
| Cash flow/total debt | = | (129.2 + 125 + 20) / 975= | .281 | |
| Retention rate | = | 1 - (40 / 114.2) | = | .65 |

Eddie's current performance appears in line with its historical performance and the industry average except with respect to below-average profitability (return on capital and return on equity) and below-average leverage (debt to equity and debt to total capital).

4(a).

|  |  | **1985** | **1989** |
|---|---|---|---|
| Operating Margin | = | (Operating Income - Depreciation) / Sales | |
|  | = | (38 - 3) / 542 | (76 - 9) / 979 |
|  | = | 6.46% | 6.84% |
| Asset Turnover | = | Sales / Total Assets | |
|  | = | 542 / 245 | 979 / 291 |
|  | = | 2.21x | 3.36x |
| Interest Burden | = | Interest Expense / Total Assets | |
|  | = | 3 / 245 | 0 / 291 |
|  | = | 1.22% | 0 |
| Financial Leverage | = | Total Assets / Common Shareholders' Equity | |
|  | = | 245 / 159 | 291 / 220 |
|  | = | 1.54x | 1.32x |
| Tax Rate | = | Income Taxes / Pre-Tax Income | |
|  | = | 13 / 32 | 37 / 67 |
|  | = | 40.63% | 55.22% |

The recommended formula is:

Return on Equity (ROE) = [(Op. Margin x Asset Turnover) - Int. Burden] x Financial Lev. x (100% - Income Tax Rate)

$$1985 = \left[ \left( \frac{38-3}{542} \right) \times \frac{542}{245} - \frac{3}{245} \right] \times \frac{245}{159} \times (1-.4063)$$

$$= \left[ (6.46\% \times 2.21\%) - 1.22\% \right] \times 1.54x \times .5937 = 11.94\%$$

$$1989 = \left[ \left( \frac{76-9}{979} \right) \times \frac{979}{291} - 0 \right] \times \frac{291}{220} \times (1-.5522)$$

$$= \left[ (6.84\% \times 3.36\%) - 0 \right] \times 1.32x \times .4478 = 13.58\%$$

Two alternative approaches are also correct.

- [Op. Margin -(Int. Burden / Asset Turnover)] x Financial Lev. x Asset Turnover x (100% - Income Tax Rate)

- [( Financial Lev. x Asset Turnover x Op. Margin) - (Financial Lev. x Interest Burden)] x (100% - Income Tax Rate)

4(b).

i) Asset turnover measures the ability of a company to minimize the level of assets (current and fixed) to support its level of sales. The asset turnover increased substantially over the period thus contributing to an increase in the ROE.

ii) Financial leverage measures the amount of financing outside of equity including short and long-term debt. Financial leverage declined over the period thus adversely affected the ROE. Since asset turnover rose substantially more than financial leverage declined, the net effect was an increase in ROE.

# CHAPTER 13

## An Introduction to Security Valuation

# Answers to Questions

1. The top-down valuation process begins by examining the influence of the general economy on all firms and the security markets. The next step is to analyze the various industries insight of the economic environment. The final step is to select and analyze the individual firms within the superior industries and the common stocks of these firms. The top-down approach thus assumes that the first two steps (economy-market and industry) have a significant influence on the individual firm and its stock (the third step). In contrast, the bottom-up approach assumes that it is possible to select investments (i.e. firms) without considering the aggregate market and industry influences.

2. It is intuitively logical that aggregate market analysis precede industry and company analysis because the government and federal agencies can exert influence on the aggregate economy via fiscal (changes in government spending, taxes, etc.) and monetary (changing money supply, interest rates, etc.) policy. Further, inflation, another aggregate economic variable, must be considered because of its major impact on interest rates and the spending and saving/investment of consumers and corporations. Therefore, a major division is the asset allocation among countries based upon the differential economic outlook including exchange rates (the outlook for the currency).

   Again, industry analysis should precede individual security analysis since there are several factors that are generally national in scope but have a pervasive effect on some industries--e.g., industry-wide strikes, import/export quotas, etc. In addition, alternative industries feel the impact of economic change at different points in the business cycle--e.g., industries may lead or lag an expansion. Further, some industries are cyclical (e.g., steel, auto), some are stable (utilities, food chains, etc.).

   The thrust of the argument is that very few if any industries perform well in a recession, and a "good" company in a "poor" industry may be difficult to find.

3.   All industries would not react identically to changes in the economy simply because of the different nature of business. The auto industry for instance tends to do much better than the economy during expansions but also tends to do far worse during contractions as consumers' consumption patterns change. In contrast, the earnings of utilities undergo modest changes during either expansion or recession since they serve a necessity and thus their sales are somewhat immune to fluctuations. Also, some industries "lead" the economy while others only react late in the cycle (e.g., construction).

4.   Estimating the value for a bond is easier than estimating the value for common stock since the size and the time pattern of returns from the bond over its life are known amounts. Specifically, a bond promises to make interest payments during the life of the bond (usually every 6 months) plus payment of principal on the bond's maturity date. With common stock, there are no such guarantees.

5.   The required rate of return on an investment is primarily determined by three major factors: (1) the economy's real risk-free rate (RFR), (2) the expected rate of inflation (I), and (3) a risk premium (RP). While this basic framework will apply no matter what country you choose to invest in, there will be significant differences in these factors among different countries over time. Among the specific reasons why an investor may have different required returns for U.S. and Japanese stocks are:

The real risk-free rate: For all countries, this rate should be an approximation of the economy's real growth rate. However, the real growth rate among countries might be significantly different due to differences in the growth rate of the labor force, growth rate in the average number of hours worked, and differences in the growth rate of labor productivity.

The expected rate of inflation: Again, there are differences between the U.S. and Japanese inflation rate that are bound to imply a difference between the required return between the two countries.

The risk premium: The risk premium is derived from business risk, financial risk, liquidity risk, exchange rate risk, and country risk. Each of these components are influenced by differences in general economic variability, political conditions, trade relations, and operating leverage employed within the countries. It is necessary to evaluate these differences in risk factors and assign a unique risk premium for each country.

6. The nominal risk-free rate (RFR) is composed of two factors: (1) real risk-free rate and (2) expected rate of inflation. As mentioned in the answer to question #5, the real risk-free rate for all countries is an approximation of the economy's real growth rate. It is highly unlikely that two countries will have the same real risk-free rate due to differences in the growth rates. Also, the expected rate of inflation will vary from country to country. Taking these factors into account, one would not expect the U.S. nominal risk-free rate to be the same as that in Germany. As Table 13.4 illustrates, Germany's nominal risk-free rate is expected to be lower than that of the U.S. in 1995.

7. No, the Indonesian and United Kingdom stocks should have significantly different risk premiums. Specifically, Indonesian stocks should have much larger risk premiums because they are relatively new securities, lack liquidity, and in many cases the underlying firms are involved in highly risky ventures (i.e. business risk). On the other hand, United Kingdom stocks typically are issued by established firms, quite liquid, and the underlying firms are typically engaged in less speculative activities.

8. No, the Singapore stock should be more risky than the United States stock based upon similar reasoning as presented in question #7.

# Answers to Problems

1. Assume semiannual compounding

| | |
|---|---|
| Par value | $10,000 |
| Coupon Payment (every six months) | $700 |
| Number of periods | 20 |
| Required return | 6% |

Therefore,

| | |
|---|---|
| Present value of interest payments | $ 8,028.94 |
| Present value of principal payment | $ 3,118.05 |
| Present value of bond | $11,146.99 |

2. If the required return rises to 16 percent then,

| | |
|---|---|
| Number of periods | 20 |
| Required return | 8% |

Therefore,

| | |
|---|---|
| Present value of interest payments | $6,872.70 |
| Present value of principal payment | $2,145.49 |
| | $9,018.19 |

3.

| | |
|---|---|
| Annual dividend | $9.00 |
| Required return | 11% |

Therefore, the value of the preferred stock is:

$$\text{Value} = \frac{\$9.00}{.11} = \$81.82$$

At a market price of $96.00, the promised yield would be $9.00/$96.00 = 9.375%, which is less than your required rate of return of 11%. Therefore, you would decide against a purchase at this price. The maximum price you will be willing to pay is $81.82.

4.
| Earnings per share: last year | $10.00 |
|---|---|
| Dividends per share: last year | $6.00 |
| Estimated earnings per share: this year | $11.00 |
| Required rate of return | 14% |
| Expected sales price at end of year | $132.00 |

Since the last dividend payout ratio = $6.00/$10.00 = 60%, and assuming you maintain the same payout ratio, then dividends per share at the end of the year is: EPS x Payout = $11.00 x 60% = $6.60.

Therefore, the present value of BBC's share is:

$$\text{Value} = \frac{\$6.60}{(1 + .14)} + \frac{\$132.00}{(1 + .14)} = \$5.79 + \$115.79 = \$121.58$$

This $121.58 is the maximum price you would be willing to pay for BBC's stock.

5.
| Earnings per share: last year | $10.00 |
|---|---|
| Dividends per share: last year | $6.00 |
| Required rate of return | 10% |
| Expected sell price | $110.00 |

$$\text{Value} = \frac{\$6.60}{(1 + .10)} + \frac{\$110.00}{(1 + .10)} = \$6.00 + \$100.00 = \$106.00$$

13 - 7

This $106.00 is the maximum price you would be willing to pay for BBC's stock.

6.  Dividends at the end of this year:     $6 x 1.08 = $6.48
    Required rate of return                12%
    Growth rate of dividends               8%

$$\text{Value} = \frac{\$6.48}{.12 - .08} = \$162.00$$

Thus, you would be willing to pay up to $162.00 for BBC's stock.

7.  Estimated earnings per share   $11.00
    Dividend payout ratio          60%
    Required rate of return        12%
    Growth rate of dividends       10%

$$\text{P/E of BBC Company} = \frac{.60}{.12 - .10} = 30x$$

Thus, the maximum price you would be willing to pay for BBC's stock is: 30 x $11 = $330.00

8.  Dividend payout ratio          40%
    Return on equity               16%

    Growth rate    = (Retention rate) x (Return on equity)
                   = (1 - payout ratio) x (Return on equity)
                   = (1 - .40) x (.16)
                   = .60 x .16
                   = 9.6%

9.      Dividend payout ratio      40%
        Dividend growth rate      9.6%
        Required rate of return      13%

$$\text{P/E of SDC Company} = \frac{.40}{.13 - .096} = 11.76 \text{ x}$$

10.     Dividend payout ratio      50%
        Required rate of return      13%

$$\begin{aligned} \text{Growth rate (new)} &= (1 - .50) \times (.16) \\ &= .50 \times .16 \\ &= .08 \end{aligned}$$

$$\text{P/E of SDC Company (new)} = \frac{.50}{.13 - .08} = 10.00 \text{x}$$

11.     $$\text{ROE} = \frac{\text{Net Income}}{\text{Sales}} \times \frac{\text{Sales}}{\text{Total Assets}} \times \frac{\text{Total Assets}}{\text{Equity}}$$

       =     Profit Margin x Total Asset Turnover x Leverage.

As the above equation illustrates, ROE can be increased through increases in profit margin, total asset turnover, or leverage. As an example of each, suppose ABC company saw an increase in demand for their product, knowing that they have a clearly superior product to others in the industry and their customers are extremely loyal, they will raise prices, thus generating more net income per sale, and have greater profit margin. As can be seen from the formula, holding other things constant, ABC will achieve a greater ROE.

Likewise, suppose demand for the product has increased on an industry wide basis. ABC knows if they raise their prices they may lose sales to the competition. As a result they decide to increase their leverage to increase ROE.

The final method of increasing ROE is by increasing overall efficiency and thus increasing the dollar value of sales to assets on hand.

The student should provide a numerical example of each of these effects.

12. Although grocery chains realize a very low profit margin because of heavy competition (around 1%), they do enjoy a very high asset turnover ratio, thereby enabling them to achieve a ROE of about 12%.

13. Student Exercise

14. 
| Required rate of return (k) | 16% |
|---|---|
| Return on equity (ROE) | 40% |
| Retention rate (RR) | 90% |
| Earnings per share (EPS) | $5.00 |

$$\text{Then growth rate} = \text{RR} \times \text{ROE} = .90 \times .40 = .36$$

$$\text{P/E} = \frac{\text{D/E}}{k - g} = \frac{.10}{.16 - .36}$$

Since the required rate of return (k) is less than the growth rate (g), the earnings multiplier cannot be used (the answer is meaningless).

However, if ROE = .19 and RR = .60 then
growth rate = .60 x .19 = .114

$$\text{P/E} = \frac{.40}{.16 - .114} = \frac{.40}{.046} = 8.696 = 8.70x$$

If next year's earnings are expected to be:

$5.57 = $5.00 x (1 + .114)

Applying the P/E:   Price  = (8.70) x ($5.57)    = $48.46

Thus, you would be willing to pay up to $48.46 for Pear Computer Company stock.


15(a).  Projected dividends next 3 years:

Year 1 ($1.25 x 1.08) = $1.35
Year 2 ($1.35 x 1.08) = $1.46
Year 3 ($1.46 x 1.08) = $1.58

Required rate of return    14%
Growth rate of dividends    8%

The present value of the stock is:

$$V \;=\; \frac{1.35}{1.14} \;+\; \frac{1.46}{(1.14)^2} \;+\; \frac{1.58}{(1.14)^3} \;+\; \frac{40}{(1.14)^3}$$

$$=\; \frac{1.35}{1.14} \;+\; \frac{1.46}{1.2996} \;+\; \frac{1.58}{1.4815} \;+\; \frac{40}{1.4815}$$

$$=\; 1.18 \;+\; 1.12 \;+\; 1.07 \;+\; 27.00 \;=\; \$30.37$$

15(b). Growth rate                  8%
Required rate of return      14%

$$V = \frac{1.35}{.14 - .08} = \frac{1.35}{.06} = \$22.50$$

15(c). Assuming all the above assumptions remain the same, the price at end of year 3 will be:

$$P3 = \frac{D4}{k - g} = \frac{1.25 \times (1.08)^4}{.14 - .08} = \frac{1.25 \times 1.3605}{.06} = 28.34$$

16.    Student Exercise

# CHAPTER 14

## The Analysis of Alternative Economies And the Security Markets

# Answers to Questions

1.  The reason for the strong relationship between the aggregate economy and the stock market is obvious if one considers that **stock prices reflect changes in expectations** for firms and the results for individual firms are affected by the overall performance of the economy. In essence, you would expect earnings of firms to increase in an expansion. Then, if the P/E ratio remains constant or increases because of higher expectations and there is no reason why it should not, you would expect an increase in stock prices.

2.  Stock prices turn before the economy for two reasons: First, investors attempt to estimate **future** earnings and thus current stock prices are based upon future earnings and dividends, which in turn are determined by expectations of future economic activity. The second possible reason is that the stock market reacts to various economic series that are **leading** indicators of the economy – e.g., corporate earnings, profit margins, and money supply.

3.  A diffusion index, by specifying the percent of reporting units experiencing a given result, indicates how pervasive a given movement in a series is. Consider the Net Change in Inventory series for four years of an expansion, assuming there were 200 companies that constitute the sample.

    | Year of Expansion | Number of Companies with Increases |
    |-------------------|------------------------------------|
    | 1 | 120 |
    | 2 | 175 |
    | 3 | 145 |
    | 4 | 120 |

    It is of considerable interest to the analyst to know whether as few as 52 percent of companies increased inventories as opposed to, say, 95 percent, rather than merely know that there was an increase in the series. Notably, the diffusion indexes almost always reach a peak or bottom before the corresponding aggregate series.

4.     Virtually all research has shown the existence of a strong relationship between money supply and stock prices as is evident from high $R^2$s when money supply is used to explain stock price changes.  However, it is not possible to use money supply changes to predict changes in stock prices, and this is **not** contradictory, since the stock market apparently reacts immediately to changes in money supply or investors attempt to **predict** this important variable.  As a result, it is impossible to derive excess profits from watching current or recent past changes in the growth rate of the money supply.

5.     Excess liquidity is the year-to-year percentage change in the M2 money supply less the year-to-year percentage change in nominal GNP.  The economy's need for liquidity is given by its nominal growth.  Any growth in M2 greater than that indicates excess liquidity that is available for buying securities, which would drive up prices.

6.     The excess liquidity argument in question #5 suggests that stock prices should rise.  On the other hand, monetary growth in excess of GNP growth may lead to expected inflation.  The rise in expected inflation should cause the nominal RFR to rise, in turn, causing the required return to rise.  This should lead to a decline in stock prices.

7.     If the market fully anticipates the rise in inflation, the long bond rate should rise to 10%.  If we assume annual coupons, the 15-year 8% bond will go from a price of $1,091.03 to $847.89.

8.     Most of the inputs in determining the price of a bond are known – for instance, the promised coupon payments, the principal amount, and the dates on which those payments will be received.  The one variable to be estimated is the required return, which can be found easily by comparing the bond in questions to a similar existing bond.

       In contrast, the payments on common stock are not known, nor the dates on which they might be received.  Further, the required return is more difficult to estimate.

9.     Based on the economic projections, there will be a low correlation of stock prices among the various countries.  As a result, the investor can reduce risk by diversifying his holdings among various countries.  The relationships

between the various countries' economic variables are reinforced in Table 14.9. This table shows a fairly high correlation of stock returns between the United States and Canada and one of the lowest relationships between the United States and Japan, although this correlation has tended to increase over time as the two economies become more interdependent.

10. Assuming a $1,000 investment, a return of 10 percent would amount to $1,100, whereas returns in the German market would amount to DM 1,695. If the exchange rate goes to 1.30 over the year, the dollar equivalent would be $1,303.84. Thus, the investor should invest in Germany. An appreciation of the dollar to 2.00 DM/$ would reduce the dollar-equivalent return of investing in West Germany to 1,824 DM/$2.0 = $912; thus, it would be more advantageous to invest in the United States.

# Answers to Problems

1.    Student Exercise

2.    CFA Exam I

2(a)1. The National Bureau of Economic Research has conducted extensive analysis of leading, coincident, and lagging indicators of general economic activity. *Business Conditions Digest* classifies economic indicators by their participation in the stage of the economic process and their relationship to business cycle movements.

The leading indicators include those economic time series that usually reach peaks or troughs before the corresponding points in aggregate economic activity. The group includes 12 series. One of the 12 leading series is common stock prices, which has a median lead of nine months at peaks and four months at troughs. Another leading series is the money supply in constant dollars which has a median lead of ten months at peaks and eight months at troughs.

2(a)2. Leading indicators have historically been a good tool for anticipating the economy. Investment managers should be aware of this information and, where possible, investment decisions might reflect projected trends. However, these indicators are by no means infallible. They often generate false signals. A downturn in leading indicators might precede only a retardation of growth rather than a full blown recession if the downturn is shallow or brief. One of the most consistent leading indicators is stock prices represented by the S & P 500 Stock Composite Index. Thus, we are dealing with indicators that are **roughly coincident** with the most significant determinant of stock returns and price changes. An efficient market should already reflect this information. Thus, the attainment of above-average returns using only these series is questionable.

2(b).  **Interest rate forecasts** are usually important in investment management for the following reasons:

Interest rates help determine the relative competitiveness of stocks versus bonds;

They have an effect on the stock returns from interest rate sensitive industries;

They help determine the maturity structure of bond portfolios;

They significantly effect investment in interest futures;

They affect the discount rate used in various equity valuation models.

2(c).   Three economic time series, indicators, or data items that might be of key relevance to an auto analyst would be disposable personal income, consumer interest rate series, and consumer confidence survey results. An increase in disposable personal income might mean more discretionary income is available with which to purchase consumer durables such as automobiles. A decline in consumer interest rates might make the effective price of a car, including borrowing charges, more affordable. Survey results that showed a high and growing level of consumer confidence about the future of the economy would likely have a positive psychological effect on consumer willingness to commit to new, large-ticket purchases.

In summary, the following variables constitute likely indicators of profits and performance in the automobile industry:

Real disposable personal income per capita – to indicate affordability of automobiles;

Installment debt as a percent of disposable income – to indicate ability of consumer to finance new car purchases;

The replacement cycle – indicating the average age of cars on the road, suggesting the inclination of consumers to consider new car purchases;

Trends in the cost of major components of auto production, including the prices charged by major suppliers.

3.    CFA Exam III

3(a). Overall, both managers added value by mitigating the currency effects present in the Index. Both exhibited an ability to "pick stocks" in the markets they chose to be in (Manager B in particular). Manager B used his opportunities **not** to be in stocks quite effectively (via the cash/bond contribution to return), but neither of them matched the passive index in picking the country markets in which to be invested (Manager B in particular).

|  | Manager A | Manager B |
|---|---|---|
| Strengths | Currency Management | Currency Management<br>Stock Selection<br>Use of Cash/Bond Flexibility |
| Weaknesses | Country Selection<br>(to a limited degree) | Country Selection |

3(b). The column reveals the effect on performance in local currency terms after adjustment for movements in the U.S. dollar and, therefore, the effect on the portfolio. Currency gains/losses arise from translating changes in currency exchange rates versus the U.S. dollar over the measuring period (three years in this case) into U.S. dollars for the U.S. pension plan. The Index mix lost 12.9% to the dollar, reducing what would otherwise have been a very favorable return from the various country markets of 19.9% to a net return of only 7.0%.

4. Student Exercise

5. Student Exercise

6. Student Exercise

# CHAPTER 15

## Bond Fundamentals

# Answers to Questions

1. A bond is said to be "called" when the issuer, at its own discretion, "calls" in the bond, and purchases it from the holder at a price stipulated in the bond indenture. When a bond is "refunded," it is called, but the firm reissues bonds for the same amount with a lower coupon rate. On a pure call (without refunding), the issue is usually retired.

2. The three factors affecting the price of a bond are coupon, yield, and term to maturity. The relationship between price and coupon is a direct one--the higher the coupon, the higher the price. The relationship between price and yield is an inverse one--the higher the yield the lower the price, all other factors held constant. The relationship between price and maturity is not so clearly evident. Price changes resulting from changes in yields will be more pronounced, the longer the term to maturity.

3. For a given change in the level of interest rates, two factors that will influence the relative change in bond prices are the coupon and maturity of the issues. Bonds with longer maturity and/or lower coupons will respond most vigorously in a given change in interest rates. Other factors likewise cause differences in price volatility, including the call features, but these factors are typically much less important.

4. A call feature and a sinking fund are bond indenture provisions that can affect the maturity of the bond issue. Specifically there are three alternative call features: (1) freely callable provision that allows the issuer to retire the bond at any time during the life of the bond issue, (2) noncallable provision that does not allow the issuer to retire the bond prior to its maturity, and (3) deferred call provision that allows the issuer to retire the bond after a designated period of time. A sinking fund requires that a bond be paid off during the life of the issue rather than at maturity.

5. Interest income from municipal bonds is normally not taxable by the federal government or by the state or city in which it is issued. Interest income on U.S. Treasury bonds is taxable at the federal level, but not by state or local

governments. Corporate bond interest is taxable at all levels as are capital gains from any of the bonds.

6.   Several institutions who participate in the market are life insurance companies, commercial banks, property and liability insurance companies, private and governmental retirement and pension funds, and mutual funds. They participate in the market because of restrictions on equity purchases (banks), the need for predictable cash flows (insurance companies), the tax exposure of the institutions, and the nature of the institution's liabilities. Commercial banks are subject to normal tax exposure and have fairly short-term liability structures, so they tend to favor intermediate term municipals. Pension funds and life insurance companies are virtually tax free institutions with long term commitments, so they generally prefer high yielding long term corporate bonds.

7.   An investor should be aware of the trading volume for a particular bond because a lack of sufficient trading volume may make selling the bond in a timely manner impossible. As a result, prices may vary widely while the investor is trying to change his position in the bond.

8.   Bond ratings provide a very important service in the market for fixed income securities because they provide the fundamental analysis for thousands of issues. The rating agencies conduct extensive analyses of the intrinsic characteristics of the issue to determine the default risk for the investor and inform the market of the analyses through their ratings.

9.   According to Table 15.1, Japanese bonds (19.2% in 1990 and 22.8% in 1994) and German bonds (11.8% in 1990 and 13.0% in 1994) have posted the largest gains in market share. Countries with slipping market share include the U.S. (45.4% in 1990 and 43.0% in 1994) and Italy (5.5% in 1990 and 4.9% in 1994). Canada (2.9% in 1990 and 2.3% in 1994) and Sweden (1.4% in 1990 and 1.0% in 1994) have also experienced declines in market share.

10.   While approximately 50-55% of the U.S. bond market is made up of government and agency issues, these issues only account for approximately 30-35% of the German market. Approximately 35% of domestic deutschemark bonds are issued by the major commercial banks. The capital market in Germany is dominated by these commercial banks because there is no formal distinction between investment, merchant, or commercial banks as

there is in the United States.  As a result, German banks continuously raise capital through bond issues to finance various industrial operations.  Since these industrial corporations rely on the banks for loans, outstanding bonds of these domestic corporations is minimal.

11.  In the United States, government agency issues, although not direct issues of the Treasury, carry the full faith and credit of the U.S. government.  The rate of interest on these securities is higher than the rate of interest on straight Treasury bond issues.  However, some of the government agency issues are subject to state and local income tax, whereas interest received on Treasury issues is exempt from state and local levies.

12.  The difference between a foreign bond and a Eurobond can be broken down as a difference in issuer and the market in which they are issued.  For example, a foreign bond in Japan (e.g., a Samurai) is denominated in the domestic currency (yen) and is sold in the domestic market (Japan), but it is sold by non-Japanese issuers.  On the other hand, a Eurobond (e.g., a Euro-DM) is denominated in the domestic currency (deutschemark) but it is sold outside the domestic country in a number of national markets.  These bonds are typically underwritten by international syndicates.  The relative size of these two markets varies by country.

13.  The following differences exist between Eurodollar and Yankee bonds:

| Differences in: | Eurodollar | Yankee |
|---|---|---|
| Primary market trading | Outside of U.S. | U.S. |
| Major secondary market trading | Outside of U.S. | U.S. |
| Registration | None | S.E.C. |
| Underwriter | International syndicate | U.S. syndicate |
| Issuer | Any entity | Non- U.S. entity |
| Coupon | Usually annually | Semi-annually |

# Answers to Problems

1.
$$\text{ETY} = \frac{i}{1-t} = \frac{.055}{1-.28} = \frac{.055}{.72} = .07639$$

Assuming all other relevant factors are equal, the corporate bond carrying an 8 percent coupon and selling at par offers a better return than a 5 1/2 percent municipal bond (with an equivalent tax yield of 7.639 percent).

2(a). Present Value = Future Value x Present Value Factor

   PV = $1,000 x .17411 = $174.11

where .17411 is the present value factor for 6% interest (12% annually/2 interest payments per year) for 30 semi-annual periods (15 years x 2 interest payments per year)

2(b). PV = $1,000 x .14205 = $142.05

where .14205 is the present value factor for 5% interest (semi-annually) for 40 semi-annual periods.

3.
$$\text{ETY} = \frac{i}{1-t}$$

3(a). For the 15% tax bracket

$$\text{ETY} = \frac{.084}{1 - .15} = \frac{.084}{.85} = .0988$$

3(b). For the 25% tax bracket

$$\text{ETY} = \frac{.084}{1 - .25} = \frac{.084}{.75} = .1120$$

3(c). For the 35% tax bracket

$$\text{ETY} = \frac{.084}{1 - .35} = \frac{.084}{.65} = .1292$$

4(a). Present Value = Future Value x Present Value Factor

PV = 1,000 x .30832 = $308.32

where .30832 is the present value factor for 4% interest (8% annually/2 interest payments per year) for 30 semi-annual periods (15 years x 2 interest payments per year)

4(b). PV = $1,000 x 0.39012 = $390.12

where .39012 is the present value factor for 4% interest for 24 semi-annual periods.

4(c). PV = $1,000 x .31007 = $310.07

where .31007 is the present value factor for 5% interest for 24 semi-annual periods.

5(a).  PV  =  FV x PV factor
         =  1,000 x .09722
         =  $97.22

where .09722 is the present value factor for 6% interest for 40 semi-annual periods.

5(b).  PV  =  FV x PV factor
       $601 =  $1,000 x PV factor for 4% and 2N periods

Solving for the unknown (4%, 2N PV factor)  =  .601

Using the PV table, the solution is 13 semi-annual periods, or 6 1/2 years (time to maturity).

5(c).  PV  =  FV x PV factor
       $350 =  $1,000 x PV factor for X%/2 and 18 semi-annual periods
Solving for the unknown (X%/2, 18 periods PV factor)  =  .350

Using the PV table, the solution is 6% semi-annual or 12% annual interest.

# CHAPTER 16

# The Analysis and Valuation of Bonds

# Answers to Questions

1. The present value equation is more useful for the bond investor, largely because the bond investor has fewer uncertainties regarding future cash flows than does the common stock investor. By investing in bonds with relatively no default risk (i.e., government securities), the investor can value a bond based primarily on expected cash flows (coupon rate and par value), required return (market yield), and the number of periods in the investment horizon (maturity date). Each of these factors can be incorporated into the present value equation.

   By contrast, common stocks have no stated maturity date and the valuation process is predominately an estimate of future earnings. Although the present value method can be used for common stock analysis by estimating dividend payments and change in price over a given time frame, the uncertainties involved are much greater. It is also assumed that the bond is held to maturity and that all cash flows are received as promised.

   In calculating the yield to call, it is assumed that the bond is called on the nearest call date. Only the cash flows promised to be paid on or before that date are assumed to be received as promised.

2. The most crucial assumption the investor makes is the assumption that cash flows will be reinvested at the **promised yield**. This assumption is crucial because it is implicit in the mathematical equation that solves for promised yield. If the assumption is not valid, an alternative method must be used or the calculations will yield invalid solutions. It is also assumed that the bond is held to maturity and that all cash flows are received as promised.

   In calculating the yield to call, it is assumed that the bond is called on the nearest call date. Only the cash flows promised to be paid on or before that date are assumed to be received as promised.

3(a). RFR is the riskless rate of interest, RF is the risk premium for the individual firm, and I is the factor for expected inflation.

3(b). The model holds no matter what the nature of the information about business conditions. The risk of not breaking even would be reflected in the model through changes in the variable RP. This uncertainty would change the nature of the frequency distribution for earnings.

4. The *expectations hypothesis* imagines a yield curve that reflects what bond investors expect to earn on successive investments in short-term bonds during the term to maturity of the long-term bond. The *liquidity preference hypothesis* envisions an upward-sloping yield curve owing to the fact that investors prefer the liquidity of short-term loans but will lend long if the yields are higher. The *segmented market hypothesis* contends that the yield curve mirrors the investment policies of institutional investors who have different maturity preferences.

5. CFA Exam I (June 1982)

5(a). The *term structure of interest rates* refers to the relationship between yields and maturities for fixed income securities of the same or similar issuer. Expectations regarding future interest rate levels give rise to differing supply and demand pressures in the various maturity sectors of the bond market. These pressures are reflected in differences in the yield movements of bonds of different maturity.

The term structure of interest rates, or *yield curve*, will normally be upward sloping in a period of relatively stable expectations. The theoretical basis for the upward sloping curve is the fact that investors generally demand a premium, the longer the maturity of the issue, to cover the risk through time.

5(b). According to the expectations theory of yield curve determination, if borrowers prefer to sell short maturity issues at the time lenders prefer to invest in longs, which happens when interest rates are expected to fall, longer maturity issues will tend to yield less than shorter maturity issues. The yield curve will be downward sloping. This generally occurs in periods when restrictive monetary policy by the Federal Reserve System, in an attempt to control inflation and inflation expectations, causes very high short-term interest rates. In these circumstances, demand for short-term maturities is severely dampened.

5(c)  The "real" rate of interest is simply the difference between nominal interest rates and some measure of inflation, such as the current consumer price index or GNP deflator. In other words, it is an inflation-adjusted interest rate.

5(d).  The market for U.S. Treasury securities is very large and highly liquid as a result of the huge cumulative debt of the United States government over time. Features of treasury securities tend to be fairly standardized and, by definition, all from one issuer. AAA corporate bonds, on the other hand, are issued by hundreds of different corporations and there are unique features to every different issue even from the same corporation. Thus, their marketplace is much more complex in terms of assessing individual securities.

Some corporate issues are large and trade in very liquid markets. Others, however, are much smaller and tend to have much more restricted marketability. With so many issuers as well as issues, there is more room for inefficiencies to exist for short periods of time, given the diversity of the marketplace.

Any market that is less than efficient offers arbitrage opportunities. Because of these inefficiencies, issues of comparable quality, maturity, and other features can be priced differently, offering swap opportunities for bond traders or portfolio managers. Also, bonds that may appear identical for various reasons could have better trading characteristics and may warrant a certain premium because of time.

5(e).  Over the past several years, fairly wide spreads have existed between AAA-corporates and Treasuries. Investor preference for Treasuries stems from several factors. Treasury securities typically are extremely liquid and provide investors with more flexibility. Secondly, Treasury securities typically do not have restrictive call features generally encountered with high-grade corporates.

Thus, in a period of high interest rates, investors purchasing long-term securities anticipate an eventual decline in inflation and interest rates and thus prefer to lock in higher long-term yields.

6.  CFA Exam III (June 1982)

The mini-coupon bonds would be preferable to the current coupon bond for three reasons:

1)    A mini-coupon bond will have a **longer duration** than the current bond because of the smaller coupon.  Its price will be **more volatile** for a given change in market interest rates, and this is a plus under the assumption of a decline in interest rates over the next three years.

2)    The mini-coupon bonds have **less reinvestment risk** because more of the return comes from the price change over time, which is assumed to increase at the YTM rate.  In contrast, the total coupon for the 14 percent bond must be reinvested at the 13.75 percent rate;  this could be difficult if rates are declining during this period.

3)    The mini-coupon bonds have **greater call protection** as they are callable at 103, or more than double the current market.  In contrast, if rates decline about two percent, the current coupon bond could be called at 114 (against the current market of about 102).  Between the two mini-coupon bonds, the large pension fund would buy the original issue discount bond with its lower price and higher yield to maturity.  This price discrepancy between the two bonds that are otherwise similar reflects the fact that an investor subject to income taxes has to pay a capital gain each year of the OID bond.  It is possible to also make an argument for the other mini-coupon bond on the basis of its longer duration because it has a lower yield to maturity, all else the same.  The point is, because you expect lower rates, you want the longest duration security.

7(a).  Given that interest rates are expected to decline, an investor should select bonds that will maximize price changes.  Thus, an investor should choose bonds with as long a duration as possible.

7(b).  <u>Case 1</u>:     Select Bond. B.  Duration is inversely related to both coupon and yield to maturity.  Bond B wins on both counts.

<u>Case 2</u>:     Select B and C.  Duration is positively related to maturity and inversely related to coupon.  B and C is preferred on both counts.

<u>Case 3</u>:     Select B and F.  Duration is positively related to maturity and negatively related to yield to maturity.  B and F have the longer duration.

8.      Select Portfolio A. First, it has a slightly longer duration, offering greater potential price appreciation. Second, the convexity is greater which also implies greater price change. Third, the portfolio is noncallable, so there is no danger of the bonds being removed from the portfolio by the issuers as rates fall.

9(a).   Call-adjusted duration takes into account the probability of a call and its impact on the actual duration of a bond. If a bond is noncallable, duration is based on all cash flows up to and including maturity. If interest rates drop and a call becomes likely, then duration should be calculated based on the time to call, which can be substantially sooner than maturity.

        The range for duration now is 8.2 to 2.1 years. Because the bond is trading at par, its duration should be near 8.2 years.

9(b).   If rates increase, then duration will drop (recall that duration is inversely related to yield to maturity.) However, call is now very unlikely, so call-adjusted duration will stay near the high end of the range.

9(c).   If rates fall to 4%, call becomes highly probable, so call-adjusted duration will drop to the low end. (Remember here that duration to call is now greater than 2.1 years because of the inverse relationship between duration and yield to maturity).

9(d).   Negative convexity refers to slow price increases of callable bonds as interest rates fall. Indeed, at some point the price change will be zero. This is due to the call price placing a ceiling on the price of a callable bond.

10.     The two methods are <u>modified</u> and <u>Macaulay</u> duration

        Macaulay duration measures the average life of a bond, ignoring any options embedded in the security. Modified duration measures the price sensitivity of a bond to the change in yield to maturity.

        Modified duration is the more widely used method particularly for corporate and mortgage backed issues.

11.  **Option-adjusted duration:** Option-adjusted duration (OAD) is the duration of a callable bond after adjusting for the call option. The formula for OAD is:

$$OAD = (Price_{NCB}/Price_{CB}) \times Dur_{NCB} \times (1 - Delta)$$

where
$Price_{NCB}$ = price of noncallable bond
$Price_{CB}$ = price of callable bond
$Dur_{NCB}$ = modified duration of the noncallable bond
Delta = delta of the call option

As the equation shows, OAD depends on three elements:

1.  **The ratio of the price of the noncallable bond to the price of the callable bond.** The difference between the price of a noncallable bond and a callable bond is equal to the price of the call option. The higher (lower) the price of the call option, the greater (smaller) the ratio. The OAD will depend on the price of the call option.

2.  **The modified duration of the corresponding noncallable (option-free) bond.**

3.  **The delta of the call option.** The delta, which varies between 0 and 1, measures the change in the price of the call option when the price of the underlying bond changes.

OAD permits the analyst to evaluate different fixed-income securities with embedded options (such as a callable bond) by analyzing each of these above components. For a callable bond, for example, using modified duration is inappropriate because the expected cash flow changes as the yield changes. OAD covers the call option component, which is important in assessing callable bonds. Unlike modified duration, which calculates duration risk for option-free bonds, OAD also considers the value and price sensitivity of the option. The OAD of a callable bond will be less than the modified duration of a noncallable bond anywhere between a deep-discount bond and a premium bond with a high coupon rate relative to the prevailing market yield.

**Effective duration.** Modified duration is a measure of the sensitivity of a bond's price to interest rate changes, if the expected cash flow does not change with interest rates. Effective duration allows for changes in the cash flow if interest rates change. The formula for effective duration is:

**Effective duration** $= (P_- - P_+)\big/[(P_0)(y_+ - y_-)]$

where
$P_0$ = initial price (per \$100 of par value)
$P_-$ = price if yield is decreased by x basis points
$P_+$ = price if yield is increased by x basis points
$y_-$ = initial yield minus $x$ basis points
$y_+$ = initial yield plus $x$ basis points

Effective duration can be used to analyze mortgaged-backed securities for changing prepayment rates of cash flows as interest rates change. Effective duration also allows investors to compare the risk (duration) and return (cash flow) between a bond with embedded options and one without any options. Other applications of effective duration include the analysis of asset-backed securities and bonds having call/put options and sinking-fund provisions.

12(a). Description of Adjustment

1. **Historical real interest rate.** The historical real interest rate should be adjusted to remove distortion caused by the U.S. government's "pegging" of interest rates at artificially low levels in the 1940s and early 1950s, when Treasury-bill rates averaged a 0.53 percent return (1941-50). If the government had not pegged interest rates during this period, the rate probably would have been higher than observed, and the "true" long-term average rates would be higher. This situation suggests an upward adjustment to historical real interest rates.

2. **Bond maturity premium.** The observed bond maturity premium should be adjusted to remove bias caused by the pronounced upward trend in inflation and nominal interest rates during the period 1926-87, when investors systematically experienced capital losses on long-term bond holdings. Arnott-Sorenson estimated the loss on long-term bonds at 0.8 percent a year. Therefore, an upward adjustment to the long-term bond maturity premium is also indicated to remove the trend.

**Justification**: The justification for each of these adjustments is that the data contain systematic, long-lasting artificial biases. Such biases must be removed if these data items are to be useful for forming valid expectations.

12(b). Adjustments are justified when existing or prospective circumstances relating to the economic or market factors to be considered differ from those reflected in the historical data. Key circumstances to consider when forming expectations about future returns are:

1.  **Current yield curve and rate of inflation**. In deriving expected returns, an investor might adjust the historical returns of different asset classes to consider the current yield curve and inflation rate. Over time, prospective returns may converge on historical experience, but the expectations embedded in current data must also be considered in deriving best expectations of the future.

2.  **"Halo" or markdown effect**. A halo effect may develop around an asset class that has done unusually well over a prolonged period, resulting in a historical record needing adjustment. Market participants do not easily forget bad investment experience with a particular asset class. Therefore, investors might want to adjust historical returns on an asset class that has done badly over a prolonged period to eliminate any embedded bias.

3.  **Distinct period**. The historical return data since 1926 include many distinct eras with different capital market and inflation experiences. An investor might want to reflect the possibility that the forecast period might differ substantially from the historical norm or might closely resemble a subperiod.

4.  **New dimensions in environment**. The environment of today's capital markets has dimensions to it such that history may be of little use. These dimensions include the savings/investment and import-export disequilibria in the U.S. economy, the globalization and integration of capital markets, and rapid innovation in financial instruments. An investor may want to consider these dimensions in forecasting future returns.

5.  **Different growth prospects**. If the economic growth prospects today differ from history, an investor should consider this circumstance when forming expectations about future returns.

6.  **Unavailability of complete or comparable data**. The lack of availability of complete or comparable data on a given asset class (e.g., real estate, venture capital, and non-U.S. investments) does not justify ignoring them. An investor might use available results plus knowledge of the risk/return characteristics of that asset class to derive useful expected return data and, thus, include that class in the universe of available asset classes.

7.   **Link between risk tolerance and value of capital assets.** Sharpe points out that a direct link exists between the collective risk tolerance of investors and the per capita value of capital assets. An increase in this measure should cause risk premia (maturity, default, equity) to decline, and vice versa. An investor who believes market participants have not considered this may want to adjust historical risk premia appropriately.

13.   Two alternative interpretations of this question are possible.

Alternative 1

In this alternative, the yields shown in the table in the question are assumed to be current yields to maturity and except for the 30 year bonds, all of the Treasury Zero have higher yield to maturity than equivalent maturity Treasury Coupons. One explanation of the higher yield to maturity on the Zeros is that they have significantly higher durations, and hence higher risk, than equivalent maturity Coupon bonds. Secondly, investors who are subject to income taxes must pay annual income taxes on the imputed income on the Zeros even though they receive no current income. Thus Zeros have higher "promised yields" because they have higher risk and tax disadvantages.

Alternative 2

In this alternative, the yields shown in the table in the question are assumed to be the returns actually realized by the investor at maturity. One explanation of the higher realized return on the Zero is that interest rates declined in the holding period, and there was no reinvestment rate risk on the Zeros (i.e., no coupons to reinvest), while the coupon payments on the other Treasuries were reinvested at the lower interest rates. A second explanation of higher realized yields on the Zeros is that even though transactions costs are usually higher on the initial purchase on Zeros as compared to Coupon Treasuries, the periodic brokerage commissions on the reinvested semi-annual coupons may have reduced the realized yield.

14(a). The call provision generally causes the offering yield of a bond to be higher, all other things being equal. The call is an option, exercisable by the issuer. From the issuer's viewpoint, the call feature is valuable when prevailing market rates drop below the coupon rate on the existing bonds. Refinancing at a lower rate would lower interest costs to the company. Between the first call date and maturity the company has this right and, therefore, the call is valuable to the company. Investors are willing to grant this valuable option to the issuer, but only for a price which reflects the likelihood the bond will be called. Therefore, callable bonds sell for a higher offering yield and lower price by the value of the option.

14(b). <u>Duration</u>

Adding a call feature to a proposed bond issue will shorten the duration of the bond.

Duration may be lowered because the call feature can potentially accelerate the payments, dependent on what happens to interest rates. When interest rates are high and the option is deep out-of-the-money, a call is unlikely, and the call-adjusted duration of the callable bond will be slightly lower than the duration of the noncallable bond. With decreasing rates, the likelihood of call increases, and the callable bond's duration decreases, relative to the duration of the noncallable bonds.

The resulting duration measure will be greater than duration to call and less than duration to maturity.

An additional impact is that the call feature increases the uncertainty of duration relative to a non-callable bond (NCB).

<u>Convexity</u>

Relative to a NCB, the call feature reduces the convexity (call-adjusted convexity) of the callable bond.

The call feature reduces the convexity across all interest rates, but the reduction is minimal at high rates when the call is out of the money and is greatest as the market price approaches the strike price and the call becomes more likely.

In fact, the call feature may induce negative convexity as the market price approaches and exceeds the strike price. When the call is more likely to be exercised, the market price won't appreciate much above the call price.

14(c). To use callable bonds and still maintain duration and convexity targets, the value and price sensitivity of the option must be taken into account. The managers will need to calculate call-adjusted duration and convexity for callable bonds and modified duration and convexity for option-free (noncallable) bonds to use them both in the same strategy.

14(d). Some advantages of including callable bonds are as follows:

- Callable bonds have higher offering yields (or more income or more cash flow) than comparable non-callable bonds.
- The larger supply of callable bonds make it easier to maintain duration and convexity targets.

Some disadvantages are:

- The reinvestment risk of having the bonds called away and having to invest at lower rates.
- Management time needed to rebalance when securities called or when rates change.
- Uncertainty about cash flows.

# Answers to Problems

1(a). Assuming annual compounding

$$AYC = \frac{70 + \dfrac{1,100 - 1,000}{4}}{\dfrac{1,100 + 1,000}{2}} = \frac{70 + 25}{1050} = \frac{95}{1050} = 9.05\%$$

1(b). Assuming annual compounding, AYC = 9.18%

$$\$1,000 = 70 \times (3.2270) + 1,100 \times (.7038)$$

$$= 225.89 + 774.18$$

$$= \$1,000.07 \text{ (rounding)}$$

where 3.2270 is the present value of annuity factor and .7038 is the present value factor (both calculated for four periods at a 9.18 percent interest rate per period).

1(c). Assuming annual compounding, 5% interest, 21 years remaining

$$\text{Price} = [70 \times (12.82115)] + [1,000 \times (.35894)]$$

$$= 897.48 + 358.94$$

$$= \$1,256.42$$

where 12.82115 is the present value of annuity factor and .35894 is the present value factor (both calculated for 21 periods at a 5 percent interest rate per period).

2(a).  Assuming semiannual compounding

$$\text{AYM} = \cfrac{40 + \cfrac{1{,}000 - 1{,}012.50}{24}}{\cfrac{1{,}000 + 1{,}012.50}{2}} = \frac{40 - .52}{1006.25} = \frac{39.48}{1006.25} = 3.92\% \text{ (semiannual)}$$

3.92% x 2 = 7.84% annual

2(b).  Assuming semiannual compounding, AYM = 7.84% (= 2 x 3.92%)

where 15.37262 is the present value of annuity factor and .39739 is the present value factor (both calculated for 24 periods at a 3.92 percent interest rate per period).

2(c).  Assuming semiannual compounding, callable in 3 years with 8% premium, AYC = 9.86% ( 2 x 4.93%)

$1,012.50   = 40 x (5.08707) + 1,080 x (.74921)
            = 203.48 + 809.15
              $1,012.63 (rounding)

where 5.08707 is the present value of annuity factor and .74921 is the present value factor (both calculated for 6 periods at a 4.93 percent interest rate per period).

3.

| (1) Period | (2) Cash Flow | (3) PV at 5% | (4) PV of Flow | (5) PV as % of Price | (6) (1) x (5) |
|---|---|---|---|---|---|
| 1 | $   40 | .9524 | $ 38.10 | .04014 | .04014 |
| 2 | 40 | .9070 | 36.28 | 03822 | .07644 |
| 3 | 40 | .8638 | 34.55 | .03640 | .10920 |
| 4 | 40 | .8227 | 32.91 | .03467 | .13868 |
| 5 | 40 | .7835 | 31.34 | .03302 | .16510 |
| 6 | 1,040 | .7462 | 776.05 | .81756 | 4.90536 |
|  |  |  | $949.23 | 1.00000 | 5.43492 |

The duration equals 5.43492 semiannual periods or 2.71746 years.

3(a).

$$\text{Modified duration} = \frac{2.71746}{1 + (.10/2)} = \frac{2.71746}{1.05} = 2.588 \text{ years}$$

3(b).  Percentage change in price

$$= -Dmod \times \Delta i$$

$$= -(2.588) \times (-50/100)$$

$$= 1.294 \text{ percent}$$

The bond price should increase by 1.294% in response to a drop in the bonds YTM from 10% to 9.5%. If the price of the bond before the decline was $949.23, the price after the decline in the YTM should be approximately $949.23 x 1.01294 = $961.51.

4.  Assuming semiannual compounding, 10 years, zero coupon, $1,000 par value, 12% YTM

Purchase Price = $1,000 (.31180) = $311.80
where .31180 is the present value factor for 6% interest
(12% annually/2 interest payments per year) for 20 semi-annual periods (10 years x 2 interest payments per year)


After two years, assuming semiannual compounding, 8 years remaining, zero coupon, $1,000 par value, 8% YTM

Selling Price = $1,000 (.53391) = $533.91
where .53391 is the present value factor for 4% interest
8% annually/2 interest payments per year) for 16 semi-annual periods (8 years remaining x 2 interest payments per year)

Assuming you bought the bond for $311.80 and sold it after two years for $533.91, the ARY = 28.78% annual (14.39% semiannual)

311.80       = 533.91 x (.58405)
             = $311.83 (rounding)

where .58405 is the present value factor (calculated for 4 semiannual periods (2 years) at a 14.39% interest rate per period.


5(a).  Assuming semiannual interest payments

$$\text{Modified duration} = \frac{5.7}{1 + (.095/2)} = \frac{5.7}{1.0475} = 5.442 \text{ years}$$

Percentage change in price    =    -Dmod x $\Delta$i

    =    - (5.442) x (+150/100)

    =    -8.163 percent

A misestimate of the price change will arise because the modified-duration line is a linear estimate of a curvilinear function. That is, convexity measures the rate of change in modified duration as yields change. The effect of convexity on price should be added to the effect of duration on price in order to obtain an improved approximation of the change in price given a change in yield.

5(b).  Percentage change in price    =    -5.442  x  -3%

    =    + 16.33%

The 3% decline in rates may not elevate the bond price by 16.33% if the bond's call price is violated and protection against a call has elapsed.

6.    There are three components of return for international (German) bonds: coupon income, capital appreciation (or loss) as resulting from interest rate movements, and profits (or loss) from changes in currency exchange rates; in contrast, only the first two components of return (coupon income and capital appreciation, or loss) apply to domestic (U.S. government) bonds.

Since both bonds were selling at par on 1/1/91 (in both cases, the market yields on the bonds equaled their coupons), the contribution from coupon income is simply the coupon rate indicated in the table. Given we're dealing with holding period return here, its appropriate to use the beginning price of the issue to measure the current yield (coupon) component of return. Price change resulting from interest rate movements can be calculated using the <u>change in yield times the modified duration</u>, with the sign changed:

    Percent price change = - modified duration x yield change x 100

    German government bond: -0.50 x -7.0 = +3.50%

    U.S. Government Bond:  -1.25 x -6.5 = +8.13%

The percentage change from currency movements can be approximated by taking the reciprocal of the DM/U.S. exchange rate (to express the exchange rate in dollar terms) and finding the percentage change:

$$(1 / 1.50) / (1 / 1.55) = .6667 / .6452 = 1.033 = +3.3\% \text{ change}$$

Thus, the contribution to total return for the two bonds can be summarized as follows:

| | Domestic Coupon Income | + | Domestic Capital Gain | + | Currency Movements | = | Total Return |
|---|---|---|---|---|---|---|---|
| German Govt. Bond | 8.5% | + | 3.5% | + | 3.7% * | = | 15.7% |
| or approximated as | 8.5% | + | 3.5% | + | 3.3% | = | 15.3% |
| U.S. Govt. Bond | 8.0% | + | 8.1% | + | 0.0% | = | 16.1% |

As indicated in the table above, the U.S. government bond offered the superior return relative to the German government bond.

*A more accurate formula to reflect currency movements is:
[(100% + coupon income + capital change) x (currency change)]
=[(100 + 8-5% + 3.5%) x (.033)] = 3.7%

7(a). Modified duration is Macaulay duration divided by 1 plus the yield to maturity divided by the number of coupons per year:

$$\textbf{Modified Duration} = \frac{\textbf{Macaulay duration}}{\left(1 + \dfrac{\textbf{Yield}}{\textbf{k}}\right)}$$

Where k is the number of coupons per year. If the Macaulay duration is 10 years and the yield to maturity is 8%, then modified duration equals 10/(1+(.08/2))= 9.62.

7(b). For option-free coupon bonds, modified duration is a better measure of the bond's sensitivity to changes in interest rates. Maturity considers only the final cash flow, while modified duration includes other factors. These factors are the size of coupon payments, the timing of coupon payments, and the level of interest rates (yield-to-maturity).

7(c). i.      Modified duration increases as the coupon decreases.
      ii.      Modified duration decreases as maturity decreases.

7(d). Convexity measures the rate of change in modified duration as yields change. Convexity refers to the shape of the price-yield relationship and can be used to refine the modified duration approximation of the sensitivity of prices to interest rate changes. Convexity shows the extent to which bond prices rise at a greater rate (as yields fall) than they fall (as yields rise). The effect of duration on price and the effect of convexity on price should be added together to obtain an improved approximation of the change in price for a given change in yield.

8.      To compare the German bond performance versus the U.S. bond performance, one must first compute the return over the six-month period for each security. The return for each security is: Return = Income + forward discount or premium + change in bond price.

     Return on German Bond = 7.5/2 + (-.75) + Change in German Bond Price

     Return on U.S. Bond = 6.5/2 + 0 + 0 = 3.25

If Return on German Bond = Return on U.S. Bond, then:

     3.75 + (-.76) + Change in German Bond Price = 3.25

     Change in German Bond Price = **.25 %** = an increase in price of 1/4 point

9(a). The forward rate is the expected yield during some future period - e.g., the forward rate for year three is the one year rate expected to prevail in year three (three years from now). To calculate the forward rate for a three year bond two years from now, you would use the following formula:

$$\left(1 + {}_{t+m}r_{n-m,t}\right)^{n-m} = \left(1 + {}_{t}R_n\right)^n \Big/ \left(1 + {}_{t}R_m\right)^m$$

where:      r = the forward rate for the period n-m

$R_n$ = the observable yield for a security with maturity n

$R_m$ = the observable yield for a security with maturity m

In this case, we are looking for the forward rate for a three year bond, two years from now (i.e., the forward three year rate for the period from two to five years). Therefore, the computation would be as follows:

$$= \frac{(1 + {}_tR_5)^5}{(1 + {}_tR_2)^2}$$

which in this example would be:

$$= \frac{(1 + .077)^5}{(1 + .079)^2} = 7.566\%$$

9(b).  The January 19XX term structure indicates an upward sloping yield curve. The <u>pure expectations hypothesis</u> would contend that investors are expecting higher short-term rates in the future and, therefore, the forward rate curve would be even steeper than the currently prevailing yield curve which is the geometric average of these future short-term rates. The market segmentation hypothesis would contend that there is greater demand for short-term securities by those who have an interest in this segment of the market. Put another way, those institutions that tend to invest in the short-term segment of the yield curve have greater funds at the present time compared to those who have an interest in long-term securities. The liquidity hypothesis would imply that this upward sloping yield curve is a natural by-product of risk averse investors who require a higher yield to invest in longer term securities because of the higher risk involved - i.e., the greater volatility of longer maturity securities.

9(c).  The term structure over this period experienced what is referred to as a "snap down" in that the short-term rates went up, but the long-term rates went down substantially. As a result, a portfolio with a maturity of two years (and a duration of less than two) would have experienced a fairly small price decline because the yields for one and two year bonds went up. Therefore, this portfolio would have had a small decrease in value during this transition. In sharp contrast, the long-term rates went down substantially and, therefore, a portfolio with a maturity of 10 years (which would have a duration of about 6 years) would have experienced greater volatility than the two year maturity portfolio, but also positive price changes during this period because all the long maturity bonds experienced a decrease in yields. Therefore, this portfolio would have experienced an increase in value.

9(d).  In January 19XX, the spread between short-term and long-term was about 135 basis points compared to the normal spread of 170 basis points. Under these conditions, you would expect this spread to increase during the ensuing period, and this could happen in several ways. Assuming no change in the general level of rates, you could either expect short rates to decline or long rates to increase. Alternatively, if you expected an increase in rates, you would envision that long rates would experience a larger increase in order to reestablish the normal spread. Finally, if you expected a decline in rates, you would expect long rates to decline by less than short rates to reestablish the norm. The point is, in all scenarios, you would expect the change in long rates to be less than optimal. Put another way, this set of expectations would discourage you from aggressively investing in long-term securities. Obviously, this portfolio decision would have been suboptimal based upon what happened because the long bonds had the very best performance because of the "snap down" in the yield curve. This example reflects the point made in the Meyer article that when making a decision with regard to yield spreads, it is also necessary to have some expectations regarding the future level of interest rates. If you really expected that interest rates would decline substantially in the future, you would have possibly anticipated the change in the shape of the yield curve or been willing to invest in long bonds simply because of the greater volatility during a period of declining interest rates.

10(a).  If yield-to-maturity (Y-T-M) on Bond B falls 75 basis points:

-75 basis points = -75/100 = -.75 $\Delta$ in Y-T-M

Pro. Price $\Delta$  = (-modified duration) ($\Delta$ in Y-T-M) + (1/2) (convexity) ($\Delta$ in Y-T-M)$^2$

$\qquad$ = (-6-8)(-.75) + (1/2)(.6)(.75)$^2$

$\qquad$ = 5.1 + .169

$\qquad$ = 5.27

So the projected price will rise to $105.27 from its current $100 price.

10(b). For Bond A, the callable bond, neither maturity nor cash flow is certain. The analysis of callable bonds can take one of four approaches. The first is to ignore the call feature and analyze on a "to maturity basis. All calculations for yield, duration, and convexity are distorted. Durations are too long and yields are too high.

A second approach is to treat the premium bond selling above the call price on a "to call" basis. The duration is unrealistically short and yields too low.

The most effective approach is to use an option evaluation approach. The callable bond can be decomposed into two separate securities - a non-call bond and an option.

Price of callable Bond = Price of non-callable Bond - Price of Option

Since the option will always have some positive value, the callable bond will always have a price which is less than the non-callable security.

An alternative, but less rigorous approach, is to use horizon analysis. The horizon approach considers the three sources of potential dollar return in analyzing a callable bond. The investor is required to estimate an investment holding period, a reinvestment rate, and a call date.

11(a). <u>Final Spot Rate:</u>

$$1000 = \frac{70}{(1+y_1)^1} + \frac{70}{(1+y_2)^2} + \frac{70}{(1+y_3)^3} + \frac{70}{(1+y_4)^4} + \frac{1070}{(1+y_5)^5}$$

$$1000 = \frac{70}{(1.05)^1} + \frac{70}{(1.0521)^2} + \frac{70}{(1.0605)^3} + \frac{70}{(1.0716)^4} + \frac{1070}{(1+y_5)^5}$$

$$1000 = 66.67 + 63.24 + 58.69 + 53.08 + \frac{1070}{(1+y_5)^5}$$

$$1000 - 241.68 = \frac{1070}{(1+y_5)^5}$$

$$758.32 = \frac{1070}{(1+y_5)^5}$$

$$(1+y_5)^5 = \frac{1070}{758.32}$$

$$y_5 = \sqrt[5]{1.411} - 1 = 7.13\%$$

<u>Final Forward Rate:</u>

$$\frac{(1.0713)^5}{(1.0716)^4} - 1 = \frac{1.411}{1.3187} - 1 = 1.0699 - 1 = 7.00\%$$

11(b). Yield-to-maturity is a single discounting rate for a series of cashflows to equate these flows to a current price. It is the internal rate of return.

Spot rates are the unique set of individual discounting rates for each period. They are used to discount each cashflow to equate to a current price. Spot rates are the theoretical rates for zero coupon bonds.

Spot rates can be determined from a series of yields-to-maturity in an internally consistent method such that the cashflows from coupons and principal will be discounted individually to equate to the series of yield-to-maturity rates.

Yield-to-maturity is not unique for any particular maturity, whereas spot rates and forward rates are unique.

16 - 24

Forward rates are the implicit rates that link any two spot rates. They are a unique set of rates that represent the marginal interest rate in a future period. They are directly related to spot rates, and therefore yield-to-maturity. Some would argue (expectations theory) that forward rates are the market expectations of future interest rates. Regardless, forward rates represent a break-even or rate of indifference that link two spot rates. It is important to note that forward rates link spot rates, not yield-to-maturity rates.

11(c). The spot rate at 4 years is 7.16%. Therefore, 7.16 is the theoretical yield to maturity for the zero coupon U.S. Treasury note. The price of the zero coupon at 7.16% is the present value of $1000 to be received in 4 years.

Annual compounding:              PV = 758.35 also can be approximated
                                 from "Present Value of $1 Table"

Semi-Annual compounding:         PV = 754.73

12.     Duration is a weighted average term-to-maturity of a security's cash flows, where the weights are the present value of each cash flow as a percentage of the present value of all cash flows. Compared to a bond with a higher coupon, a bond with a lower coupon provides a larger proportion of its total cash flows at maturity. Hence, it has a longer duration, and exhibits greater percentage price volatility in the face of interest rate changes. Thus the US$-pay SLMA, with its lower coupon, will have a longer duration and increase more in value if rates fall by 100 basis points. Currency fluctuations do not affect directly measures of volatility; the price increases would be in local currency terms.

**13(a). Calculation of One-Year Forward Rate for January 1, 1996:**

$$\left(1+R_4\right)^4 = \left(1+R_3\right)^3\left(1+f_{1,3}\right)$$

$$\left(1+.055\right)^4 = \left(1.05\right)^3\left(1+f_{1,3}\right)$$

$$f_{1,3} = \frac{\left(1+.055\right)^4}{\left(1.05\right)^3} - 1$$

$$f_{1,3} = \frac{1.2388}{1.1576} - 1$$

$$f_{1,3} = 0.701 \text{ or } 7.01\%$$

OR

| Date | Calculation of Forward Rate (Linking Method) |
|------|----------------------------------------------|
| 1/1/93 | 3.5% |
| 1/1/94 | $(1.045)^2 = (1.035)(1+f)$<br>f = 0.0551 or 5.51% |
| 1/1/95 | $(1.05)^3 = (1.035) \times (1.0551) \times (1+f)$<br>f = 0.0601 or 6.01% |
| 1/1/96 | $(1.055)^4 = (1.035) \times (1.0551) \times (1.0601) \times (1+f)$<br>f = 0.0701 or 7.01% |

13(b). The conditions would be those that underlie the pure expectations theory of the term structure: (1) risk neutral market participants who are willing to (2) substitute among maturities solely on the basis of yield differentials. This behavior would rule out liquidity or term premia relating to risk as well as market segmentation based on maturity preferences.

13(c). Under the expectations hypothesis, lower implied forward rates would indicate lower expected future spot rates for the corresponding period. Since the lower expected future rates embodied in the term structure are nominal rates, either lower expected future real rates or lower expected future inflation rates would be consistent with the specified change in the observed (implied) forward rate.

13(d). Multiple scenario forecasting is a technique for developing a set of expectations that reflects the effects that different realizations of key economic variables will have on capital market returns. By providing a mechanism that reveals information about market participants expectations for future interest rate levels (and about changes in these expectations), the term structure can be a useful source of inputs in the process of assembling scenario forecast.

The decline in anticipated futures short-term nominal rates could be depicted either by revising the scenario outcome, (the states) to reflect the possibility of lower future rates or by reweighting the probabilities attached to the scenarios to increase the odds associated with lower future rates.

To maintain consistency, it would also be necessary to take into account changes in other variables that might be induced by lower future interest rates.

The contrast in effects between lower anticipated inflation and a lower real rate of interest will have implications for the development of scenarios.

14. The calculations necessary for obtaining the expected returns are shown below:

Bill:  Coupon = 12.5/4 = 3.125% for the period
       1500 * 1.03125 = 1546.875
       With currency effect: 1546.875/1526 = 1.01368 - 1 = 1.368%

Note:  Coupon = 10/4 = 2.5% for the period
       With duration effect:
100bp * 6 mod dur = 6%
1500 (1.025 + .06) = 1627.50
With currency effect: 1627.50/1526 = 1.06651 - 1 = 6.651%

An alternate approach for obtaining the expected returns is:

Bill:  Yield 12.5%/4 =                                    3.125%
       Currency (1500/15261) - 1                          -1.704
       Return in $ =                                      **1.421%**

Note:  Yield 10.0%/4 =                                    2.500%
       100 basis point change in expected return over
       3-month horizon x 6.00 modified duration =         6.000
       Currency (1500/15261) - 1 =                        -1.704
       Return in $ =                                      **6.796%**

15(a). Current yield = Annual dollar coupon interest / Price

= 70 / 960

= 7.3%.

The annual yield to maturity (YTM) is

$$P = \sum_{t=1}^{n} \frac{C}{(1+y)^t} + \frac{M}{(1+y)^n}$$

where

$P$ = price of the bond,

$C$ = semiannual coupon,

$M$ = maturity value,

$n$ = number of periods, and

$y$ = semiannual yield to maturity.

That is,

$$960 = \sum_{t=1}^{10} \frac{35}{(1+y)^t} + \frac{1000}{(1+y)^{10}}$$

$y$ = 4.0% semiannual return,

YTM = 8% per year.

Horizon yield (also called total return) accounts for coupon interest, interest on interest, and proceeds from sale of the bond.

1. Coupon interest + interest on interest

$$= C \left[ \frac{(1+r)^n - 1}{T} \right]$$

where,

$C$ = semiannual coupon,

$r$ = semiannual reinvestment rate, and
$n$ = number of periods.

That is,

$$= 35\left[\frac{(1.03)^6 - 1}{0.03}\right] = 226.39$$

2.  Projected sale price at the end of three years is $1,000 because bonds that yield the required rate of return always sell at par
3.  Sum the results of Steps 1 and 2 to obtain $1.226.39.
4.  Semiannual total return =

$$= \left[\frac{1226.39}{960}\right]^{1/6} - 1 = 4.166\%$$

5.  Double the interest rate found in Step 4 for the annual total rate of return of 8.33 percent.

15(b). The shortcomings of the yield measures are as follows: (1)Current yield does not account for interest on interest (compounding) or changes in bond price during the holding period. It also does not allow for a gain or loss from a bond purchased at a discount or premium. (2) Yield to maturity assumes that the bond is held to maturity and that all coupon interest can be reinvested at the yield-to-maturity rate. Because yields change constantly, that assumption is incorrect. However, yield to maturity is the industry standard for comparing one bond with another. (3) Total return (as calculated) assumes that all coupons can be invested at a constant reinvestment rate and requires assumptions about holding period, reinvestment rate, and yield on the bond at the end of the investor's holding period. Although it is a more complete measure of return, it is only as accurate as its inputs.

16(a). In U.S. dollars, one share of Euro Disney sells for 86.80 x 0.1761 = $15.29. The exchange value is 19.651 x 15.29 = $300.37.

16(b). Disadvantages to Disney resulting from redeeming the zero-coupon note and replacing some of the funds with proceeds from the issue of 100-year bonds include: (1) Notes with a yield to maturity of 6 percent are replaced with bonds at a higher yield to maturity, 7.55 percent. (2) No annual cash payment is required for the zero-coupon note, but annual cash payments are required for the 100-year bond. (3) The new bonds are not callable until the year 2023 (30 years of call protection for a holder of the bond), whereas the zero-coupon note has no call protection. (4) Only with the zero-coupon note does Disney get a cash tax savings from a deduction for interest without an associated cash outflow for interest. (5) Of lesser importance, transaction costs (investment banking fees, etc.) associated with the replacement may be significant.

17. The essence of the answer is to price each bond's cash flows using the spot curve (Table 2).

The nonarbitrage price of bond A is

$$\frac{10}{1.05} + \frac{10}{(1.08)^2} + \frac{110}{(1.11)^3} = 98.53$$

The market price of Bond A is 98.40,13 cents (13.2 basis points of market price) less than the nonarbitrage price.

The nonarbitrage price of Bond B is

$$\frac{6}{1.05} + \frac{6}{(1.08)^2} + \frac{106}{(1.11)^3} = 88.36$$

The market price of Bond B is 88.34, only 2 cents (2.3 basis points of market price) less than the nonarbitrage price.

*Conclusion.* Despite having the lower yield to maturity (10.65 percent versus 10.75 percent), Bond A is the better value because the excess of its nonarbitrage price over market price is greater than for Bond B.

# CHAPTER 17

# Bond Portfolio Management Strategies

# Answers to Questions

1. An indexing portfolio strategy is one in which the investor selects a bond portfolio that matches the performance of some bond-market index. The basic justification for this strategy is that many empirical studies have shown that portfolio managers on average can't match the risk-return performance in the bond market using active portfolio management.

2. A *pure yield pickup swap* is selling a bond and buying another one with a higher coupon. Normally, both current yield and yield-to-maturity are enhanced. A *substitution swap* is the swapping of one bond for another between which a yield spread imbalance exists. The investor expects the imbalance to disappear through the mechanism of having the yield on the purchased bond drop (through a price increase) to the level of the swapped bond, leading to attractive capital gains. A *tax swap* is simply a bond swap which enables an investor to realize capital losses on one bond to offset capital gains which she has realized on some other investment.

3. These active management strategies include interest rate anticipation, credit analysis, and spread analysis. *Interest rate anticipation* is the riskiest strategy because it relies on forecasting uncertain future interest rate behavior. The strategy involves altering the maturity (duration) structure of the portfolio to preserve capital when an increase in interest rates is anticipated and achieve capital gains when they are expected to decline. A *credit analysis* strategy involves attempting to project changes in quality ratings assigned to bonds. It is necessary to analyze internal changes in the firm and external changes in the environment to project rating changes prior to the actual announcement by rating agencies. *Spread analysis* involves monitoring the yield relationships between various bond sectors to take advantage of abnormal relationships by executing various sector swaps. Liquidity is a key factor in this strategy, as abnormal relationships are only believed to be temporary.

4. Two important variables when analyzing junk bonds include: 1) the use of cash flows in relation to debit obligations, and 2) a detailed analysis of

potential asset sales. The *cash flow analysis* is important in determining the firm's ability to make interest payments, as well as maintain cash for research and growth in periods of economic decline. Cash flow can also affect the firm's borrowing capacity to provide flexibility and needed working capital. In many cases, asset sales are a critical part of the strategy for a leveraged buyout. In order to analyze the market value of these assets it is necessary to determine whether there are any prior liens against the assets, as well as the true liquidation value and a reasonable time period for the sale.

5.   The advantage of the cash-matched portfolio is that it is a relatively conservative strategy in which cash flows generated from the portfolio are designed to exactly match liability schedules in both timing and amount. Such a portfolio is often difficult to construct as a result of certain call features often associated with the higher-yielding deep discount bonds. On the other hand, if the portfolio manager limits himself to only Treasury bonds, he will likely forego significant added returns that could be achieved with other investments, thus adding to the net cost of funding the liability stream.

6.   Interest rate risk comprises two risks -- a price risk and a coupon reinvestment risk. Price risk represents the change that interest rates will differ from the rates the manager expects to prevail between purchase and target date. Such a change causes the market price for the bond (i.e., the realized price) to differ from the expected price. Obviously, if interest rates increase, the realized price for the bond in the secondary market will be below expectations, while if interest rates decline, the realized price will exceed expectations.

Reinvestment risk arises because interest rates at which coupon payments can be reinvested are unknown. If interest rates change after the bond is purchased, coupon payments will be reinvested at rates different than that prevailing at the time of the purchase. As an example, if interest rates decline, coupon payments will be reinvested at lower rates than at the time of purchase and their contribution to the ending wealth position of the investor will be below expectations. Alternatively, if interest rates increase, there will be a positive impact as coupon payments will be reinvested at rates above expectations.

7.    A portfolio of investments in bonds is ***immunized*** for a holding period if the value of the portfolio at the end of the holding period, regardless of the course of interest rates during the holding period, is at least as large as it would have been had the interest rate function been constant throughout the holding period. Put another way, if the realized return on an investment in bonds is sure to be at least as large as the computed yield to the investment horizon, then that investment is immunized. As an example, if an investor acquired a portfolio bond when prevailing interest rates were 10% and had an investment horizon of four years, then the investor would expect the value of the portfolio at the end of four years to be 1.4641 times the beginning value. This particular value is equal to 10% compounded for four years.

A bond manager would want to immunize the portfolio in the instance where he/she had a specified investment horizon and had a definite required or promised yield for the bond portfolio. In the case where this required or expected yield was below current prevailing market rates, it would be worthwhile for the bond managers to immunize the portfolio and therefore "lock in" the prevailing market yield for this period. Put another way, it is used when the bond portfolio manager is willing to engage in non-active bond portfolio management and accept the current prevailing rate during the investment horizon.

8.    As mentioned, the purpose of immunization is to mitigate the price risk and reinvestment risk associated with changes in interest rates over the investment horizon. Assuming a constant flat yield curve over the investment horizon, there is no need to immunize the portfolio. The investor can obtain investment objectives by simply purchasing bonds scheduled to mature at the end of his investment horizon. With no change in interest rates, the stated yield-to-maturity at the time of purchase should equal the realized yield at the time the bonds mature.

9.    Investment horizon a year later       = 3
      Duration of portfolio a year later    = 3.2

While the term-to-maturity has declined by a year, the duration has only declined by .8 years. This means that, assuming **no changes in market rates**, the portfolio manager must rebalance the portfolio to reduce its duration to three years.

*17 - 5*

10. The objective of immunization centers around mitigating the two components of interest rate risk--price risk and coupon reinvestment risk. Keeping this in mind, many feel that a zero coupon bond is the ideal financial instrument to use for immunization because it eliminates these risks, and thus eliminates the need to rebalance the portfolio. Reinvestment risk is eliminated because it is assumed the value of the bond will grow at the stated discount rate, and price risk is eliminated because if you set the duration equal to your time horizon, you will receive the face value of your bond at maturity.

11. Several characteristics of duration make it impossible to set a duration equal to the initial time horizon of a portfolio and ignore it thereafter. First, because duration declines more slowly than term-to-maturity, even if one assumes no changes in interest rates, the portfolio manager must periodically rebalance the portfolio. Second, if there is a change in market rates, the duration of the portfolio will change. If the deviation becomes large compared to original duration of the portfolio, the manager will again have to rebalance. Third, the technique assumes that when market rates change, they will change by the same amount and in the same direction. Since this is not true of the real world, the manager must assure that the portfolio is composed of various bonds with durations that bunch around the desired duration of the portfolio. Finally, developing the portfolio can be a problem since there can always be a problem of acquiring the desired bonds in the market.

12. A contingent immunization strategy allows the investor an opportunity to obtain a higher return on his portfolio if he is willing to accept greater uncertainty and a possibly lower ending wealth value. By specifying a floor return lower than the current market rate, the investor gives up the certainty involved with immunizing the portfolio at the current rate. However, the investor gains the benefit of his portfolio being actively managed in such a way as that *potential returns* may be achieved over the investment horizon that are above the then-current market rate at the beginning of the horizon.

13. Exam III (June 1983)

13(a). Interest rate risk comprises two risks -- a price risk and a coupon reinvestment risk. *Price risk* represents the chance that interest rates will differ from the rates the manager expects to prevail between purchase and target date. Such a change causes the market price for the bond (i.e., the realized price) to differ from the expected price. Obviously, if interest rates increase, the realized price for the bond in the secondary market will be below expectations, while if interest rates decline, the realized price will exceed expectations.

*Reinvestment risk* arises because interest rates at which coupon payments can be reinvested are unknown. If interest rates change after the bond is purchased, coupon payments will be reinvested at rates different than that prevailing at the time of the purchase. As an example, if interest rates decline, coupon payments will be reinvested at lower rates than at the time of purchase and their contribution to the ending wealth position of the investor will be below expectations. Contrariwise, if interest rates increase there will be a positive impact as coupon payments will be reinvested at rates above expectations.

13(b). A portfolio of investments in bonds is immunized for a holding period if the value of the portfolio at the end of the holding period, regardless of the course of interest rates during the holding period, is at least as large as it would have been had the interest rate function been constant throughout the holding period. Put another way, if the realized return on an investment in bonds is sure to be at least as large as the computed yield to the investment horizon, then that investment is immunized. As an example, if an investor acquired a portfolio bond when prevailing interest rates were 10% and had an investment horizon of four years, then the investor would expect the value of the portfolio at the end of four years to be 1.4641 x the beginning value. This particular value is equal to 10% compounded for four years.

A bond manager would want to immunize the portfolio in the instance where he/she had a specified investment horizon and had a definite required or promised yield for the bond portfolio. In the case where this required or expected yield was below current prevailing market rates, it would be worthwhile for the bond managers to immunize the portfolio and therefore "lock in" the prevailing market yield for this period. Put another way, it is when the bond portfolio manager is willing to engage in non-active bond portfolio management and accept the current prevailing rate during the investment horizon.

13(c). As set forth by a number of authors, the technique used to immunize a portfolio is to set the duration of the portfolio equal to the investment horizon for the portfolio. It has been proven that this technique will work because during the life of the portfolio, the two major interest rate risks (price risk and reinvestment risk) offset each other at this point in time. The zero coupon bond is an ideal immunization instrument because, by its very nature, it accomplishes these two purposes when the maturity of the zero coupon bond equals the investment horizon because the duration of a zero coupon bond is equal to its maturity period. In contrast, when you match the maturity of the bond to the investment horizon, you are only taking account of the price risk whereby you will receive the par value of the bond at the maturity of the bond. The problem is that you are not sure of how the investment risk will work out. It obviously can be that rates rise in which case you will receive more in reinvestment than expected. Alternatively, if rates decline, you will not benefit from the price advantage and, in fact, will lose in terms of the reinvestment assumptions.

13(d). The zero coupon bond is a superior immunization security because it eliminates both interest rate risks--price and reinvestment.

A zero coupon bond is a perfect immunizer when its duration (or maturity, as they are the same) is equal to the liability or planning horizon of the portfolio. Given adequate availability, the portfolio manager would match these elements and no further activity is necessary to the end of the horizon.

The zero coupon bond is superior to a coupon paying instrument because the lack of cash flow prior to maturity eliminates any coupon reinvestment and, therefore, the risk of realized return changes due to uncertainty of these levels. Price risk is also nonexistent regardless of the timing or nature of yield curve shifts.

13(e). The primary difference between contingent and classical immunization is the role of active management. Classical immunization precisely matches the duration of the portfolio with the horizon of the particular liability. Management of such a portfolio is limited to periodic rebalancing necessitated by yield curve shifts, yield changes, and time effects on duration. Contingent immunization is an active form of management, initially, and can continue in this mode until the manager's results are unfavorable to the extent that a predetermined target return is unlikely to be achieved. At this point, the active mode is triggered to a classical passive immunization to "lock in" the minimum desired return.

Contingent immunization achieves its risk control by establishing two parameters: (1) The minimum return target for more specifically the difference between the minimum return target and the immunization return than available in the market, and (2) the acceptable range for the terminal horizon date of the program. The chart below illustrates the potential rewards from contingent immunization based on possible moves in interest rates. It is interesting to note the similarity of this curve to that of option strategies.

Potential Return (%)

Immediate Yield Change from 12%
(Percent Points)

Careful monitoring of the value achieved by the manager in the portfolio is important. A return or portfolio value line can be established, initially, which traces the required dollar value of the portfolio at any given point in time and would be a minimum level necessary for the portfolio to reach its minimum return target. If the return or value falls to this, the "safety net" is activated.

A key facet of contingent immunization is the benefit from flexibility or loosening of rigid conditions. Substantial flexibility is granted the portfolio's manager if either the horizon time is widened to a range rather than a single point or if the minimum return is meaningfully below that available currently through classical immunization.

By granting this flexibility and being willing to accept a slightly lower than current market return, the plan sponsor or portfolio manager has the opportunity to achieve much greater returns through interest rate anticipation, swapping and other facets of active management.

This approach is attractive to a portfolio manager who believes his/her skills will provide "excess returns" yet establish a downside risk control that assures achievement of a minimum target return.

14.   CFA Exam III (June 1986)

14(a). With an immunized portfolio the goal is to provide a minimum dollar amount of assets at a single horizon.

*Contingent immunization* is primarily an active strategy. However, a minimum return is required. Should the portfolio deteriorate to the point where this return is threatened, there is a switch to full immunization of the portfolio.

The purpose of a *cash-matched dedicated portfolio* is to have a portfolio which will generate cash flows that specifically match the required *stream* of cash outflows. Therefore, it is necessary to match maturities and amounts over a time period, not a single time period. This is accomplished by planning maturities and interim cash flows from the portfolio.

The purpose of a *duration-matched dedication portfolio* is likewise to match the cash flows from the portfolio to the required cash outflows over time. The major difference from the cash-matched dedication is that you recognize that you do this by matching the weighted average duration of the obligations with the duration of your investment portfolio.

14(b). When managing an *immunized* portfolio, it is necessary to maintain the duration of the portfolio equal to the investment horizon. The problem is that this requires *rebalancing* because 1) duration declines slower than term to maturity, and 2) duration is affected by changes in market yields -- i.e., there is an inverse relationship between yield and duration.

14(c). With a cash-matched dedication portfolio it is necessary to make several major decisions.

   (1). Timing of initiation. Usually, the client wants to initiate the portfolio immediately. Let the client prevail unless the portfolio manager considers a delay advisable.

   (2). Payments time intervals. Specify when the required payments are to be made -- yearly, semiannually, quarterly.

   (3). How to avoid call risk. Is this accomplished by having deep-discount bonds or non-callable securities?

   (4). What is your reinvestment rate assumption for the interim flows? You should be very conservative in your estimate to avoid negative surprises.

14(d). Three basic components should be specified for contingent immunization:

   (1). Immunized Base Return -- the return which could be earned if the portfolio is immunized at today's rates.

   (2). Investment Objective – the return goal which exceeds the Immunized Base Return to be achieved by active management.

   (3). Assured Minimum Return – the minimum allowable return consistent with the needs of the client. This is the trigger for full immunization.

   In addition to the above, the client and manager should agree on the flexibility to be allowed the manager in an active strategy. The agreement should specify *the time horizon* and *duration variance*.

14(e). Once the portfolio is established, the *cash-matched dedicated* portfolio probably requires the least supervision over time. You do not have to rebalance the immunized portfolio or adjust the duration of the duration-matched dedicated portfolio.

15. CFA Exam III (June 1988)

Restructuring opportunities are not a function of time, but rather a result of changing market conditions. Conditions that are generally favorable to restructuring include:

(1). Availability of more efficient issues. When you originally structured the portfolio program, you used the issues that were available. Over time, more issues become available through trading or new issues come to market that do a better job of fitting the requirements of the portfolio. As a result, you can substitute issues that do a better job (i.e., are more efficient) of meeting the goals of the portfolio.

(2). Changes in the shape of the yield curve. If the yield curve changes (e.g., goes from positively sloped to negative), it might be possible to shift out of a pure cash matched policy to one where you receive the cash flows earlier and can invest them at a higher rate of return to exceed expectations. The question becomes: What was the assumed reinvestment rate compared to the current rates, given the prevailing yield curve?

(3). Changes in quality or sector spreads. This would involve changes in the price relationship between quality groups (e.g., agencies versus Treasuries, AAA versus AA) or sectors (e.g., industrials versus utilities). You could envision an instance where the yield spread of AAA corporates to treasuries that were in the portfolio declined and the spread for FNMA issue increased which would allow you to swap the AAA corporate for the FNMA issue. This swap would provide a portfolio of equal quality and probably all a cash takeout.

16. CFA Exam III (June 1988)

16(a). You would generally expect it to be easier to match the performance of a bond index as contrasted to a stock index because of the aggregate homogeneity of the bond market compared to the stock market. As a result you could match the performance of the bond index with substantially fewer issues. As an example, in order to match the performance of the S&P 500 Stock Index, it generally requires anywhere from 300 to 450 issues. In contrast, one could do a fairly good job of tracking a bond index that would include thousands of issues with less than 100 bonds simply because bonds are so heavily influenced by the general movements in interest rates. Therefore, although you might need bonds with different characteristics to match the index (e.g., industry and quality characteristics), it would not be necessary to have numerous issues with each of the desired characteristics.

16(b). While it might be possible to match the bond index with fewer issues, the selection and operational process of running the bond index fund would be more difficult. First, it is going to **require more characteristics to derive the desired diversification**. While the equity market only requires serious consideration of capitalization and risk decile, bonds have many characteristics that can effect return including maturity, duration, credit quality, capitalization, coupon, industrial classification, sinking fund, and a call features. Thus, it will be necessary to determine the makeup for each of these characteristics and attempt to match it in the portfolio.

A second factor would be the **difficulty of trading bonds** as opposed to stocks. In the case of a stock index you are typically dealing with very large capitalization stocks traded on an exchange or involved in an active over-the-counter market. In contrast, the secondary corporate bond market is not nearly as liquid and so it is difficult to buy and sell for the bond index fund.

Finally, there is greater difficulty in **reinvestment of the cash flows** from a bond index fund rather than a stock index. Because of heavier cash flows from a bond index fund you are going to have more frequent buying programs. These can be a blessing because it allows you to change the makeup of the fund, but also it could be difficult to avoid changing the fund with small buying programs. The point is, it is going to require balancing cash flow purchases among all relevant bond characteristics to avoid changing the bond index fund portfolio.

17. CFA Exam III (June 1988)

17(a). Assuming that Kaufmann does not take currency hedging into account in his analysis, he would have to project portfolio returns in each country based on (1) coupon, (2) changes in interest rates (bond prices), and (3) changes in currency. Estimated changes in the money supply, GNP/GDP, and inflation are already factored into estimated interest and exchange rates.

One method to determine investment weighting would be to estimate the income from the bond, change in bond price, and foreign currency change. Assuming a duration of 8 for the bond portfolio, the calculations are as follows:

|  | INCOME | BOND PRICE | CURRENCY | EXPECTED RETURN | RECOMMEND |
|---|---|---|---|---|---|
| U.S. | 8.8% | (1.6%) | N/A | 7.2% | Overweight/ Neutral |
| Japan | 6.1 | 0 | 0.8 | 6.9 | Underweight/ Neutral |
| West Germany | 6.1 | (7.2%) | 4.0 | 2.9 | Underweight |
| United Kingdom | 9.8 | 2.4 | (1.7) | 10.5 | Overweight |

In the above solution, the conclusion will vary, depending upon the duration of the portfolio and the coupon income.

In a more simplistic analysis, Kaufmann could evaluate whether the factors of real rates, direction of rates, and exchange rates are positive or negative.

Real rates in each country are as follows:

| United States | 5.2% |
|---|---|
| Japan | 3.1% |
| West German | 4.8% |
| United Kingdom | 4.7% |

Real interest Rates are highest in the United States and lowest in Japan, with West Germany and the United Kingdom in the middle.

|  | REAL RATES | OF RATES | EXCHANGE RATE | RECOMMEND |
|---|---|---|---|---|
| U.S. | + | -/0 | N/A | Overweight/ Neutral |
| Japan | - | 0 | +/0 | Underweight |
| West Germany | 0 | -/0 | N/A | Overweight |
| United Kingdom | 0 | + | 0 | Overweight |

| 0 | = | Neutral |
|---|---|---|
| + | = | Positive |
| ++ | = | Very Positive |
| - | = | Negative |
| -- | = | Very Negative |

Given all of the above factors, Kaufmann would overweight the United Kingdom. Interest rates are expected to decline, the exchange rate is not expected to change dramatically, and real interest rates are moderate. West Germany would likely be underweighted, since interest rates are anticipated to rise dramatically, offsetting any benefits from currency. Japan and the United States would have rankings between the other two. For the United States, exchange rates are not a factor, so relatively high rates that are not projected to rise dramatically would probably warrant a neutral or slight overweighting. In Japan, rates are anticipated to be stable, and since currency is only a very slight positive factor, this country's bonds should be weighted neutrally or slightly underweighted.

17(b). If hedging is used, then changes in currency will not be part of the return analysis. In this case, the decision would probably not change. The United Kingdom still has the most appealing outlook.

18(a). The three issues that Robert and Neil should address are the following:

1) <u>The starting yield level relative to the U.S.</u> If the spread is positive, this provides a cushion against unfavorable moves in either interest rates in the foreign market or in the value of the foreign currency. If the spread is negative, the foreign market must make up the difference by outperforming in local currency terms or by experiencing an appreciation in its currency (or both).

2) <u>The prospects for internal price movements relative to the U.S. bond market</u>. In other words, what is the likely trend in yield spreads between the foreign market and the U.S.? Unlike in the U.S., where yields in different sectors will generally move in the same direction, albeit at different rates, yields in foreign markets may move in opposite directions to the U.S., due to differences in economic, social and political factors in those foreign markets.

3) <u>The prospects for currency gain or loss versus the dollar</u>. The factors Robert and Neil should look at to assess prospects for the Deutschemark and the Australian dollar include:
   a) trends in the balance of payments
   b) inflation and interest rate differentials
   c) the social and political atmosphere, particularly as it relates to foreign investment
   d) the extent of central bank intervention in the currency markets.

18(b). The two reasons for investing in a mixture of international bonds are (1) the opportunity for superior rates of return and (2) diversification. With respect to return, economic and interest rate cycles tend not to move in parallel worldwide. As a result, being able to invest in a host of different markets presents opportunities for above-average return in comparison to having access to only one individual and relatively homogeneous market. Similarly, as regards diversification, foreign bond markets are not perfectly correlated with the U.S. bond market. This means that the volatility of return for a portfolio of global bonds will be less than for a portfolio comprised only of U.S. bonds.

The ERISA account does have a 10% position in Canadian bonds, but the close interrelationship of the Canadian economy and its capital markets makes Canada highly correlated with the U.S. In that sense, the Canadian position does not afford the return and diversification opportunities that other foreign bond markets would offer.

19(a). Market liquidity should be a major consideration when investing in high-yield bonds. It has been demonstrated on many occasions that high yield bon(1s possess substantially less liquidity than Treasury securities and high grade corporate bonds. This lack of liquidity has been very evident following credit problems for several individual issues. Apparently tied to some default announcements, there were days when there was almost no trading at all in the high-yield bond market. Even though high-yield bonds are less liquid than Treasury and high-grade corporate bonds, it is important to recognize that they are still more liquid than corporate bank loans or private placement bond issues in the debt continuum.

The pricing of high-yield bonds has likewise come under some scrutiny from those accustomed to the continuous pricing available in equities, the reasonably good pricing available for Treasury issues, and the frequent quotes typically available for high-grade corporate bonds. Even though some high-yield issues have been listed on either the New York or American exchanges, which implies that there should be more pricing available, it is universally recognized that the volume of bond transactions on the exchanges is only a very limited proportion of total trading since almost all of the large, important trades are done over-the-counter, and these transactions are not reported. Also, there are important differences between quoted prices and the actual price that would be received if an attempt to trade a fairly large block of a high-yield issue was made.

Because high-yield bonds are generally less liquid and are more difficult to price, this should enter into the pricing of these securities (i.e., it is necessary to include a liquidity/pricing premium as part of your required rate of return in addition to the credit risk premium). Second, because of the relative illiquidity, when adding these to a portfolio, it must be recognized that they cannot be used for short-term trading. Alternatively, a portfolio manager may decide that he/she wants to invest in high-yield bonds, but will limit investments to the set of high-yield bonds that enjoy fairly active, liquid markets with relatively frequent pricing.

19(b). The reason that Treasury bonds and high-grade corporate bonds are so highly correlated (in excess of .98) is because the major factor causing changes in their rates of return are aggregate market interest rates (i.e., the yield curve for Treasury securities). In terms of the Capital Asset Pricing Model (CAPM), the fact that these rates of return move together means that they possess very high systematic risk (i.e., all rates of return are being driven by one major aggregate market variable which in this case is market interest rates). The rates of return for high-yield bonds are likewise influenced by market interest rates, but they also have a very large unique component which is the performance of the company and the credit quality of the issue. In terms of the CAPM, this unique risk possessed by high-yield bonds would be described as "unsystematic risk." Notably, this unsystematic risk can be diversified away in a large portfolio. This implies that while it is essential to diversify a portfolio of high-yield bonds to eliminate the unsystematic risk, it also means that such bonds are good additions to a portfolio with high systematic risk, as described above.

Because the rates of return for high-yield bonds are not very highly correlated with rates of return for Treasuries and high-grade corporate bonds, they would be an excellent addition to such a portfolio because they would help reduce its overall risk. This would be like adding common stocks to such a bond portfolio. In addition, if the expected rates of return on these securities were higher than those on treasuries and high-grade corporates, you could be in a position of not only reducing the overall risk of the portfolio, but also increasing its average rate of return. The fact is, for most of the years prior to 1989, the total rates of return on high yield bonds was consistently higher than comparable returns on Treasuries or high-grade corporate bonds.

19(c). The duration for high-yield bonds would be much lower than the duration for high-grade corporates because of the impact of all three of the major factors that influence duration: maturity, coupon and market yield. The average maturity of high-yield bonds is shorter than high-grade corporates simply because of the inherent risk which causes investors to demand shorter maturities - e g, 10 to 15 year maturities for high-yield bonds compared to 15 to 25 years for high-grade corporates. The average maturity for high-yield bonds is lower than for high-grade corporates, and duration is positively related to maturity.

Second, because of the risk of high-yield bonds, they have a higher required rate of return which is reflected in a higher coupon for these securities, and there is an inverse relationship between the coupon and the duration of the security.

Third, not only is the coupon high, but the market yield to maturity on these securities would likewise be high. Again, there is an inverse relationship between the discount rate used to compute duration (i.e., the yield to maturity) and the duration of the bond.

20(a). <u>Concept</u>

To evaluate the uses of convexity and duration. Option theory is not required to answer this question as this is probably a Level III concept at this point. However, many candidates will incorporate it into their answer.

(1) Kemp should be generally concerned about the ability of the new portfolio structure to outperforrn the old in a falling interest rate environment. He should ask about the degree of negative convexity being added through use of the callable bonds. Treasury bonds will rise more in price, based on a mathematical model, versus a callable corporate. Since the move forecasted is relatively large, convexity will become quite important.

(2) Kemp should ask about the yield calculations being used for the corporate bonds. If it is "yield-to-maturity" and the bonds are selling at a premium, he should ask for spreads on a "yield-to-call" basis. Results from a yield-to-maturity basis - both spreads and calculations will be unrealistic.

(3) Kemp may want to encourage the bond group to state the swap on an option adjusted spread basis. This is the most effective approach to describe the characteristics of callable bonds. Each bond is broken into two portions - the non-callable and the option owned by the issuer.

20(b). Given the outlook for significantly lower rates, it is important to minimize negative convexity. He should look for non-callable corporates and lower the coupon level of the purchases to accomplish this.

He also should take a close look at the option adjusted spreads received on any corporate to see if it is worth reducing convexity in a bull market. There may be some doubt if this is realistic.

If he does proceed with corporate bonds, they should insist on adhering to the use of utilities where event risk is lower. While maturity is a major determinant of volatility, credit spreads can also add significant risk to the duration. Utility bonds are less likely to be subject to this.

21. *Competition.* In an industry where large firms have pricing power, a small firm could be at a significant disadvantage, particularly if it has higher unit costs than the large firms. A price war to capture market share could drive small competitors out of business. To the extent that a small company can differentiate its product and, therefore, control a segment of the market, this size factor is less important. However, this market niche must be monitored to ensure that it remains under the control of the small company.

Greater competition within the industry could affect the future cash flows of a company because of price wars or market-share-volume declines. Cash flow could also be negatively affected if a company responds to competition by increasing R&D expenses and capital expenditures to retain market share. Whether driven by declining gross revenues or increased expenditures, competition could lead to a compression of margins, declining earnings, and reduced cash flow from operations. This reduction exposes bondholders to the potential of a company being unable to service its debt obligations.

*Liquidation.* The liquidation value of the assets must be determined or approximated. Assets are occasionally spun off to the equity owners of the company. The bondholders could, under those circumstances, experience a sudden and substantial deterioration in the credit quality of the issuer because of the lower asset level. The bondholder should have specific identification of collateral to ensure the bond's value and marketability. The analyst must also be aware of the location of the company assets. Finally, the bondholder must be cognizant of asset protection in the event of a takeover. Assets that originally provided protection for the bondholder could be usurped to secure new debt that is senior to the original bondholder's issue.

*Management.* The management team must be evaluated for depth. Is there a strong financial manager? What is management turnover? What is the managers' experience/track record? Also important is their record of honesty and integrity in dealing with bondholders. How good are the financial controls? Is there a strong marketing manager? Significant ownership by management is generally viewed positively because of the resulting large personal incentive to build a growing, profitable company.

# Answers to Problems

1. Modified duration $= 7/1.10 = 6.36$ years

   Percentage change in portfolio $= +2 \times -6.36 = -12.72$ percent

   Value of portfolio $= \$50$ million $\times (1 - .1272) = \$43.64$ million

2(a). $\$200$ million $\times (1.06)^2 = \$224.72$ million

2(b). Since modified duration will equal the remaining horizon (5 years), the change in bond price must be $+10\%$ -- or (-5) "times" (-2%). The new value of the portfolio would then be $\$247.192$ million -- or $\$224.72$ million "times" (1.10).

3(a).
### Computation of Duration (assuming 10% market yield)

| (1) | (2) | (3) | (4) | (5) PV as % | (6) |
|-----|-----|-----|-----|-----|-----|
| Year | Cash Flow | PV @ 10% | PV of Flow | of Price | (1) x (5) |
| 1 | 120 | .9091 | 109.09 | .1014 | .1014 |
| 2 | 120 | .8264 | 99.17 | .0922 | .1844 |
| 3 | 120 | .7513 | 90.16 | .0838 | .2514 |
| 4 | 120 | .6830 | 81.96 | .0762 | .3047 |
| 5 | 120 | .6209 | 695.41 | .6464 | 3.2321 |
| Sum | 1120 | | 1075.79 | 1.0000 | 4.0740 |

Duration = 4.07 years

3(b).

## Computation of Duration (assuming 10% market yield)

| (1) | (2) | (3) | (4) | (5) | (6) |
|-----|-----|-----|-----|-----|-----|
| | | | | PV as % | |
| Year | Cash Flow | PV @ 10% | PV of Flow | of Price | (1) x (5) |
| 1 | 120 | .9091 | 109.09 | .1026 | .1026 |
| 2 | 120 | .8264 | 99017 | .0922 | .1864 |
| 3 | 120 | .7513 | 90.16 | .0848 | .2544 |
| 4 | 1120 | .6830 | 764.96 | .7194 | 2.8776 |
| Sum | | | 1063.38 | 1.0000 | 3.4210 |

Duration = 3.42 years

3(c). The duration of the portfolio should always be equal to the remaining time horizon and duration declines slower than term-to-maturity assuming no change in market interest rates as shown in a and b above.

4(a).

## Computation of Duration (assuming 8% market yield)

| (1) | (2) | (3) | (4) | (5) | (6) |
|-----|-----|-----|-----|-----|-----|
| | | | | PV as % | |
| Year | Cash Flow | PV @ 12% | PV of Flow | of Price | (1) x (5) |
| 1 | 100 | .9259 | 92.59 | .0868 | .0868 |
| 2 | 100 | .8573 | 85.73 | .0804 | .1608 |
| 3 | 100 | .7938 | 79.38 | .0745 | .2234 |
| 4 | 1100 | .7350 | 808.50 | .7583 | 3.0332 |
| Sum | | | 1066.20 | 1.0000 | 3.5042 |

Duration = 3.5 years

4(b).

## Computation of Duration (assuming 12% market yield)

| (1) | (2) | (3) | (4) | (5) | (6) |
|-----|-----|-----|-----|-----|-----|
| | | | | PV as % | |
| Year | Cash Flow | PV @ 12% | PV of Flow | of Price | (1) x (5) |
| 1 | 100 | .8929 | 89.29 | .0951 | .0951 |
| 2 | 100 | .7972 | 79.72 | .0849 | .1698 |
| 3 | 100 | .7118 | 71.18 | .0758 | .2274 |
| 4 | 1100 | .6355 | 699.05 | .7442 | 2.9768 |
| Sum | | | 939.24 | 1.0000 | 3.4691 |

Duration = 3.47 years

4(c). A portfolio of bonds is immunized from interest rate risk if the duration of the portfolio is always equal to the desired investment horizon. In this example, although nothing changes regarding the bond, there is a change in market rates which causes a change in duration which would mean that the portfolio is no longer perfectly immunized.

5(a). $300 million x $(1.06)^{10}$ = $537,254,310

5(b). PV of $537.25 million for 4 years @ 12 percent
537.25 (.627) = $336.86 million

PV of $537.25 million for 3 years @ 10 percent
537.25 (.746) = $400.79 million

PV of $537.25 million for 2 years @ 14 percent
537.25 (.763) = $409.92 million

5(c). 340 - 336.86 = $3.14 million safety margin
375 - 400.79 = $25.79 million deficiency
360.2 - 409.92 = $49.72 million deficiency

6.

|  | CURRENT BOND | CANDIDATE BOND |
|---|---|---|
| Dollar Investment | 839.54 | 961.16 |
| Coupon | 90.00 | 110.00 |
| i on One Coupon | 2.59 | 3.16 |
| Principal Value at Year End | 841.95 | 961.71 |
| Total Accrued | 934.54 | 1,074.87 |
| Realized Compound Yield | 11.0125 | 11.4999 |

Value of swap: 48.6 basis points in one year

$P_0$ = 45 x (16.04612) + 1,000 x (.11746) = 839.54

$P_0$ = 55 x (15.53300) + 1,000 x (.10685) = 961.16

$$P_0 = 45 \times (15.80474) + 1{,}000 \times (.13074) = 841.95$$

$$P_0 = 55 \times (15.31315) + 1{,}000 \times (.11949) = 961.71$$

where 16.04612 is the PVA factor and .11746 is the PV factor, both for 40 periods at 5.5 percent per period.

15.53300 is the PVA factor and .10685 is the PV factor, both for 40 periods at 5.75 percent per period.

15.80474 is the PVA factor and .13074 is the PV factor, both for 38 periods at 5.5 percent per period.

15.31315 is the PVA factor and .11949 is the PV factor, both for 38 periods at 5.75 percent per period.

7.

|  | CURRENT BOND | CANDIDATE BOND |
| --- | --- | --- |
| Dollar Investment | 868.21 | 849.09 |
| Coupon | 90.00 | 90.00 |
| i on One Coupon | 2.36 | 2.36 |
| Principal Value at Year End | 869.40 | 869.40 |
| Total Accrued | 961.76 | 961.76 |
| Total Gain | 93.55 | 112.67 |
| Gain per Invested Dollar | .10775 | .12370 |
| Realized Compound Yield | 10.50 | 12.856 |

Value of swap: 235.7 basis points in one year

$$P_0 = 45 \times (17.57281) + 1{,}000 \times (.07743) = 868.21$$

$$P_0 = 45 \times (17.24714) + 1{,}000 \times (.07297) = 849.09$$

$$P_0 = 45 \times (17.41389) + 1{,}000 \times (.08577) = 869.40$$

17 - 24

where 17.57281 is the PVA factor and .07743 is the PV factor, both for 50 periods at 5.25 percent per period.

17.24714 is the PVA factor and .07297 is the PV factor, both for 50 periods at 5.375 percent per period.

17.41389 is the PVA factor and .08577 is the PV factor, both for 48 periods at 5.25 percent per period.

15.31315 is the PVA factor and .11949 is the PV factor, both for 38 periods at 5.75 percent per period.

8.    CFA Exam III (June 1984)

8(a).  *Active management* (or expectations management) seeks the highest return possible (above bond market returns) while not exceeding the desired risk posture.  This is done through a process consisting of:

   (1)    Formation of expectations about interest rates, credit risk and spread changes.

   (2)    Their transformation into return and risk measures via a return simulation process.

   (3)    Their implementation via an optimization routine for the actual building of the portfolio.

Reinvestment rate risk is not protected against in any systematic way and is, therefore, of real concern.  It must be considered when making all portfolio changes, as it is one of the most important components of the total return that will be achieved.

8(b).  *Classical immunization* can be defined by any of the following:

   (1).   Any investment strategy designed to minimize the risk of reinvestment over a specific time horizon.

(2).    Being assured that the assets at the end of the horizon period are greater than, or equal to, some minimum level that might have been established.

(3).    Achieving the maximum return possible with minimum reinvestment risk.

The classical immunizer spends a considerable amount of time rebalancing the portfolio to bring the duration of the portfolio back in line with the duration of the liabilities that are being immunized.  This is because classical immunization is based on three unrealistic assumptions:

(1).    a flat yield curve,

(2).    parallel yield curve shifts, and

(3).    an instantaneous change in yields.

Reinvestment rate risk is significantly reduced or almost eliminated by matching duration to the time horizon.  The price risk is in the opposite direction of the reinvestment risk, and these offsetting risks equal each other when the duration of the portfolio is equal to the investment horizon of the portfolio.

8(c)    *Dedicated portfolios* are used to generate sufficient cash to finance each of a sequence of liability payments as they come due, with virtually no interest rate risk.  This is accomplished using one of two techniques:

(1).    a cash-matched portfolio or

(2).    a duration-matched portfolio.

At least two practical problems introduce some reinvestment risk: (a) the risk that bonds in the portfolio may be called prior to maturity; and (b) in the case of cash-matching, the life of the liabilities may extend beyond the normal maturity range of bonds.  If the amount of the liabilities diminishes over time, then the reinvestment risk is further reduced.

Conventionally, a conservative reinvestment rate is chosen to represent that rate at which cash flows are assumed to be reinvested from the date they are received through coupons and maturities until the payment date of the liability being financed.

8(d). *Contingent immunization* is an active-passive strategy normally having three components:

   (1). *Immunized Base Return* - the return that can be currently achieved with little or no active management for a specific time horizon regardless of the future direction of interest rates.

   (2). *Investment Objective* - a return goal in excess of the Immunized Base Return to be achieved with active management strategies.

   (3). *Assured Minimum Return* - a return set below the immunized base return that can be assured with the future use jof immunization if active management decisions are wrong.

Due to the use of a specific time horizon, there is a real element of reinvestment rate-risk which should be addressed regularly by the portfolio manager.

All of the reinvestment rate-risk to which active management is subject exists for the contingent immunizer, unless having failed his performance goals by falling to the Assured Minimum Return. In that case, the portfolio would be immunized and reinvestment rate-risk would be eliminated subject to the same conditions discussed in B.

9. CFA Exam III (June 1985)

9(a). The required ending wealth value to equal to:

$300 million  x  1.629  (5% for ten periods)    = $488.70 million

9(b). and 9(c).

| YEAR | MARKET VALUE (MIL $) | MARKET YIELD | REQUIRED FLOOR PORTFOLIO (MIL $) | SAFETY MARGIN OF ERROR (MIL $) |
|---|---|---|---|---|
| 1 | 340.09 | 10% | 330.85 | 10.05 |
| 2 | 405.50 | 08% | 386.07 | 19.43 |
| 3 | 395.20 | 12% | 367.05 | 8.15 |

In general, the required floor portfolio is the present value of the required ending value ($88.70 million) at the current market yield.

For Year One - The required floor portfolio is the present value of $488.70 at 10% for four years (5% for eight periods).

$488.70 x .667 = $330.85

For Year Two - The required floor portfolio is the present value of $488.70 at 8% for three years (4% for six periods).

$488.70 x .790 = $386.07

For Year Three - The required floor portfolio is the present value of $488.70 at 12% for two years (6% for four periods).

$488.70 x .792 = $387.05

9(d). If the margin of error at the end of any year had been zero or negative, the portfolio manager would discontinue active management of the portfolio and immunize it. If the margin of error had been negative, the manager would immunize the portfolio and thereby minimize any further losses to the portfolio.

10(a). Advantages of the three strategies as set forth in Table 2 are as follows.

Active management

1) Active management incurs greater volatility of returns in exchange for higher potential returns. The best performing active managers in the top decile had the highest return per unit of risk (return/standard deviation) of 83.7% over the past 15 years .

2) Active managers can attempt to achieve higher returns through security selection by choosing superior securities or by avoiding poor performers. Securities not in the WGB Index can be selected by an active manager.

3) Active managers can adjust country and currency weights based on expectation of political and economic events.

4) Durations can be changed to anticipate yield curve movements.

Passive management

1) Passive management has lower expected volatility of returns than active management with a lower management fee.

2) Fewer transactions should also result in lower transaction cost

3) Small duration shifts can be used to make minor adjustments to interest rate movements

4) The historical data indicate that passive management had higher average returns per unit of risk (73.8% versus 69.4%) than active management.

5) Limitations on country allocations keep funds diversified internationally.

6) This strategy would allow the manager some limited flexibility to add value.

7) Compared with active management, PTC's Investment Committee retains more control over investment strategy and the ability to easily monitor the manager's contribution.

Indexing

1) Indexing produces returns which should closely track the returns of the WGB Index.

2) Little risk exists in picking a poor manager, as Table 2 shows little difference between top decile and bottom decile managers.

3) Indexing has the lowest management fees and, except for rebalancing, should have very low transactions costs.

4) Indexing has produced the most favorable average return per unit of risk (75.8%).

5) The value added by the investment advisor through indexing can be measured with relative ease and precision.

10(b). The primary disadvantage of active management is the risk of significant underperformance by managers who miss either interest rate, currency, or country trends. Of the three strategies, returns of active manager are the most dependent on manager selection (as shown by the difference between highest and lowest decile returns). Also, active management ha the highest fees, the highest standard deviation of returns, and the lowest average return-to-risk ratio.

The passive management strategy does not produce returns that differ greatly from the index returns but does have both higher standard deviation of returns and larger difference between highest and lowest decile managers. Also, passive management incurs higher management fees than indexing.

Indexing has the highest opportunity costs with little or no ability to outperform the index. Due to transaction costs and fees, the indexed portfolio will frequently underperform the index. The top decile return-to-standard deviation ratio is 80.5% for indexing compared to 83.9% for active managers, and indexing has virtually no flexibility to avoid poor performance in bear markets, to avoid anticipated deteriorating credits, or to invest in assets outside the index.

10(c). <u>Full replication</u> is a portfolio construction technique in which all securities repre6ented in an index are owned in proportions identical to their index weights. A key advantage of this approach is that a portfolio so constructed would track the index accurately. However, this approach may not be practical, in that most fixed income indices contain thousands of securities; some of the bonds in the index may not be liquid or attractively priced; and receipt of cash inflows requires periodic portfolio rebalancing.

The <u>stratified sampling</u> technique divides the index into cells based on parameters such as country, coupon, term-to-maturity, and duration. If required, the index could be stratified further into subsectors. Stratification is followed by selection of the security or securities to represent each cell; the process of setting up an index fund is complete when all cells in the index have been replicated. An advantage of this approach is the ability to include attractive securities in the portfolio which are not contained in the index. However, the stratified sampling approach, while simple in concept, is labor intensive and relies upon portfolio management expertise to appropriately stratify the index. Unless properly structured, the resulting portfolio may not track the index accurately. Finally, the portfolio may have to be optimized using either linear or quadratic programming to achieve the highest yield and greatest convexity.

10(d). The selection of an appropriate benchmark is a key decision in any indexing strategy. The Salomon Brothers WGB Index does not represent currency exposures that are even close to the liability exposures of Planet Trade's pension plan. For example, 23.3% of PTC's non-U.S. dollar liabilities are in Australia which has only a 2% weighting in the Salomon Index.

| Country | Liabilities | Index |
|---------|-------------|-------|
| Australia | 23.3% | 2% |
| Japan | 20.0 | 37 |
| Singapore | 20.0 | 0 |
| Thailand | 13.3 | 0 |
| Spain | 13.3 | 0 |
| Malaysia | 10.0 | 0 |
| Others | 0.0 | 61 |
| | 100.0% | 100% |

Therefore, in an asset-liability management context, the recommendation is inappropriate. If accepted, the proposal would result in a mismatch between the investment assets and the liabilities of the plan.

# CHAPTER 18

## Stock Market Analysis

# Answers to Questions

1.  Although corporate earnings may rise by 12 percent next year, that information by itself is **not** sufficient to forecast an increase in the stock market. The market level is a product of both corporate earnings and the earnings multiple. The earnings multiple must likewise be projected since it is **not** stable over time.

2.  Student Exercise.

3.  The investor can **improve** his net profit margin estimate by working from the gross margin down to the net profit margin. By this procedure, the investor explicitly considers each major component that affects the net profit margin. This level of analysis provides insights into the components which do **not** behave consistently over time. Also, the gross profit margin should be easier to estimate since it has the lowest level of relative variability.

4.  The effect of a **decline** in capacity utilization should be a **decline** in the aggregate profit margin, all else the same, because it will mean greater overhead and depreciation per unit of output. Also more fixed financial charges per unit.

5.  In addition to the estimate of the changes in the hourly wage rate, an estimate of the productivity rate change is also needed to forecast the unit labor cost change. The relationship is:

    % Δ Hourly Wages - % Δ Productivity  =  % Δ Unit Labor Cost

    The unit labor cost is negatively related to the profit margin.

6.  % Δ Hourly Wages - % Δ Productivity  =  % Δ Unit Labor Cost

    7.0 - 5.0  =  2.0% increase in the unit labor cost. This increase would, holding other factors constant, decrease the aggregate profit margin.

Because it is a low rate of increase, the effect on the profit margin should be small.

7(a). An increase in the ROE with no other changes should cause an increase in the multiple because it would imply a higher growth rate. An important question is, how was the increase in ROE accomplished? If it was due to operating factors (higher asset turnover or profit margin) it is positive. If it was due to an increase in financial leverage, there could be some offset due to an increase in the required rate of return (k).

7(b). Increase, because this will increase earnings growth by raising equity turnover. It could also cause a decrease because it will increase the financial risk and, therefore, the required k.

7(c). Decrease, because this will increase growth and therefore raise the real RFR. It could also reduce inflation, which would decrease the nominal RFR, causing the multiplier to rise.

7(d). Increase, because a decrease in the dividend payout rate increases the retention rate, raising the growth rate. It could also cause a decrease because it reduces the next period's dividends.

# Answers to Problems

1. Using only the graph and drawing a line over from ten percent to the line of best fit and down to the horizontal percent change indicates an estimate of slightly under 10% for the S & P series. Alternatively, if you simply apply the slope coefficient (1.38) discussed relative to the date in Table 18.2, you will get an estimate of 13.8% (.10 x 1.38). You could use these as your high and low estimates or derive a confidence interval around the line of best fit and determine the estimate for one or two standard errors from point estimate at ten percent.

2(a).
$$P/E = \frac{.60}{.13 - .07} = \frac{.60}{.06} = 10x$$

2(b).
$$P/E = \frac{.50}{.13 - .07} = \frac{.50}{.06} = 8.3x$$

2(c)
$$P/E = \frac{.60}{.16 - .09} = \frac{.60}{.07} = 8.57x$$

2(d).
$$P/E = \frac{.60}{.10 - .06} = \frac{.60}{.04} = 15x$$

3. CFA Exam I (June 1985)

3(a). Overall, both managers added value by mitigating the currency effects present in the Index. Both exhibited an ability to "pick stocks" in the markets they chose to be in (Manger B, in particular). Manager B used his opportunities **not** to be in stocks quite effectively (via the cash/bond contribution to return), but neither of them matched the passive index in picking the country markets in which to be invested (Manger B, in particular).

|  | MANAGER A | MANAGER B |
|---|---|---|
| **STRENGTHS** | Currency Management | Currency Management<br>Stock Selection<br>Use of Cash/Bond Flexibility |
| **WEAKNESSES** | Country Selection<br>(to a limited degree) | Country Selection |

3(b).  The column reveals the effect on performance in local currency terms after adjustment for movements in the U.S. dollar and, therefore, the effect on the portfolio.  Currency gains/losses arise from translating changes in currency exchange rates versus the U.S. dollar over the measuring period (3 years in this case) into U.S. dollars for the U.S. pension plan.  The Index mix lost 12.9% to the dollar, reducing what would otherwise have been a very favorable return from the various country markets of 19.9% to a net return of only 7.0%.

4(a).  Growth $= .40 \times .09 = .036 = 3.6\%$

4(b).
$$P/E = \frac{.60}{.11 - .036} = 8.108x$$

4(c).  The market price will rise to:

Price $= 8.108 \times \$39 = \$316.21$

4(d).  Rate of Return $= \dfrac{316.21 - 700 + 22}{700} = -51.68\%$

5(a). $850 x .152      =      $129.20

$129.20 - $38      =      $ 91.20

$91.20 - $16      =      $ 75.20

$75.20 x (1 - .32)  =      $ 51.14

5(b)  <u>Optimistic:</u>

$850 x .155      =      $131.75

$131.75 - $38      =      $ 93.75

$93.75 - $16      =      $ 77.75

$77.75 x (1 - .32)  =      $ 52.87

<u>Pessimistic:</u>

$850 x .149      =      $126.65

$126.65 - $38      =      $ 88.65

$88.65 - $16      =      $ 72.65

$72.65 x (1 - .32)  =      $ 49.40

6(a).  High      =      52.87 x 20.4545   =      $1081.43

Low      =      49.40 x  5.6522   =      $ 279.22

Consensus  =      51.14 x  7.6923   =      $ 393.38

6(b).  High      =      (1081.43/750)  -1   =      + .4419

Low      =      (279.22/750)   -1   =      - .6277

Consensus  =      (393.38/750)   -1   =      - .4755

18 - 7

# CHAPTER 19

## Industry Analysis

# Answers to Questions

1.  The results of three empirical studies concluded that there are substantial differences in absolute or relative performance among industries during any given time period. This conclusion was supported even when alternative industry classifications were used, such as the Standard and Poor's *Analysts Handbook*, the SIC industrial classifications, or the 30 *Barron's* Industry Averages. In addition, industry performance differences are found in alternative time periods where the time periods may vary in length. Therefore, the investor must examine alternative industries <u>after</u> he had forecasted market movements because of the wide dispersion of industry performance around the expected market performance.

2.  Studies show that relative industry performance is **inconsistent** over time. When industries are ranked over successive time periods, there is little correlation in the rankings. This result holds for different types of markets and for alternative length time periods. These findings imply that simple extrapolation of past performance is **not** useful by itself. Therefore, the analyst must put additional effort into his industry analysis by **projecting** industry performance based upon future expectations of industry conditions. This obviously makes industry analysis more demanding.

3.  A **greater** emphasis must be placed upon industry analysis when the performance of the individual firms cluster about the industry performance. In contrast, this implies that once the industry performance is estimated, the need for individual firm analysis is **reduced** since all the firms will behave similar to the industry.

4.  Disagree. Although studies have shown a significant dispersion of individual firm performance within a given industry, they also found that the industry component can partially explain individual firm performance. Although the strength of the industry component varies among industries, industry analysis is still an important step before company analysis. The important implication is that individual company analysis is more important for industries where individual company returns are widely dispersed. The

point is, the dispersion among companies within industries indicates a need for company analysis **after** industry analysis.

5. For given time periods, there were significant differences in risk among alternative industries. An analysis of Beta coefficients for the 30 *Barron's* industry groups indicated a wide range of systematic risk. The substantial dispersion in risk for alternative industries implies that the analyst must examine and attempt to estimate the risk levels for alternative industries.

6. While there is substantial dispersion in industry risk during a given time period, studies indicate reasonably **stable** beta coefficients **over time**. This implies that past industry risk analysis may be useful in estimating future industry risk.

7. The fourth stage is stabilization and market maturity. It is characterized by sales growth rates roughly in line with the economy's growth rate. A 20% growth rate for the industry would be well above the growth rate for the market. You should go back and (a) check your assumptions and (b) check your arithmetic

8. An industry in the "rapid accelerating growth" phase of the industrial life cycle would be most advantageous to prospective investors. During this stage, profits can more than double as sales and efficiency improve dramatically.

9. An industry experiencing the kind of explosive growth characteristic of stage two (rapid accelerating growth) is computer software.

10. Input-output analysis is one of three popular methods for forecasting industry sales. For autos, industries supplying steel, glass, tires and upholstery fabrics should be scrutinized as well as the spending capabilities/habits of consumers. For computers, the suppliers of critical components would have to be studied along with the spending capabilities/habits of potential users.

11. A substitute product for steel would limit the prices firms in that industry could charge. The degree of limitation would depend on how closely the substitute product was in price and function to steel.

# Answers to Problems

1.  Student Exercise

2.  Student Exercise

3.  Student Exercise

4.  Student Exercise

5.  Student Exercise

6.  Student Exercise

7.  Student Exercise

8(a). Relevant data items from Table 1 that support the conclusion that the retail auto parts industry as a whole is in the stabilization phase of the industry life cycle are:

1. The population of 18-29 year olds, a major customer base for the industry, is gradually declining.

2. The number of households with income less than $35,000, another important customer base, is not expanding.

3. The number of cars 5-15 years old, an important end market, has recorded low annual growth (or actual declines in some years), so the number of units that potentially need parts is not growing.

4. Automotive aftermarket industry retail sales have been growing slowly for several years.

5. Consumer expenditures on automotive parts and accessories have grown slowly for several years.

6. Average operating margins of all retail autoparts companies have steadily declined.

8(b). Relevant items of data from Table 1 that support the conclusion that Wigwam Autoparts Heaven, Inc. (WAH) and its major competitors are in the growth stage of their life cycle are:

1. Sales growth of retail autoparts companies with 100 or more stores have been growing rapidly and at an increasing rate.

2. Market share of retail autoparts stores with }90 or more stores has been increasing but is still less than 93 percent, leaving room for much more growth.

3. Average operating margins for retail autoparts companies with 100 or more stores are high and rising.

Because of industry fragmentation (i.e., most of the market share is distributed among many companies with only a few stores), the retail autoparts industry apparently is undergoing marketing innovation and consolidation. The industry is moving toward the "category killer" format, in which a few major companies control large market shares through the proliferation of outlets. The evidence suggests that a new "industry within an industry" is emerging in the form of the 'category killer' large chain-store company. This industry subgroup is in its growth stage (i.e. rapid growth with high operating profit margins) despite the fact that the industry is in the stabilization stage of its life cycle.

# CHAPTER 20

## Company Analysis And Stock Selection

# Answers to Questions

1.  An example of a growth company would be McDonald's. Not only does the firm enjoy above-average increases in sales and earnings, it also retains a high percentage of earnings to fund superior investment projects. Since McDonald's P/E ratio is not below the industry average, it could not be considered undervalued and, therefore, would not qualify as a growth stock.

2.  An example of a cyclical stock would be Harley-Davidson. A cyclical stock is stock that has returns which are more volatile than the overall market. The motorbike maker had a recent beta of 1.6.

3.  The biotechnology firm may be considered a growth company because (1) it has a growth rate of 21 percent per year which probably exceeds the growth rate of the overall economy, (2) it has a very high return on equity, and (3) it has a relatively high retention rate. However, since a biotechnology firm relies heavily on continuous research and development, the above-average risk will require a high rate of return. Therefore, it is unlikely that the stock would be considered a growth stock due to the extremely high price of the stock relative to its earnings.

4.  Student Exercise

5.  Student Exercise

6.  Student Exercise

7.  Student Exercise

8.  Price/Book Value (P/BV) is used as a measure of relative value because, in theory, market price P should reflect book value (BV). In practice, the two can differ dramatically. Some researchers have suggested that firms with low P/BV ratios tend to outperform those with high P/BV ratios.

9.    A high P/BV ratio such as 3.0 can result from a large amount of fixed assets being carried at historical cost. A low ratio, such as 0.6, can occur when assets are worth less than book value, for instance, bad real estate loans by banks.

10.   The price/cash flow ratio (P/CF) has become more popular because of the increased emphasis on cash by various analysts and because of the increased availability of cash flow numbers. Differences could result from differences in net income or non-cash items.

11.   The major components of EVA include the firm's net operating profit less adjusted taxes (NOPLAT) and its total cost of capital (in dollars) including the cost of equity. A positive EVA implies that NOPLAT exceeds the cost of capital and that value has been added for stockholders.

12.   Absolute EVA makes it difficult to judge whether a firm is succeeding relative to past performance or if the growth rate can support additional capital. To overcome those shortcomings and to facilitate the comparison of firms of different size, it is preferable to compute an EVA return on capital ratio: EVA/Capital.

13.   While the EVA measures a firm's internal performance, the MVA reflects the market's judgment of how well the firm performed in terms of the market value of debt and equity vis-a-vis the capital invested in it. Since the latter measure is affected by external factors such as interest rates, it is not surprising that the EVA and MVA share a weak relationship.

14.   The two factors that determine a firm's franchise value are (1) the difference between the expected return on new opportunities and the current cost of equity and (2) the size of those new opportunities relative to the firm's current size. In the absence of a franchise value, an equity cost of 11% would translate into a (base) P/E ratio of 9.1 (or 1/.11).

15.   Above average earnings growth is a characteristic of a growth company. Additionally, a rather high retention rate of 80 percent implies that the firm will have the resources to take advantage of high-return investment opportunities. These factors lend support to classifying the firm as a growth company. However, as a result of the high retention rate, investors will continue to require a high return on investment. Only if the firm can

20 - 4

continue to achieve returns above its cost of capital will the firm continue to be classified as a growth company.

16.    In a perfectly competitive economy, if other companies see a particular firm achieving returns consistently above risk-based expectations, it is expected that these other companies will enter that particular industry or market and eventually drive prices down until the returns are consistent with the inherent risk. In other words, the competition would not allow the continuing existence of excess return investments and so competition would negate such growth. The computer industry is a good example of increased competition resulting in lower profit margins. The theory implies that in truly competitive environments, a true growth company is a temporary classification.

17.    Because the dividend model assumes a constant rate of growth for an infinite time period, the point is that a true growth company is earning a rate of return above its cost of capital and this should not be possible in a competitive environment. Therefore, it is impossible for a true growth firm to exist for an infinite time period in a purely competitive environment. Changes in non-competitive factors, as well as changes in technology will tend to cause various growth patterns. Therefore, we will consider special valuation models that allow for finite periods of abnormal growth and for the possibility of different rates of growth.

18.    The growth duration model attempts to compute the implied growth duration for a growth firm given differential past growth rates for the market and for the firm and also alternative P/E ratios. These major assumptions of the model are: (1) equal risk between the securities compared; (2) no significant differences in the payout ratio of different firms; and (3) the stock with the higher P/E ratio has the higher growth rate. While the assumption of equal risk may be acceptable when comparing two larger, well-established firms to each other or to a market proxy, it is probably not a valid assumption when comparing a small firm to the aggregate market. Likewise, the assumption of no significant differences in payout ratios could present a problem. For example, many growth firms have low initial payout ratios in order to use retained earnings for future investment projects. It might be inappropriate to compare a well-established company with a new start-up firm on the basis of an equal payout ratio. Finally, while the model assumes that the stock with the higher P/E ratios has the higher growth rate, in many cases you will find that this is not true.

19.	The projected growth rate for the company (15%) is above that of the market (8%); however, the growth company also has a lower P/E ratio than the aggregate market. This implies that the stock of the growth company might be undervalued. It would be necessary to investigate the company further to determine if the firm's stock is a growth stock. It is still necessary to estimate the average payout ratio and the ROE and its components for both the firm and the aggregate market in order to make a proper comparison of the growth company to the aggregate market. This should help you determine if it is currently a true growth company and if this performance can be sustained.

20.	Walgreen seems to illustrate "simple long-run growth" since r>k and b>0. Its failure to observe a constant retention rate precludes "dynamic growth".

21.	GM is likely an example of "expansion" since r=k and b>0.

22.	In order to use the Mao three-stage growth model, one must make estimates for the retention rate, the required return, the return on growth investments, and the length of time each stage (dynamic growth, simple growth, and declining growth) will last.

23.	The computation of book value is:

(assets - liabilities) / # of shares

Accounting conventions can affect this computation by increasing or decreasing any of the three components: assets, liabilities, or number of shares.

**Increasing or Decreasing Assets**

- Accountant's use of historic cost does not recognize the replacement value of assets and is, therefore, not an accurate measurement of an assets value. This is particularly true of real estate assets.
- Several assets with real economic value are ignored by accountants. Internally developed goodwill, management expertise, market share, and technological innovation are just a few of the assets ignored by accountants.

- Some assets that are on the balance sheet should not be recognized. Purchased goodwill is an accounting convention that is often placed on or stays on the balance sheet when there is no economic reason for it to exist.
- Assets can change value for any of the following reasons:
  - Different estimates result in different values (estimates of different asset lives can affect depreciation calculations and then the book value of an asset)
  - Different accounting standards can result in changes in balance sheet values (the decision to adopt SFAS 106 immediately or over 20 years)
  - Adoption of different accounting choices can affect asset values
    - LIFO/FIFO inventory
    - Straight line/accelerated depreciation
    - Short-term/long-term marketable securities
    - Purchase/pooling acquisitions
    - Cost/equity recognition
    - Lower of cost or market
    - Capitalization of costs
    - Pension options
    - Deferral of taxes
    - Foreign currency translations
    - Revenue recognition choices

**Increasing or Decreasing Liabilities**

- Off-balance-sheet liabilities will change book value. Contingent liabilities and off-balance-sheet financing are two such liabilities that sometimes are not included on the balance sheet that should be included.
- Changes in the value of existing liabilities can affect book value. When interest rates change long-term debt which is on the balance sheet does not change even though the economic value of these liabilities do change.

**Increasing or Decreasing # of Shares**

- The existence of warrants or options can increase the number of shares depending upon the decision to include them in the computation of book value or not.
- The purchase or sale of shares at a value different from book value will change book value.

24(a). Some arguments <u>for</u> a high dividend payout policy are:

  1. **Limited investment opportunities**. If a firm has cash flows greater than those needed to fund projects with positive net present values, it should return the capital to shareholders as higher dividends.

  2. **Clientele effect**. Some investors require some income from investments. The higher the dividend, the greater the proportion of investors who will be satisfied with the income of a given investment.

  3. **Certainty of dividends versus capital gains**. The "bird in hand" argument says that (a) cash dividends are a definite return whereas capital appreciation is less certain, or (b) investors should apply a lower discount rate to cash dividends versus capital appreciation because dividends are more certain.

  4. **Tax effects**. Corporate and tax exempt investors in some tax jurisdictions pay no income tax on dividends.

  5. **Informational content**. Management uses the dividend payout policy to communicate the long-term prospects of the corporation.

Some arguments <u>against</u> a high dividend payout policy are:

  1. **No effect on value**. A firm's investment decisions determine its profitability. Dividend policy does not affect investment decisions, but it does affect the amount of outside financing needed by a firm.

  2. **Less cash available for investments**. Paying high dividends reduces the cash available to finance profitable investment projects. With less internal financing, a firm may resort to external financing to finance projects, which may reduce earnings per share because of greater interest expense or more shares outstanding.

  3. **Taxes**. Investors can defer taxes on capital appreciation until realized but pay taxes on dividends (except tax-exempt investors) even if dividends are reinvested. Also, double taxation exists on corporate profits and dividends paid to investors.

4. **Violation of an indenture**. High dividend payouts may violate bond indentures or loan covenants.

5. **Financial distress**. Paying high dividends while financing investment projects may force the firm to increase its leverage ratios and lead to a higher level of risk. This could eventually lead to financial distress.

24(b). The constant growth dividend discount model, $P_0 = D_1/(k - g)$, implies that a stock's value, $P_0$, will be greater

1. the larger its expected dividend per share, $D_1$;
2. the lower the market capitalization rate, k, (also called the required rate of return);
3. the higher the expected growth rate of dividends, g.

The director has ignored the denominator used to convert the dividend to a present value. The denominator consists of two variables, both of which dividend policy could influence. One variable is the market capitalization rate, k, which risk affects. Investors may view a higher dividend payout as increasing risk because a higher payout may lead to an increase in a firm's leverage ratios. The other variable is the expected growth rate of dividends, g, which is likely to be lower if firms pay higher dividends in the short run. In summary, a higher dividend payout may increase k and lower g. Therefore, the statement by the director that the use of dividend discount models by investors is "proof" that "the higher the dividend, the higher the stock price" is potentially misleading and possibly inaccurate.

24(c). (i) **Internal (implied, normalized, or sustainable) growth rate**

The internal growth rate of dividends, g, is calculated as:

g = ROE x b,

where ROE = return on equity b = plowback or earnings retention ratio (1 - dividend payout ratio).

As the dividend payout ratio increases, the expected growth rate in dividends decreases. If the firm pays out all earnings as dividends, the expected growth rate in dividends would be zero. Valuation would also decrease to the degree investors would pay a lower ratio of price to earnings for the lower growth rate calculated in this manner.

## (ii) Growth in book value

A higher dividend payout ratio would slow the increase in book value (all other factors being equal) because the retained earnings included in stockholders' equity would increase at a slower rate (reflecting the higher dividend payout).

# Answers to Problems

1.    Student Exercise

2.    Student Exercise

3.    Student Exercise

4(a).   $r_i$   =   .07 + 1.75 (.15 - .07)   =   .21   =   21%

4(b).   $r_i$   =   .07 + 1.75 (.10 - .07)   =   .1225 =   12.25%

5.    Student Exercise

6.
$$\ln \frac{24}{16} \approx T \ln \frac{1 + .14 + .02}{1 + .06 + .04}$$

$$= \ln (1.50000) \overset{\approx}{=} T \ln (1.05455)$$

$$.40547 = T (.05311)$$

$$T = \frac{.40547}{.05311} = 7.63 \text{ years}$$

7(a).   $\ln(x) = 10 \ln \dfrac{1.18}{1.08}$

$\ln (x) = 10 \ln (1.09259)$

ln (x) =        10 (.08855) =        .8855

x       =      2.42

Thus, the P/E ratio would be 33.9 (2.42 x 14).

7(b)   ln (x) =       $5 \ln \dfrac{1.18}{1.08}$ =      $5 \ln (1.09259)$

ln (x) =       5 (.0855)   =      .44275

x     =      1.56

The P/E would be 14 x 1.56     =      21.8

8(a).  <u>Company A</u>

$$\ln \dfrac{24}{12} \approx T \ln \dfrac{1 + .18 + .02}{1 + .07 + .05}$$

$$= \ln (2) \overset{\approx}{=} T \ln (1.071429)$$

$$.69315 = T (.068993)$$

$$T = \dfrac{.69315}{.06899} = 10.0 \text{ years}$$

### Company B

$$\ln \frac{20}{12} \approx T \ln \frac{1 + .15 + .03}{1 + .07 + .05}$$

$$= \quad \ln (1.6667) \overset{\approx}{=} T \ln (1.05357)$$

$$.51085 \quad = \quad T (.05218)$$

$$T \quad = \quad \frac{.51085}{.05218} \quad = \quad 9.79 \text{ years}$$

8(b).

$$\ln \frac{20}{12} \approx T \ln \frac{1 + .18 + .02}{1 + .15 + .03}$$

$$= \quad \ln (1.2) \overset{\approx}{=} T \ln (1.0169)$$

$$.18232 \quad = \quad T (.01681)$$

$$T \quad = \quad \frac{.18232}{.01681} \quad = \quad 10.85 \text{ years}$$

8(c). After computing the implied growth durations, the analyst must decide whether the projected growth rates can be sustained over the periods implied in the model. If the implied growth duration is greater than you believe is reasonable, you would likely advise against buying the respective stock.

9. CFA Exam II (June 1981)

9(a). Three factors that must be estimated for any valuation model are:

The expected stream of returns – which is specified for bonds in terms of interest (coupon) and principal payments but is uncertain for common stocks, as dividends are not contractual or precisely predictable.

The time pattern of expected returns – specified for bonds, in terms of semi-annual interest payments and principal payments annually (sinking fund) or at maturity but is uncertain for common stocks because, although dividends may be paid annually, a stock is in effect "perpetual."

Maturity value of a bond is known while the sale price for stock involves an estimate of earnings in that year and the P/E that will then prevail. The required rate of return on the investment adjusted for risks is uncertain for both stocks and bonds. For bonds, this generally depends upon the prevailing risk-free rate. For common stocks, given the security market line prevailing at a point in time and the estimate of the stock's beta with the market portfolio of risky assets, it is possible to derive the return that should be required for the investment.

9(b). The problem in using a dividend valuation model is that growth is a changing phenomenon and cannot be projected to infinity, as indicated in each of the following three types of companies:

(1) Constant growth in dividends is unrealistic for a corporation that is subject to cyclical swings in its business.

(2) Maturing companies might be experiencing a slowing in the rate of growth of dividends, although some such companies maintain dividend growth by increasing the payout ratio, but this is a short-term phenomenon.

(3) Small, rapidly growing companies are not able to sustain above-average rates of growth indefinitely.

10. CFA Exam I (June 1985)

The analyst would recommend investing in the lease obligation since, for each dollar invested, the present value of the future cash flows generated by the lease is greater than the present value of the cash flow that will be realized when the stock is sold.

### Present Value of Common Stock

| Year | | Cash Flow | PV 10% | $ PV |
|---|---|---|---|---|
| 1 | | $ -0- | .909 | -0- |
| 2 | | $ -0- | .826 | -0- |
| 3 | $100,000 x (1.1 x 1.1 x 1.1) = | $133,100 | .751 | $100,000 |
| | | | | $100,000 |

### Present Value of Lease Cash Flow

| Year | | Cash Flow | PV 10% | $ PV |
|---|---|---|---|---|
| 1 | | $ -0- | .909 | $ -0- |
| 2 | | | .826 | -0- |
| 3 | ($100,000 x $25,000) | 15,000 | .751 | $101,385 |
| | | $135,000 | | $113,775 |

Ratio of common stock PV for $1 invested = 1.00
Ratio of lease PV for $1 invested ($113,775/$100,000) = 1.14

11(a). The dividend discount model is

$$P = \frac{d}{k - g}$$

Where
P - value of the stock today
d - annual dividend stream
k - discount rate
g - constant dividend growth rate

Solving for k: $(k - g) = d / P$ ; then $k = d/P + g$

So k becomes the estimate for the long-term return of the stock.

k = ($.60 / $20.00) + 8% = 3%  8% = 11%

11(b). Many professional investors shy away from the dividend discount framework analysis due to its many inherent complexities.

1)  The model cannot be used where companies pay very small or no dividends and speculation on the level of future dividends could be futile. (Dividend policy may be arbitrary.)

2)  The model presumes one can accurately forecast long term growth of earnings (dividends) of a company. Such forecasts become quite tenuous beyond two years out. (A short-terrn valuation may be more pertinent.)

3)  For the variable growth models, small differences in g for the first several years produce large differences in the valuations.

4)  The correct k or the discount rate is difficult to estimate for a specific company as an infinite number of factors affect it which are themselves difficult to forecast, e.g., inflation, riskless rate of return, risk premium on stocks and other uncertainties.

5)  The model is not definable when g > k as with growth companies, so it is not applicable to a large number of companies.

6)  Where a company has low or negative earnings per share or has a poor balance sheet, the ability to continue the dividend is questionable.

7)  The components of income can differ substantially, reducing comparability.

11(c).  Three alternative methods of valuation would include:
1)  Price/Earnings ratios
2)  Price/Asset value ratios (including market and book asset values)
3)  Price/Sales ratios
4)  Liquidation or breakup value
5)  Price/cash flow ratios

12(a). The formula for the constant growth discounted dividend model is shown below:

$$Price = \frac{D_0(1+g)}{k-g}$$

Where $D_0$ = current dividend per share

For Eastover:

$$Price = \frac{1.28(1+.08)}{0.11 - 0.08} = 43$$

This compares with its current stock price of 28. On this basis, it appear that Eastover is undervalued.

12(b). The formula for the two-stage discounted dividend model is as follow:

$$Price = \frac{D_1}{1+k} + \frac{D_2}{(1+k)^2} + \frac{D_3}{(1+k)^3} + \frac{P_3}{(1+k)^3}$$

For Eastover:     $g_1 = .12$
          $g_2 = .08$

| | | | | | | |
|---|---|---|---|---|---|---|
| $D_0$ | = | 1.20 | | | | |
| $D_1$ | = | 1.20 | * | 1.12 | = | 1.34 |
| $D_2$ | = | 1.20 | * | $(1.12)^2$ | = | 1.50 |
| $D_3$ | = | 1.20 | * | $(1.12)^3$ | = | 1.69 |
| $D_4$ | = | $D_3$ | * | (1.08) | = | 1.82 |
| $P_3$ | = | 1.82 / (.11 - .08) | | | = | 60.67 |

$$Price = \frac{1.34}{1.11} + \frac{1.50}{(1.11)^2} + \frac{1.69}{(1.11)^3} + \frac{60.67}{(1.11)^3} = 48.03$$

This approach indicates that Eastover is even more undervalued than was the case with the constant growth approach.

An alternative solution to the two-stage model is:

$$Price = \frac{D_1}{1+k} + \frac{D_2}{(1+k)^2} + \frac{P_2}{(1+k)^2}$$

$D_0$ = 1.20

$D_1$ = 1.20 * 1.12 = 1.34

$D_2$ = 1.20 * $(1.12)^2$ = 1.50

$D_3$ = 1.20 * $(1.12)^3$ = 1.69

$P_2$ = 1.69 / (.11 - .08) = 56.33

$$Price = \frac{1.34}{1.11} + \frac{1.50}{(1.11)^2} + \frac{56.33}{(1.11)^2} = 1.21 + 1.22 + 45.72 = 48.15$$

This answer differs from previous answer because of round off error.

12(c). Constant growth model:

Advantages:

1)     logical, theoretical basis
2)     simple to compute
3)      inputs can be estimated

Disadvantages:

1)     very sensitive to inputs of growth
2)     g and k difficult to estimate accurately
3)     result is meaningless if g > k
4)     constant growth is an unrealistic assumption
5)     assumes growth will never slow down
6)     dividend payout must remain constant
7)     not usable for firm not paying dividend
8)     assumes stock price will increase at g

Improvements with the two-stage model:

1.      The two-stage model is more realistic. It accounts for low, high, or zero growth in the first stage, followed by constant long-term growth in the second stage.

2.      The model can solve for stock value when the growth rate in the first stage exceeds the required rate of return.

13(a).  In order to determine whether a stock is undervalued or overvalued, analysts often analyze price-earnings ratios (P/Es) and price-book value ratios (P/Bs) as compared to those of the market as represented by the S&P 500 Index. The formulas for these calculations are:

Relative P/E = P/E of specific company / P/E of S&P500

Relative P/B = P/B of specific company / P/B of S&P500

To evaluate EO and SHC using the relative P/E model, Mulroney should calculate the five year average P/E for each stock, and divide that number by the 5 year average P/E for the S&P 500. This gives the average relative P/E. Mulroney should then compare the average historical relative P/E to the current relative P/E, which is the current P/E on each stock, using 1992 estimated E.P.S., divided by the current P/E of the market, again using the 1992 estimate.

For the price/book model, Mulroney should make similar calculations, i.e., divide the five year average price/book ratio for a stock into the five year average price/book for the S&P 500, and compare the result to the current relative price/book (using 1991 estimated book value, as that is all that is available).

The results are shown below:

|                |                       | EO      | SHC    | S&P500  |
|----------------|-----------------------|---------|--------|---------|
| P/E Model:     | 5 yr. avg. P/E        | 16.6x   | 11.9x  | 15.2x   |
|                | Relative 5 yr. P/E    | 1.09x   | 0.78x  |         |
|                | Current P/E           | 17.5x   | 16.0x  | 20.20x  |
|                | Current relative P/e  | 0.87x   | 0.79x  |         |
| Price/Book:    | 5 yr. avg. price/book | 1.50x   | 1.10x  | 2.10x   |
|                | Relative 5 yr. p/b    | 0.71x   | 0.52x  |         |
|                | Current price/book    | 1.62x   | 1.49x  | 2.60x   |
|                | Current relative p/b  | 0.62x   | 0.57x  |         |

From this analysis, it is evident that EO is trading at a discount to its historical 5 year relative P/E ratio, whereas Southampton is trading right at its historical 5 year relative P/E. With respect to price/book, Eastover is trading at a discount to its historical relative price/book ratio, whereas SHC is trading modestly above its 5 year relative price/book ratio. As noted in the preamble, however, Eastover's book value is understated due to the very low historical cost basis for its timberlands. The fact that Eastover is trading at below its 5 year average relative price to book ratio even though its book value is understated makes Eastover seem especially attractive on a price/book basis.

13(b). Disadvantages of relative P/E model:

1) measures relative, not absolute, value
2) accounting earnings estimate for next fiscal year may not be representative of sustainable earnings
3) no standardization on which earnings to use
4) changing accounting standards may make historical comparisons difficult
5) requires estimating earnings growth for next fiscal year

Disadvantages of relative P/B model:

1) book value may be under or overstated -- particularly for a company like Eastover, which has valuable lumberlands on its books carried at low historical cost
2) book value may not be representative of earning power or future growth potential
3) changing accounting standards may make historical comparisons difficult

14(a). The formula for a multistage DDM model with two distinct growth stages consisting of a first stage with five years of above-normal constant growth followed by a second stage of normal constant growth is:

$$P_0 = \frac{D_1}{(1+r)^1} + \frac{D_2}{(1+r)^2} + \frac{D_3}{(1+r)^3} + \frac{D_4}{(1+r)^4} + \frac{D_5}{(1+r)^5} + \frac{\dfrac{D_6}{(r-g)}}{(1+r)^5}$$

$$P_0 = \frac{\$2.29}{(1.10)^1} + \frac{\$2.75}{(1.10)^2} + \frac{\$3.30}{(1.10)^3} + \frac{\$3.96}{(1.10)^4} + \frac{\$4.75}{(1.10)^5} + \frac{\dfrac{\$5.08}{(0.10-0.07)}}{(1.10)^5}$$

$$P_0 = \$117.62$$

Note: Though referred to as a multistage DDM, the use of the so called "H-Model" is incorrect in this application. The H-Model assumes that the growth rate declines in a linear fashion from the above-normal growth rate of 20% to the normal growth rate of 7%. The problem as stated, depicts a situation in which the growth rate drops abruptly from 20% to 7% after five years.

14(b).

| | | | | |
|---|---|---|---|---|
| Philip Morris P/E (12/31/91) | = | $80.25 / $4.24 | = | **18.9x** |
| S&P500 P/E (12/31/91) | = | $417.09 / $16.29 | = | 25.6x |
| Philip Morris relative P/E | = | 18.9x / 25.6x | = | **0.74x** |

14(c).

| | | | | |
|---|---|---|---|---|
| Philip Morris book value (12/31/91) | = | $12,512 / 920 | = | $13.60 |
| Philip Morris P/B (12/31/95) | = | $80.25 / $13.60 | = | **5.90x** |
| S&P500 P/B (12/31/95) | = | $417.09 / $161.08 | = | 2.59x |
| Philip Morris relative P/B | = | 5.90x / 2.59x | = | **2.28x** |

## 15(a). <u>**Multistage Dividend Discount Model**</u>

### Advantages

1. Excellent for comparing greatly different companies.
2. Solid theoretical framework.
3. Ease in adjusting for risk levels.
4. Dividends relatively easy to project.
5. Dividends not subject to accounting.
6. Flexibility in use and more realistic than constant growth model.

### Disadvantages

1. Need to forecast well into the future.
2. Problem with non-dividend paying companies.
3. Most investors aren't looking to collect a stream of dividends.
4. Problem with high growth companies ($g > k$).
5. Problems projecting "forever after" ROE and payout ratio.
6. Small changes in assumptions can have big impact.
7. Need technology for more advanced models.
8. Quality of payouts may differ.

## <u>Absolute and Relative Price/Earnings Ratio</u>

### Advantages

1. Widely used by investors.
2. Easy to compare with market and other companies in specific industries.

### Disadvantages

1. Difficult with volatile companies.
2. Need to determine what is "normal."
3. Difficult to project earnings.
4. Effect of accounting differences.
5. Many factors influence multiples.
6. Can be used only for relative rather than absolute measurement.
7. Point in time "snapshot."
8. Doesn't address quality of earnings.
9. Problem with companies with no income.

## Absolute and Relative Price/Book Ratio

### Advantages

1. Incorporates some concept of asset values.
2. Easy to compute even for companies with volatile or negative earnings.
3. Easy to compare with market and specific industries.

### Disadvantages

1. Subject to differing accounting rules.
2. Effected by non-recurring items and share repurchases.
3. Subject to historical costs.
4. Book may be poor guide to actual asset values.
5. Ignores future earnings prospects and growth potential.

15(b). Support can be given to either position.

Philip Morris is undervalued because:

1. DDM indicates intrinsic value above current market price.
2. Given forecasts of dividends over two stages, DDM is best to use for this situation and should be given more weight.
3. P/E below market despite past growth and forecast of superior future growth.
4. P/E relative below 10-year average.
5. P/B for Philip Morris is high due to share repurchases and FAS 106 having much greater effect than other companies on average.

Philip Morris is overvalued because:

1. P/B considerably higher than market.
2. P/B relative higher than 10-year average.
3. DDM discount rate used should be higher than market's 10% due to large potential risks in cigarette manufacturing business.
4. P/E on Philip Morris should be low relative to market and past growth due to risks inherent in its business.

**16(a). Constant growth dividend discount model:** $D_1/(k-g) = P_0$

Litchfield:   $0.90/(0.10 - 0.08) = 45.00$
Aminochem: $ 1.60/(0.11 - 0.07) = 40.00$

**16(b). Expected return:** $R_f + \beta(R_m - R_f) = k$
Litchfield:   5% + 1.2(20% - 5%) = 23%
Aminochem: 5% + 1.4(20% - 5%) = 26%

**16(c). Internal growth rate:** $[(E-D)/E] \, [E/BV] = g$
Litchfield:    [($4.00 - $0.90)/$4.00)($4.00/$30) = 10.3%
                   BV = $300/10 = $30
Aminochem: ($3.20 - $1.60/$3.20)($3.20/S16) = 10.0%
                   BV = $320/20 = $16

**16(d). Recommendation**: Aminochem (AOC) is a more attractive investment than Litchfield (LCC) based on the answers to parts A, B, and C, and the information provided in Table 1.

**Justification**: Using the constant growth dividend discount model (DDM) (computed in Part A), the stock price of AOC is more attractive at a price of $30 (well below its DDM value of $40) than LCC at a price of $50 (above the DDM value of $45).

AOC has the higher expected return (computed in Part B) because it has a higher beta and the market (S&P 500) is expected to rise.

LCC's internal growth rate (computed in Part C) is higher than that of AOC, but LCC's higher price-to-earnings ratio of 12.5 (S50/S4) versus 9.4 ($30/$3.20) for AOC is not justified by the small difference in growth rate.

# CHAPTER 21

## Technical Analysis

# Answers to Questions

1. The principle contention of technicians is that stock prices move in trends which persist for long periods of time. Because these trends persist they can be detected by analyzing past prices.

2. Technicians expect trends in stock price behavior because they believe that new information that causes a change in the relationship between supply and demand does not come to the market at one point in time--i.e., they contend that some investors get the information before others. Also, they believe that investors react gradually over time to new information. The result is a gradual adjustment of stock prices.

3. The problems encountered when doing a fundamental analysis of financial statements are: (1) much of the information in financial statements is not useful; (2) there are comparability problems for firms using alternative accounting practices; and (3) there are important psychological factors not included in financial statements. Also, with technical analysis it is not necessary to invest until the move to a new equilibrium begins.

4. The disadvantages of technical analysis are: (1) past price patterns may not be repeated in the future; (2) the intense competition of those using the trading rules will render the technique useless; (3) the trading rules require a great deal of subjective judgment; and (4) the values that signal action are constantly changing.

5. The mutual fund cash position of 12 percent is relatively high. This would indicate a bullish market because: (1) the theory of contrary-opinion states that mutual funds are the odd-lot trader of the institutional market and typically make the wrong decision by holding excess cash near a trough when they should be fully invested; and (2) the large cash positions of mutual funds represent potential buying power.

6. Credit balances result when investors sell securities and leave the proceeds with their broker with the intent of reinvesting the funds shortly. Therefore, they can be considered a source of potential buying power. Given this line of reasoning, a decline in credit balances would indicate a decline in potential buying power which is bearish. Another line of reasoning is based on

*21 - 3*

contrary opinion. It is assumed that these balances are generally maintained by small investors who draw them down to invest at the peak, so this is bearish for the contrary opinion technician.

7.   This index indicates what proportion of investment advisory services are bearish and 61 percent is a fairly high ratio. To a contrary opinion technician this is bullish because so many of the services are bearish.

8.   When the ratio of specialist short sales to total short sales is equal to 70 percent, it is relatively high. The technician would consider this bearish because specialists are aggressively selling short and they make good decisions--i.e., you want to follow the smart money. In contrast, if odd-lot short sales increase, it would be bullish because the odd-lotter is typically wrong so when they become very bearish it is probably near the trough.

9.   Debit balances represent borrowing by sophisticated investors, therefore, higher debit balances indicate optimism on the part of these investors. The problem with the debit balance measure is that it only represents borrowing through brokers and it ignores the amount of borrowing from alternative sources.

10.  The Dow Theory contends that stock prices move in waves. Specifically, these waves may be grouped into three categories based upon the period of the wave: (1) major trends for long periods (tides); (2) intermediate trends (waves); and (3) short-run movements for very short periods (ripples). The major trend (the tide) is most important to investors. An intermediate reversal occurs when some investors decide to take profits.

11.  Volume is important to the technician because it is an indicator of the breadth of the changes in supply and demand for a stock. The direction of a price movement accompanied by high volume is more important than if the same price change is associated with light volume. If prices decline (advance) on heavy volume it is bearish (bullish) since it indicates numerous sellers (buyers).

12.  The breadth of the market index is a time series calculated as the cumulative number of net advances or net declines. It indicates a peak or trough in stock prices prior to the peak (or trough) in the aggregate price series by indicating a broadly based decline in the majority of individual stocks. The technician would expect that at a turning point this decline (advance) in the breadth index would be moving in the opposite direction of a rising (falling) market

*21 - 4*

price index series -i.e., the aggregate price series would still be rising (falling) when most individual stocks are beginning to decline (advance).

13. Technicians following the breadth of market rules might interpret the event as indicative of a possible market peak. Since the DJIA is a value-weighted series confined to 30 large well-known stocks, the past trading period indicates that while the large stocks are still advancing, the majority of individual issues are declining. Due to the technical analyst's belief that information is disseminated on an unequal basis, the technicians would interpret a net cumulative decline as a sign of a market turn that has not been interpreted yet by small investors who hold funds of the large, well-known stocks.

14. A support level is a price range where considerable demand is expected, while a resistance level is a price range where a large supply is expected. Support and resistance levels exist due to the behavior of a number of investors who are closely monitoring the market and will trade quickly at attractive price levels. Specifically, a support level occurs after a stock has increased in price followed by a brief period of profit-taking at which time some investors who did not get in on the first round decide to take the opportunity to get in. A resistance level occurs after a stock has declined and when it experiences a recovery, some investors who missed selling at a price peak take the opportunity to sell.

A price break through a resistance level on strong volume would be considered very bullish. This is because as the price rises to the target price set by investors, the supply increases usually causing the price increase to reverse. Thus, a price breakthrough on strong volume would be bullish because it would mean the excess supply is gone.

15. A moving average line indicates the major trend of a security's price. When daily prices break through the long term trend from below on heavy volume it is considered a bullish action. The move above the trend line may indicate a new upward change in the trend.

16. If current prices break through the 50-day MA line from above on heavy volume, technicians would anticipate a reversal of a rising trend and become bearish. If the 50-day MA line crosses the 200-day line from above on good volume, technicians would again expect a reversal in rising prices and become bearish.

17. Relative strength is the ratio of a firm's stock price to a market price series. If the relative strength ratio is increasing during a bear market it means that the stock is not declining as much as the aggregate market. Under such favorable conditions, the technician would expect the stock to likewise outperform the market in the ensuing bull market.

18. Technicians recognize that there is no single technical trading rule that is correct all the time--even the best ones miss certain turns or give false signals. Also, various indicators provide different information for alternative segments of the market. Therefore, you don't want to depend on any one technique, but look at several and derive a consensus.

# Answers to Problems

1.  Student Exercise

2.  Student Exercise

3.  Student Exercise

4.  40
    39
    38 X 0
    37 X 0
    36 X 0
    35 X 0
    34 X 0
    33 X 0
    32 X 0
    31 X 0
    30 X 0 X
    29 X 0 X
    28 X 0 X
    27 X 0 X
    26 X 0 X
    25 X
    24 X
    23 X

The minimal horizontal movement evident in the chart above suggests the absence of any consolidation. Rather, the chart implies a buying opportunity at the current stock price of 32 inasmuch as the stock has advanced from 26 to 32 without a <u>significant</u> reversal.

# CHAPTER 22

## Equity Portfolio Management Strategies

# Answers to Questions

1.  Passive portfolio management strategies have grown in popularity because investors are recognizing that the stock market is fairly efficient and that the costs of an actively managed portfolio are substantial.

2.  Numerous studies have shown that the majority of portfolio managers have been unable to match the risk-return performance of stock or bond indexes. Following an indexing portfolio strategy, the portfolio manager builds a portfolio that matches the performance of an index, thereby reducing the costs of research and trading.

    In an indexing strategy, the portfolio manager's evaluation is based upon how closely the portfolio tracks the index or "tracking error," rather than a risk-return performance evaluation.

3.  There are a number of active management strategies discussed in the chapter including sector rotation, the use of factor models, quantitative screens, and linear programming methods.

    Following a sector rotation strategy, the manager over-weights certain economic sectors, industries or other stock attributes in anticipation of an upcoming economic period or the recognition that the shares are undervalued.

    Using a factor model, portfolio managers examine the sensitivity of stocks to various economic variables. The managers then "tilt" the portfolios by trading those shares most sensitive to the analyst's economic forecast.

    Through the use of computer databases and quantitative screens, portfolio managers are able to identify groups of stocks based upon a set of characteristics.

    Using linear programming techniques, portfolio managers are able to develop portfolios that maximize objectives while satisfying linear constraints.

4.  Three basic techniques exist for constructing a passive portfolio: (1) full replication of an index is where all securities in the index are purchased proportionally to their weight in the index; (2) in sampling the portfolio managers purchases only a sample of the stocks in the benchmark index; and (3) quadratic optimization or programming techniques utilize computer programs that analyze historical security information in order to develop a portfolio that minimizes tracking error.

5.  Managers attempt to add value to their portfolio by: (1) timing their investments in the various markets in light of market forecasts and estimated risk premiums; (2) shifting funds between various equity sectors, industries, or investment styles in order to catch the next "hot" concept; and (3) stockpicking of individual issues (buy low, sell high).

6.  The job of an active portfolio manager is not easy. In order to succeed, the manager should maintain his/her investment philosophy, "don't panic." Since the transaction costs of an actively managed portfolio typically account for 1 to 2 percent of the portfolio assets, the portfolio must earn 1-2 percent above the passive benchmark just to keep even. Therefore, it recommended that a portfolio manager attempt to minimize the amount of portfolio trading activity. Numerous portfolio turnovers will result in diminishing portfolio profits due to growing commission costs.

7.  The four asset allocation strategies are: (1) integrated asset allocation strategy, which relies on current market expectations; (2) strategic asset allocation strategy, which utilizes long-run projections; (3) tactical asset allocation strategy, which assumes that investor's objectives and constraints remain constant over the planning horizon; and (4) insured asset allocation strategy, which presumes changes in investor's objectives and constraints as market conditions change.

8.  Systematic and unsystematic risk are the two components of risk in an equity portfolio. Systematic risk or market risk is defined as the portfolio's exposure to price fluctuations caused by changes in the overall equity market. Unsystematic risk is defined as the portfolio's exposure to industries, sectors, or firms that is different from the benchmark.

9.  Hedge ratio is the appropriate number of futures contracts that must be bought or sold in order to hedge a position. Futures contracts are used in

22 - 4

order to maintain the desired exposure to stocks (in this case) when the portfolio experiences a cash inflow or outflow.

10. Stock-market index portfolios are probably more difficult to construct and maintain because securities must frequently be bought and sold in order to reflect cash inflows and outflows, company mergers and acquisitions, etc.

11. There are tradeoffs between using the full replication and the sampling method. Fully replicating an index is more difficult to manage and has higher trading commission costs, when compared to the sampling method. However, tracking error occurs from sampling, which should not be the case in the full replication of the index.

12. The portfolio manager could emphasize or overweight, relative to the benchmark, investments in natural resource stocks. The portfolio manager could also purchase options on natural resource stocks.

# Answers to Problems

1.  $50 million x 1.2 x 1.10 = 66 million

2.

| Month | Portfolio (R$_i$) | R$_i$ – E(R$_i$) | S&P 500 (R$_m$) | R$_m$ – E(R$_m$) | [R$_i$ – E(R$_i$)] [R$_m$ – E(R$_m$)] |
|---|---|---|---|---|---|
| Jan | 5.0% | 4.7583 | 5.2% | 5.0333 | 23.9500 |
| Feb | -2.3 | -2.5417 | -3.0 | -3.1667 | 8.0488 |
| March | -1.8 | -2.0417 | -1.6 | -1.7667 | 3.6071 |
| April | 2.2 | 1.9583 | 1.9 | 1.7333 | 3.3943 |
| May | 0.4 | 0.1583 | 0.1 | -0.0667 | -0.0106 |
| June | -0.8 | -1.0417 | -0.5 | -0.6667 | 0.06945 |
| July | 0.0 | -0.2417 | 0.2 | 0.0333 | -0.0080 |
| Aug. | 1.5 | 1.2583 | 1.6 | 1.4333 | 1.8035 |
| Sept. | -0.3 | -0.5417 | -0.1 | -0.2667 | 0.1445 |
| Oct. | -3.7 | -3.9417 | -4.0 | -4.1667 | 16.4239 |
| Nov | 2.4 | 2.1583 | 2.0 | 1.8333 | 3.9568 |
| Dec. | 0.3 | 0.0583 | 0.2 | 0.0333 | 0.0019 |
| Sum | 2.9 | | 2.0 | | 62.0067 |

$E(R_i) = 2.9/12 = .2417$        $E(R_m) = 2.0/12 = .1667$

$Var_i = 60.3490/12 = 5.0291$    $Var_m = 64.7865/12 = 5.3989$

$\sigma_i = \sqrt{5.0291} = 2.2426$     $\sigma_m = \sqrt{5.3989} = 2.3236$

$COV_{i,m} = 62.0067/12 = 5.1672$

$$R_{i,m} = \frac{5.1672}{(2.2426)(2.3236)} = .9916 \quad R^2 = (.9916)^2 = .9833$$

$$B_i = \frac{5.1672}{5.3989} = .9571$$

$$\alpha = E(R_i) - (B_i \times E(R_m))$$

$$= .2417 - (.9571)(.1667) = .0822$$

With a $R^2$ value of .9833, one can conclude that the passive portfolio did closely track the S&P 500 benchmark. The tracking errors were +0.9% (with sign) and 3.3% (without sign).

3.   The annual geometric mean for the equity risk premium is 6.3 percent. Trading costs of 1.5 percent is equal to 23.8% of the equity risk premium.

Since (8.21 - 1.57) / 120.3% equals 0.33 standard deviation and 0.33 SD corresponds with an area of 0.1293 under a normal curve, the probability of exceeding the 1.5% trading costs is 0.1293 + 0.5000 -- or 0.63.

4.   The value of the S&P 500 futures contract is equal to $500 times the S&P 500 index value.

$$\$500 \times 470.50 = \$235,250$$

4(a).   $$\frac{\$3 \text{ million}}{\$235,250} \times 1.05 = 13.39 \text{ contracts}$$

13 contracts (rounded) would be purchased to hedge cash inflow.

4(b).   $$\frac{-\$8 \text{ million}}{\$235,250} \times 1.05 = -35.71 \text{ contracts}$$

36 contracts would be sold to hedge cash outflow.

5(a).   $$1.15 = (.95 \times 1.05) + \frac{F \times \$235,250}{\$100 \text{ million}} \times 1.0$$

$1.15 = .9975 + .0023525 \, F$

$.1525 = .0023525 \, F$

$64.82 = F$     (65 contracts must be purchased)

5(b).   $$1.30 = (.95 \times 1.05) + \frac{F \times \$235,250}{\$100 \text{ million}} \times 1.0$$

$1.30 = .9975 + .0023525 \, F$

$.3025 = .0023525 \, F$

$128.59 = F$     (129 contracts must be purchased)

5(c).   $$.95 = (.95 \times 1.05) + \frac{F \times \$235,250}{\$100 \text{ million}} \times 1.0$$

$.95 = .9975 + .0023525 \, F$

$-.0475 = .0023525 \, F$

$-20.19 = F$     (20 contracts must be sold)

5(d).   $$0 = (.95 \times 1.05) + \frac{F \times \$235,250}{\$100 \text{ million}} \times 1.0$$

22 - 8

$0 = .9975 + .0023525 \text{ F}$

$-.9975 = .0023525 \text{ F}$

$-424.02 = \text{F}$     (424 contracts must be sold)

6(a).  One S&P 500 futures contract = $500 x 493.45 = $246,725

6(b).  $0 = (1.0 \times 1.3) + \dfrac{\text{F} \times \$246,725}{\$1.5 \text{ million}} \times 1.0$

$0 = 1.3 + .1647 \text{ F}$

$-7.893 = \text{F}$

In order to make the portfolio market neutral, it is
necessary to sell 8 (rounded) futures contracts.

6(c).  If the market drops by 10 percent, S&P 500 goes from 493.45
to 444.11.

    i.    <u>In futures market</u>

        Sold 8 S&P 500 contracts @ $500 x 493.45     = $1,973,800
        Bought 8 S&P 500 contracts @ $500 x 444.11 =   1,776,440
                                            ---------------
                        Profit in futures     $  197,360

    ii.    <u>Unhedged stock portfolio</u>

        A 10 percent market decline equals a 13% portfolio decline
        assuming a beta of 1.3.

        $1,500,000 x (.10 x 1.3) = ($195,000) loss in portfolio value

$1,500,000 - $195,000 = $1,305,000 new portfolio value

   iii.    <u>Hedged portfolio</u>

           Profit in futures         = $197,360
           Loss in portfolio value   = ($195,000)
                                 --------------
                Profit         $   2,360

A perfectly hedged portfolio should be market neutral, that is, no profits or losses. In this case, a small profit occurred due to rounding (to the next highest integer) in part 6(b).

6(d).   If the market increases by 10%, the S&P 500 goes from 493.45 to 542.795.
       i. <u>In the futures market</u>
       Sold 8 S&P 500 contracts @ $500 X 493.45     = $1,973,800
       Bought 8 S&P 500 contracts @ $500 X 542.795  =  <u>2,171,180</u>
                              Loss in futures   = $   191,380

       ii. <u>Unhedged stock portfolio</u>

       $1,500,000 X (.10  X 1.3) = $195,000 gain in portfolio value

       $1,500,000 + 195,000 = $1,695,000 new portfolio value

       iii. <u>Hedged portfolio</u>

       Loss in futures         = $197,380
       Gain in portfolio value  =  <u>195,000</u>
       Net loss             = $   2,380

The small loss was attributable to rounding, In the absence of rounding, a perfectly hedged portfolio will produce zero profit or loss.

7(a).   One S&P 500 futures contract = $500 x 477.75 = $238,875

7(b). $\quad 0 \quad = (1.0 \times 1.1) + \dfrac{F \times \$238,875}{\$2.3 \text{ million}} \quad\quad \times \quad 1.0$

$\quad\quad 0 \quad = 1.1 + .1039 \, F$

$\quad -10.59 = F$

In order to make the portfolio market neutral, it is necessary to sell 11 (rounded) futures contracts.

7(c). i. <u>In futures market</u>

If the market drop by 10 percent, S&P 500 goes from 477.75 to 429.98

| | | |
|---|---|---|
| Sold 11 S&P 500 contracts @ $500 x 477.75 | = | $2,627,625 |
| Bought 11 S&P 500 contracts @ $500 x 429.98 = | | 2,364,890 |
| | Profit in futures | $ 262,735 |

ii. <u>Unhedged stock portfolio</u>

A 13% portfolio decline is equivalent to $299,000 loss in portfolio value ($2,300,000 x .13 = $299,000)

$2,300,000 - $299,000 = $2,001,000 new portfolio value

iii. <u>Hedged portfolio</u>

| | |
|---|---|
| Profit in futures | = $262,735 |
| Loss in portfolio value | = ($299,000) |
| Loss | ($ 36,265) |

Because of unsystematic risk the stock portfolio declined by 13 percent, rather than the 11 percent which was covered by the hedge (1.1 beta x .10 market decline).

7(d).  i.    <u>In futures market</u>

If the market increases by 10 percent, S&P 500 goes from
477.75 to 525.53

| | |
|---|---|
| Sold 11 S&P 500 contracts @ $500 x 477.75 | = $2,627,625 |
| Bought 11 S&P 500 contracts @ $500 x 525.53 | =   2,890,415 |
| | ---------------- |
| Loss in futures | ($  262,790) |

ii.    <u>Unhedged stock portfolio</u>

A 15% portfolio increase is equivalent to $345,000
increase in portfolio value ($2,300,000 x .15 = $345,000)

$2,300,000 + $345,000 = $2,645,000 new portfolio value

iii.    <u>Hedged portfolio</u>

| | |
|---|---|
| Loss in futures | = ($262,735) |
| Gain in portfolio value | =   345,000 |
| | --------------- |
| Gain | $  82,265 |

Because of unsystematic risk the stock portfolio increased by 15
percent, rather than just the 11 percent which was covered by the
hedge (1.1 beta x .10 market decline).

22 - 12

# CHAPTER 23

## Forward And Futures Contracts

# Answers to Questions

1.  If WEC invests in Bunds, they can use the current spot rate to calculate how many bonds they will receive today for $30 million. We can assume WEC is satisfied with the Bund interest rate and motivated primarily by a desire to diversify and reduce interest rate risk. Even if they could guarantee the Deutschemark value of the bonds they will hold, however, they would still face exchange rate risk. A currency futures contract sets the rate for future exchange of marks for dollars. With a prior agreement, like a futures contract, WEC can guarantee their exchange rate six months hence.

Short futures positions will incur losses as the exchange rate rises and gains as the exchange rate falls. The dollar value of the Bunds will change in the opposite direction. A perfect hedge would have WEC buy just enough futures (face value in marks) to cover the marks they will repatriate.

Undesirable Characteristics:
Even a perfect fixed futures hedge does not preserve the entire $30 million. The futures settlement rate for six months hence is almost surely less favorable than the exchange rate today. WEC can hedge but probably will lock in a loss, even without transactions costs. This loss is part of the opportunity cost of hedging - forgoing the chance of exchange rate gains in return for preventing exchange rate losses.

Fixed currency hedges are rarely perfect because German mark futures contracts are for a fixed amount (currently 125,000 DM) and may not be an integer multiple of the number of marks purchased today. A typical fixed futures hedge is either slightly over or under hedged.

Currency futures positions require margin. Losses must be paid daily. If WEC does not liquidate gains on the Bunds to fund losses on the futures, they may need extra cash some time during the six months.

Fixed currency hedging also presents problems when the Bunds mature beyond the six month holding period. WEC will not know exactly how many marks it will need to repatriate six months hence. Hedging by shorting a fixed number of contracts is rarely done unless the foreign investment is a pure discount security.

2. There are two types of basis risk that this hedge is exposed to. The first is from changes in the shape of the yield curve. Since the company wishes to hedge a seven year issue's cost with a ten year contract, the hedge is exposed to changes in the relative level of interest rates between the seven and ten year maturities. Specifically, if the seven year treasury rate rises more relative to the ten year rate then the hedge will not completely neutralize the position and lose money for the firm. The second source of basis risk is from the quality spread over treasuries in the Eurobond market. Since the company will have to sell its bonds with a spread over the treasury rate, changes in this spread will also effect the quality of the hedge. Specifically, increases in the spread will lead to losses for the firm.

3. When the index futures price is below its theoretical level, the arbitrage involves buying the futures contract and selling the underlying index of stocks short. When the index futures price is above its theoretical level, the arbitrage involves selling the futures contract and buying the underlying index of stocks. The practicalities of selling the index short make the first type of arbitrage more difficult. First, there is an up-tick rule for short sales that prevents short sales from being possible for all of the index's stocks at the current market price. This is because, on average, about half of the market prices will have just moved down a tick and the up-tick rule prevents short sales until they trade up a tick. Second, margin requirements and limitations on the use of proceeds from short sales demand the use of more capital than long positions in the underlying stocks. Finally, for some stocks there may not be shares available to borrow and then short, or shares borrowed may be recalled by the original owner prior to the arbitrageur's preferred time to close the position.

4. Because the funds from one country could be converted to another currency and then through the use of forward contracts converted back to the original currency at the same rate, an arbitrage opportunity is available. Investors from the Country B could borrow at the lower rate, convert into the currency of Country A, earn a higher rate of return on the money, and then pay back their loan pocketing the difference in interest payments. The market forces from these transactions would tend to either equalize interest rates or change the forward exchange rates so that the currency of Country A trades at a forward discount.

5. Before entering into a futures or forward contract, hedgers have exposure to price changes in the underlying asset. To hedge this risk, hedgers enter into

contracts that most closely offset this price risk. The problem is that for most hedgers there is not a contract that exactly matches there exposure. Perhaps, the commodity they use is a different grade or needed in a different location than specified in the contract, so differences in prices between the actual asset the company is exposed to and the asset in the contract may exist and change over time. Likewise, a portfolio manager hedging a stock portfolio may hold a portfolio that is not perfectly correlated with the index future he/she is using to hedge with. To minimize basis risk it is necessary to find the contract that's price is most highly correlated with the price of the asset to be hedged.

6(a).   To hedge price risk, you could enter into a long position in 100,000 gallons worth of gasoline futures.

6(b).   Since you will have to post margin on the futures contract, the price swings in the futures contract will effect how much you earn on the capital posted as margin. If gas prices go up, your margin account will be credited and you will earn more interest. If gas prices go down, your account will be debited and you will earn less interest. If prices go down substantially, you will be required to post additional margin, and therefore tie up additional capital. How this effects your pricing of the forward contract you have sold depends on your opportunity cost of capital.

6(c).   In this case, by using futures you will not be able to match the quantity or time of delivery in the forward contract you sold. This gives rise to two types of risk. Since you will be forced to over or under hedge, you will be exposed to the general price movements in gas one way or the other. Next, if you synthetically create a three month expiration using half two-month and half four-month contracts, then you will be exposed to relative price changes in the two futures contracts in the near term. Later, after the two-month contract expires, you will be forced to hedge a shorter term position with a longer term contract, so again relative near-term and longer-term price differentials will lead to basis risk.

7.   Both Eurodollar and Treasury Bill futures are designed so that the long position benefits from a decline in the respective reference dates (relative to the contract yield) while the short position benefits from a rate increase. In both cases, the purpose of the hypothetical price index is to translate rate declines into price increases—and vice versa—which is a more natural way to think of the contract holder's position. Despite the fact that the underlying

rate for these contracts are quoted on different conventions, they can both use the same price index calculation because all that really matters at maturity (or contract unwind) is the number of basis points the settlement price differs from the original contract price, with each basis point begin worth \$25 (= (\$1,000,000) x (90/360) ).

8.   First, enter into a forward position agreeing to exchange pesos for dollars in two months. Then, enter into another forward contract agreeing to exchange those dollars for Swiss francs, also in two months.

9.   There are many different reasons some futures contracts succeed and some fail, but the most important is demand. If people need a particular contract to expose themselves to or hedge a price risk, then the contract will succeed. Most people use treasury bond futures to gain exposure to or hedge general long-term interest rate risk. The only additional advantage of futures on corporate bonds would be that the investors could gain exposure to changes in the credit spread. Apparently there is little demand for this, either because investors do not want to hedge or gain exposure to this risk or because the underlying market is not liquid enough to support futures. Either way, the lack of futures is motivated by a lack of demand in the asset or futures contract. The lack of chicken contracts most likely derives from a similar lack of demand. It could be that chicken prices are highly correlated with other existing contract prices, so investors do not need the additional chicken contract. Perhaps there are too many different types of chickens to have a single contract that would attract enough trading volume.

There are other reasons beyond demand. For example, contract specifications can be difficult to standardize, and there must be two sides of a market (buyers and sellers) for the particular asset. But, demand for exposure to that price risk seems to be the primary determinant.

10.  The fourth factor affecting the price of a stock index futures contract is the risk-free interest rate, usually measured by the Treasury bill rate. Futures prices increase with increases in the risk-free interest rate. Investors can create portfolios having identical levels of risk by either investing directly in a diversified equity portfolio or purchasing an equivalent position in stock index futures and placing the remainder in risk-free assets. The stock portfolio earns the price appreciation of the stocks plus their dividend yield; the futures portfolio earns the price appreciation of the futures plus the risk-free interest rate. Since futures are marked to the market, the futures price

will equal the spot price of the stocks at the futures contract's expiration date. Market forces (arbitrage activity) results in stock index futures being priced such that their price is equal to the future value of the current spot price, using the "cost of carry" as the discount rate. The cost of carry is the risk-free interest rate minus the dividend yield on the stock portfolio.

If the risk-free interest rate subsequently increases, it becomes more profitable to purchase the futures/Treasury bill combination than to invest directly in the stocks themselves, because of the higher return on the Treasury bills now available. As a result, the price of the futures contract will be bid up until it is again equal to the future value of the current spot price of the equivalent stock portfolio. There is, thus, a direct and positive relationship between the risk-free interest rate and futures prices.

11.   It is most likely that a single position in an index futures market would be the best hedge. There are several reasons for this. The most important is cost. Since there are no exchange traded futures for individual stocks, entering 50 different positions would have to be done through an over-the-counter derivatives dealer. This typically would mean higher transaction costs to cover the fees from setting up the one-off deal, the lower liquidity of individual stocks, and the increased commissions for the dealer. Another disadvantage is the liquidity of the position. Index options are very liquid and can be closed out quickly with little trading cost. Closing the 50 different positions would entail paying many of the start-up costs twice. Finally, it is easy to short an index future but rather hard and more expensive to short the underlying stocks (see question 3) which the OTC dealer would have to do to hedge the position in the 50 different stocks. The only advantage to the 50 different positions is that they would provide a nearly perfect hedge, whereas there would be some basis risk in the index futures position. Since the portfolio is well diversified, this should not be a major problem.

# Answers to Problems

**1(a).**

|           | Price    | Adjustment | Margin | Maintenance |
|-----------|----------|------------|--------|-------------|
| March 9   | $173.00  | 0          | 3000   | 0           |
| April 9   | $179.75  | -675       | 2325   | 0           |
| May 9     | $189.00  | -925       | 3000   | 1600        |
| June 9    | $182.50  | 650        | 3650   | 0           |
| July 9    | $174.25  | 825        | 4475   | 0           |

Net loss of $4475 - ($3000 + $1600) = -$125

including maintenance:

Total Return      = -125/3000
                       = -4 17

**1(b).** Cost of Carry = 1.5%+8%=9.5%

Theoretical spot price on March 9

$$S = PV(F)$$
$$S = 173*exp(1.095*.3333)$$
$$S = \$167.61$$

Implied May 9 price
$$S = \$189*exp(-.095*.16667)$$
$$S = \$186.03$$

**1(c).** Futures (Forwards) unwind without (with) discounting net differential, so

|        | Short Futures | Long Forward | Net |
|--------|---------------|--------------|-----|
| May 9  | -(189 - 173) x 100 = ($1,600) | (189-173) x 100 x exp(-0.8x.166667) = $1,578.81 | -21.19 |
| June 9 | -(182.5 - 173) x 100 = ($950.00) | (182.5 - 173) x 100 x exp(-0.8 x 0.08333) = $943.69 | -6.31 |

This implies that the forwards underhedge with equal notional amounts of forwards and futures.

2(a). Client A would need to go short 10,000 units of the June 1 contract at $24.95 and long 15,000 units of the September 1 contract at $25.85 The change in value of the two contracts to Client A is

$$= (24.95\text{-}25.85) \times 10{,}000 + (25.85\text{-}25.65) \times 15{,}000$$
$$= (\$2{,}500.00)$$

So, you would receive this amount since this is the amount of their losses.

2(b). You would need to add in the interest received on the margin balance.

2(c). If Client B called to default, it would not be to your advantage since they had a long position at $26.40 and the price has declined to $25.85. So you would lose 25,000 x ($26.40-$25.65) = $18,750.00 at expiration, which in present value terms is $18,610.42

2(d). Yes, you were short the equivalent of 25,000-15,000=10,000 contracts so you would be harmed by a price increase.

3(a). You buy the coffee at 58.56 cents per pound. This will cost 75,000 x ( $ .5856) = $43,920. Your futures profit will be 75,000 x ($ .592 - $ .5595) = $2,437.50. This reduces the effective price at which you buy the coffee to $43,920-$2,437.50 = $41,482.50. This is an effective price per pound of $41,482.50/75,000 = $ .5531. So you paid 55.31 cents per pound.

Buying two contracts for 75,000 pounds at 55.95 cents/pound leaves 7,000 pounds unhedged and therefore purchased in the spot market for 58.56 cent/lb. The effective price per pound is therefore = (75,000 x 55.95 + 7,000 x 58.56)/82,000 = 56.17 cents/pound

The difference in price between spot and future is probably due to delivery costs.

3(b). There are a couple of types of basis risk. First the anticipated amount is not exactly hedgable because of the contract size. This means you will either have to over-hedge or under-hedge. Also you may not know the exact amount that you will really need at the future date. If you are really going to purchase the coffee somewhere else and were only using the futures to hedge (i.e. close your position before delivery) then you will be exposed to changes in the relative prices between the market you purchase in and the futures market.

4.    In setting up the hedge, the crucial assumption is the hedge ratio as follows:

$ position in Treasury bond futures / $ size of bond issue

Obviously, the easiest assumption is a "naive" hedge where it is 1 to 1 with the bond issue, and in this situation, the 1 to 1 hedge ratio provides a satisfactory offset.

|  | Case 1<br>Interest rates **rise** 50 basis points | Case 2<br>Interest rates **fall** 50 basis points |
| --- | --- | --- |
| Sell 1000 contracts | | |
|     June '83 futures at 78.875 | $78, 875, 000 | $78, 875, 000 |
| Close-out 1000 contracts | | |
|     May '83 | 75, 930, 000 | 81,840,000 |
|     Gain/loss | 2, 945, 000 | (2,965,000) |
| Present value of Increase/decrease Interest ($500,000) for 10 years at 10.5 (6.021) | (3,010,500) | 3,010,500 |
| Net gain/loss | (65,500) | 45,500 |

By hedging, United American Co. can offset some of the loss (or gain) due to the increased or decreased cost of financing due to changing interest rates. Comparison of the gain or loss on the futures contract to the present value of the increased or decreased interest payments must be made as a result of the change in the interest rate level. If United American Co. did not hedge and Case 1 occurred, then the loss would have been $3,010,500 instead of $65,500.

5(a).    The price of the bond as of August 1993 will be 97.39193% of par for a total portfolio value of $97,391,930:

$$D = \frac{1.03435}{.039435} - \frac{1.03943 + \left[40(0.04 - .039435)\right]}{0.04 \times \left[\left(1.039435^{40}\right) - 1\right] + .039435}$$

$$P_{Aug93} = \sum_{t=1}^{52} \frac{(.03625 \times 100)}{(1 + 0.37395)^t} + \frac{100}{(1 + .037395)^{52}}$$

5(b).   The duration portfolio bond:

$$D = \frac{1.037395}{.037395} - \frac{1.037395 + \left[52(0.03625 - .037395)\right]}{0.03625 \times \left[\left(1.037395^{52}\right) - 1\right] + .037395}$$

$= 27.741543 - 3.9796244$

$= 23.761919$ six month periods

$= 11.88096$ years

modified duration $= \dfrac{11.88096}{1.037395} = 11.4537$

The duration futures bond:

$$D = \frac{1.039435}{.039435} - \frac{1.039435 + \left[40(0.04 - .039435)\right]}{0.04 \times \left[\left(1.039435^{40}\right) - 1\right] + .039435}$$

$= 26.358184 - 5.6688275$

$= 20.689356$ six month periods

$= 10.3447$ years

modified duration $= \dfrac{10.3447}{1.039435} = 9.9522$

5(c).   The calculation of the hedge ratio:

$$= \frac{11.4527}{9.9522} \times 1 \times \frac{97391930}{101125}$$

$= 1.15077 \times 963.0846$

$= 1108.29$ contracts

$= 1108$ contracts

6(a). Both bonds in portfolio 1 are zero coupon bonds so,

$$D_1 = \frac{4}{10} \times 14 + \frac{6}{10} \times 3 = 7.4$$

$$ModD_1 = \frac{7.4}{1.0731} = 6.896 \text{ years}$$

$$D_2 = \frac{1.0731}{.0731} - \frac{1.0731 + 9 \times (.046 - .0731)}{.046\left[(1.0731)^9 - 1\right] + .0731} = 7.4$$

$$ModD_2 = \frac{7.4}{1.0731} = 6.896 \text{ years}$$

For both portfolios:

$$\frac{\Delta P}{P} \approx -6.896 \times .006 = -4.137\%$$

6(b). Though the two portfolios have identical durations, the actual price changes will be different because the portfolios have different convexities. In general, a "barbell" portfolio (i.e. portfolio 1) will have greater convexity, meaning that its value will fall less relative to portfolio 2.

6(c). To hedge this position

$$HR_1 = \frac{6.896}{10.355} \times [0.6 \times 1.13 + 0.4 \times 1.03] \frac{-10,000,000}{109,750} = -66.14$$

$$HR_2 = \frac{6.896}{10.355} \times [1.01] \frac{11,500,000}{109,750} = 70.48$$

Combining these two gives a net hedge ratio of 4.339. Consequently, the hedge would be to enter into a long position in 4 futures contracts.

7.

$$IFDY_{90,180} = \left[ \frac{(180 \times .0750) - (90 \times .0750)}{180 - 90} \right] \times \left[ \frac{1}{1 - \left( \frac{90 \times .0750}{360} \right)} \right]$$

$= .076433$

Since the implied forward rate, 7.6433%, is not equal to the explicit futures rate, an arbitrage opportunity is possible, depending on the size of the profit compared to the transaction costs.

- Go long (or lend) at 7.6433% between days 90 and 180 by buying the 180-day paper and selling the 90-day paper in the current spot market.
- Go short (or borrow) at 7.50% between days 90 and 180 in the futures market.

(all transactions are in British pounds)

| Date 0 | 90 | 180 |
|---|---|---|
| Buy 180-day paper in spot market | | |
| Pay 96,250 | | Get 100,000 |
| Sell 90-day paper in spot market | | |
| Get 98,125 | Pay 100,000 | |
| Sell 90-day paper forward | | |
| | Get 98,125 | Pay 100,000 |

$$96,250 = 100,000 \times \left( 1 - \frac{180 \times .0750}{360} \right)$$

$$98,1250 = 1000,000 \times \left( 1 - \frac{90 \times .0750}{360} \right)$$

On a net basis, for each set of transactions having a face value of £100,000, the arbitrageur receives £1,875 on date 0 and pays £1,875 on date 90. The profit, therefore, is the interest that can be earned on £1,875 for 90 days. For example, 90-day paper having a face value of £1,910.83 perhaps can be purchased for £1,875 (a discount yield of 7.50). The net profit of £35.83 would have to be sufficient to cover transactions costs.

8(a). Recalling the convention that the interest expense on floating-rate debt is determined in advance and paid in arrears, the relevant quarterly LIBOR expenses (rounded to the basis point) are:

*1st Quarter Expense Rate:*

4.60% (i.e., current 90-day LIBOR)

*2nd Quarter Expense Rate:*

$$IFR_{90,180} = \left[ \frac{(180 \times .0475) - (90 \times .0460)}{180 - 90} \right] \times \left[ \frac{1}{1 - \left( \frac{90 \times .0460}{360} \right)} \right] = 4.84\%$$

*3rd Quarter Expense Rate:*

$$IFR_{180,270} = \left[ \frac{(270 \times .0500) - (180 \times .0475)}{270 - 180} \right] \times \left[ \frac{1}{1 - \left( \frac{180 \times .0475}{360} \right)} \right] = 5.37\%$$

*4th Quarter Expense Rate:*

$$IFR_{270,360} = \left[ \frac{(360 \times .0530) - (270 \times .0500)}{360 - 270} \right] \times \left[ \frac{1}{1 - \left( \frac{270 \times .0500}{360} \right)} \right] = 5.98\%$$

Based on a non-amortizing loan balance of $1,000,000 and 90-day quarters, these percentages imply the following sequence of quarterly cash payments: $11,500 (= [$1,000,000][.046][90.-360]); $12,100; $13,425; and $14,950.

8(b). Although there are four interest payments due, the convention of setting LIBOR at the front-end of a borrowing period means that there are only three uncertain cash flows at the time the funding is originated. This means that the customer will have to "lock in" a 90-day LIBOR on settlement dates 90, 180, and 270 days from now.

This can be done by shorting the following strip of Eurodollar futures contracts: short one 90-day contract, short one 180-day contract, and short one 270-day contract. Notice that this problem would require a short hedge because the floating-rate borrower would need a hedge to compensate him/her when LIBOR rose (i.e., Eurodollar futures prices fall), thereby raising their underlying funding cost.

8(c). If Eurodollar prices are consistent with the series of implied forward rates, we would observe the following prices: 90-day contract: 95.16 [=100 - 4.84]; 180-day contract: 94.63; and 270-day contract: 94.02.

The annuity that would be equivalent to locking in the preceding series of quarterly cash expenses with the futures strip is calculated as the solution to:

$$
\frac{\$11,500}{\left[1+\dfrac{(.046)(90)}{360}\right]} + \frac{\$12,100}{\left[1+\dfrac{(.0475)(180)}{360}\right]} + \frac{\$13,425}{\left[1+\dfrac{(.050)(270)}{360}\right]} + \frac{\$14,950}{\left[1+\dfrac{(.053)(270)}{360}\right]}
$$

$$
= \frac{Annuity}{\left[1+\dfrac{(.046)(90)}{360}\right]} + \frac{Annuity}{\left[1+\dfrac{(.0475)(180)}{360}\right]} + \frac{Annuity}{\left[1+\dfrac{(.050)(270)}{360}\right]} + \frac{Annuity}{\left[1+\dfrac{(.053)(270)}{360}\right]}
$$

or:

$$Annuity = (50,325.8353 - 3.87895) = \$12,974.07.$$

Expressing this dollar amount on a percentage basis on terms comparable to LIBOR leaves:

$$\left[\frac{\$12,974.07}{\$1,000,000}\right]\left[\frac{360}{90}\right] = 5.19\%.$$

9.  Since you think that interest rates are going to rise, you would not want to have a net long position in T-bill or Eurobond futures. But, since you also believe that the credit spread between treasuries and LIBOR will narrow, you would want to be short this spread. Let LIBOR be expressed as the T-bill rate (R) plus a spread (S). Then creating a portfolio

    1. Shorting the T-bill future (payoff = $N*\Delta R*\Delta T$)
    2. Offsetting long position in the Eurodollar future
       (payoff = $N*\Delta(R+S)*\Delta T$).

    Combining these two payoffs gives
    Net payoff = $N*\Delta R*\Delta T - N*\Delta(R+S)*\Delta T = -N*\Delta S*\Delta T$. So the portfolio value is not related to R. Hence, if R increases and S decreases ($\Delta S<0$) then the payoff on the portfolio will be positive. If you strongly believed that interest rates were going to increase you could also profit from an additional short position in T-bill futures.

10. We can calculate the theoretical spot price for the index as $S = F*\exp[-(r-d)t]$ = $614.75*\exp[-(.08-.03)*.25] = 607.11$ Since this is larger than the actual spot price, there is a theoretical arbitrage opportunity, so program trading might take place. This would involve borrowing the money to buy 1 "index share," taking a short position in the futures, and "delivering" the share at the future date. The cash flows would be as follows:

    |  | T= now | T=90 days |
    |---|---|---|
    | 1. borrow 602.25 | +602.25 | -614.42 |
    | 2. buy 1 index | -602.25 | S |
    | 3. short future (K=614.75) | 0 | 614.75 - S |
    | 4. receive dividends on index | 0 | 4.53 |
    | Total | 0 | $4.86 |

    So the arbitrage nets $4.86 in 90 days. This may or may not cover transaction costs or overcome the fact that most investors cannot borrow at the risk-free rate.

11(a). To get a return of 4.25% by converting to CHF it must be the case that a dollar converted today, invested at rate R, and converted back at the end of a year is then worth $1.0425. So,

$$\left[\left(\frac{\$1}{.6651}\right)\times(1+R)\right]\times.6586 = 1.0425$$
$$R = 5.28\%$$

11(b). If the actual rate is 5.5% for a one-year Swiss government bond then the return on investing in CHF would be greater. This can be seen by plugging in R=.055 into the above left-hand side to get

$$\left[\left(\frac{\$1}{.6651}\right)\times(1+.055)\right]\times.6586 = 1.0447$$

11(c). An arbitrageur could borrow $250,000 domestically at 4.25%, convert it into 375,883.33 CHF, buy Swiss government bonds, and enter into a forward contract to reconvert the proceeds after a year. After a year invested at 5.5% the arbitrageur would have $396,556.91 which could be converted back into dollars at the forward rate of 0.6586 $/CHF. This would result in $261,172.38 of which $260,625 would be needed to repay the loan plus interest. So the arbitrageur would be left with a $547.38 profit, before commissions.

# CHAPTER 24

# Option Contracts

# Answers to Questions

1. A long straddle consists of a long call and a long put on the same stock and profits from dramatic price movement by the stock. A short straddle involves the sale of a call and a put on the same stock and profits from little or no stock price change. Investors going long would anticipate volatility in excess of that discounted by the options' prices while investors going short would expect volatility below that already discounted. Since volatility enhances option prices, long straddles would tend to pay higher premiums for more volatile options, whereas short straddles must accept lower premiums for less volatile options.

2. A range forward is actually an option strategy that combines a long call and a short put (or vice versa) through a costless transaction. Because the options will not have the same striking price, the combination is classified as a range forward as opposed to an actual forward, created by combining long and short options with the same striking price. It is fair to view actual forwards as a special case (or zero-cost version) of range forwards.

3. Call options give the owner the right, but not the obligation, to purchase SFr's for a pre-specified amount of domestic currency. Purchasing an at-the-money call option would guarantee the current exchange rate over the life of the option. If the SFr declines in value, the call will not be exercised since francs can be purchased more cheaply in the open market and redeeming the bond issue will be less costly.

   Contrasting characteristics: (1) Currency options are traded world-wide and enjoy a liquid market. (2) Exchange-traded currency option contracts have standard amounts, maturities, etc. (3) Over-the-counter options could be tailored to meet Michelle's needs. (4) The initial cash outflow would be the premium. (5) The use of options preserves the ability to profit. (6) No counterparty credit risk. (6) Must roll to match year obligation.

Currency forward contracts commit the seller to deliver the specified amount of currency to the buyer on a specified future date at a fixed price. A short position in a forward contract requires delivery.

Contrasting characteristics: (1) The market for forward contracts is over-the-counter and sometimes may not be as liquid as option or futures market. (2) Forward contracts may be custom-designed for specific applications. (3) Cash does not change hands until a forward contract is settled. (4) Counterparty credit risk. (5) Can best match 5-year obligation.

Currency futures are like forward contracts except the gain or loss on the contract is settled daily under the supervision of an organized exchange. A short position in the futures requires either offset or delivery at expiration.

Contrasting characteristics: (1) Futures are traded in standardized contracts and are highly liquid. (2) Cash is required for daily settlement. (3) A margin account is required. (4) Management and administration costs are higher than with a forward or option contract. (5) No counterparty credit risk. (6) Must roll to match year obligation.

4.    The other three factors affecting the value of call options and the ways that changes in them affect value are:

    (1).    <u>Increases in underlying stock volatility</u>. A call cannot be worth less than zero no matter how far the stock price falls, but rising stock prices can increase the call's value without limit. Therefore, the wider the range within which a stock's price can fluctuate (i.e. the greater its volatility), the greater the chance that the option will expire in-the-money, the higher the expected payoff from owning it, and the higher its value. A wider range of probable future prices on the underlying stock increases the probability of higher payoffs in general but because the call's value cannot decline below zero does not symmetrically increase the probability of lower payoffs.

    (2).    <u>The risk-free interest rate</u>. Call value increase with increases in interest rates (given constant stock prices) because higher interest rates make the ownership of call options more attractive. The call owner does not pay for the stock until the option is exercised; its owner can, therefore, take advantage of the time value of money by investing the funds that will later be needed to pay for the stock. A higher risk-free interest rate increases the time value benefit to the call owner, increasing the value of the call option.

    (3).    <u>The exercise price of the option</u>. Call values decrease with increases in the exercise price. When a call option is exercised, the payoff is the difference between the stock price at the time of exercise and the exercise (or strike) price. A higher exercise price decreases the expected payoff from the call, thus reducing the option's value.

5.    Put-call parity indicates that a long position in a stock combined with being short a call and long a put (with the same strike price) is a risk-free investment. In other words, no matter what the stock price at expiration, the payoff will be the same. Consequently, any investment in this portfolio should earn the risk-free return. The three-step process for valuing options is to

    1.    Determine a distribution of future stock prices,

    2.    Calculate the cash flows from the option at the future prices, and

    3.    Discount these expected cash flows to the present at the risk-free rate.

It is this final step that is relevant. Cash flows can be discounted at the risk-free rate because of the riskless replicating portfolio strategy.

6.    The Black-Scholes model is derived by showing how a portfolio of the underlying asset and risk-free bonds can be created that exactly mimics the price of an option. This involves taking a long position in the underlying asset to replicate a call option. For currency options, the underlying asset can be thought of as risk-free deposits (bonds) in the foreign currency. So, just as stocks pay dividends, foreign deposits pay interest. Therefore, we can just substitute the foreign risk-free rate for the dividend yield when pricing options on currency.

7.    If there are no transaction costs, it is only rational to exercise a call option early, immediately before a dividend payment. This is because it will always be more profitable to sell the option and buy the stock in the open market rather than exercise the option, unless there is a dividend. When a firm pays a dividend, the price of the stock usually declines by approximately the

amount of the dividend. This has two impacts on the option holder. First, the decrease in the stock price decreases the value of his option. Second, the investor does not get the dividend payment unless he actually has exercised the option and owns the stock. Consequently, if the value of the dividend is greater than C+K-S, it will be beneficial to exercise early. Note, this is most likely to happen for every in-the-money options.

For put options, it may be the case that the interest that could be earned on the proceeds from early exercise are greater than the intrinsic option value (P+S-K), so early proceeds from early exercise is optimal. Using similar logic as above, puts should always be exercised immediately after a dividend (on a dividend paying stock) because the stock's price declines after a dividend, thus making the put more valuable.

8.  In the Black-Scholes model, the expected future value of a stock is a function of the risk-free interest rate and the dividend yield. As long as the risk-free rate is greater than the dividend yield, the future expected value will be greater than today's price. The longer the time period, the higher the expected price. So, as time to expiration increases, there are two opposing forces on the value of a European put. First, the increased time to expiration increases the chances of the option being more in-the-money. This increases put value. Second, the higher expected price at expiration decreases the expected value of the put's payoff at expiration and, therefore, decreases the put value. Depending on which of these two effects is larger, the put may increase or decrease in price with an increase in time to expiration.

For a European call option, these two effects work in the same direction, since an increase in expected future price increases the value of a call. Hence, an increase in the time to expiration always increases the value of a European call.

9.  Since the price of an option is positively related to volatility, "buying low vol and selling high vol" is the same as the idea of "buy low, sell high" for any risky asset if the other parameters that affect option prices are fixed. The other factors that affect option prices can be effectively neutralized by holding the appropriate portfolio of options and the underlying asset (beyond the scope of this question). If this is the case, then the risky asset is volatile itself, not the underlying foreign currency.

10. On October 19, 1987, implied volatilities sky-rocketed. The jump in implied volatility increased the value of call options more than enough to offset the negative impact of the decline in the index level.

# Answers to Problems

1(a).

|  | Cost/Contract | x 31,250 |
|---|---|---|
| long 1.44 Call | 0.0422 | $1,318.75 |
| short 1.48 Call | 0.0255 | $796.88 |
| long 1.40 Put | 0.0260 | $812.50 |
| short 1.44 Put | 0.0422 | $1,318.75 |

| June USD/GBP | Net Initial Cost | Long Call 1.44 Profit | Short Call 1.48 Profit | Long Put 1.40 Profit | Short Put 1.44 Profit | Total Net Profit |
|---|---|---|---|---|---|---|
| 1.36 | $15.63 | 0 | 0 | 1250 | -2500 | ($1,234.38) |
| 1.4 | $15.63 | 0 | 0 | 0 | -1250 | ($1,234.38) |
| 1.44 | $15.63 | 0 | 0 | 0 | 0 | $15.63 |
| 1.48 | $15.63 | 1250 | 0 | 0 | 0 | $1,265.63 |
| 1.52 | $15.63 | 2500 | -1250 | 0 | 0 | $1,265.63 |

1(b).

This position resembles a bull vertical spread. The purchaser of this portfolio is probably moderately bullish on the exchange rate. We see this from the willingness to give up the extreme upside in exchange for limiting the downside.

1(c). This is a simple application of put-call parity

$$C - P = FX * \exp(-rf * dt) - K * \exp(-rd * dt)$$

where FX is the exchange rate,
rd (rf) is the domestic (foreign) risk-free rate,
and dt is the time to expiration.

$$C - P = 1.385*\exp(-.07*.1667) - 1.44*\exp(-.05*.1667)$$
$$= (\$0.0591)$$

2(a). A straddle-type option strategy called a conversion would involve writing (selling) 40 calls and buying 40 puts on the underlying Government bond portfolio. The investor receives the option premium less commissions for the calls and pays the option premium plus commissions for the puts.

2(b). The breakeven market prices for the underlying Government bonds are calculated as follows:

Portfolio Manager Sells Dec 112 Calls     @ 1.65
           Buys Dec 109 1/2 Puts     @ 2.25
Portfolio Manager Receives:     (.60) / $100 par value
Less Commission of:     (.10) / $100 par value
Resulting in Total Net Option Receipts of:     (.70) / $100 par value

Currently, the market price of the bond is $111.00. The breakeven market price on the upside is equal to the call exercise price plus (less) the total net option premiums received (paid). The breakeven price on the downside is equal to the put exercise price less (plus) the total net option premiums received (paid).

Upside:     112.00 - .70 = 111.30
Downside:     109.50 + .70 = 110.20

2(c). Presently the market price of the bond at $111.00 is about in the middle of breakeven range. If the bond price increases 0.27% $\left[ \dfrac{\mathbf{111.30 - 111}}{\mathbf{111}} \right]$ or

24 - 9

decreases 0.72% $\left[\dfrac{111-110.20}{111}\right]$, then the strategy would break even. These percentage price changes are much less than one standard deviation of past price changes on the underlying bonds (10% standard deviation). Thus, based on past evidence, it is unlikely that this strategy would add to return. But this is all right because this strategy is essentially a risk minimization, return protection strategy designed to lock in already achieved returns.

3(a).

| Price of ARB Stock at Expiration | Initial Cost | Profit on Call #1 Position | Profit on Call #2 Position | Net Profit on Total Position |
|---|---|---|---|---|
| 40 | ($1.72) | $0 | $0 | ($1.72) |
| 45 | ($1.72) | $0 | $0 | ($1.72) |
| 50 | ($1.72) | $0 | $0 | ($1.72) |
| 55 | ($1.72) | $5 | $0 | $3.28 |
| 60 | ($1.72) | $10 | $0 | $8.28 |
| 65 | ($1.72) | $15 | ($10) | $3.28 |
| 70 | ($1.72) | $20 | ($20) | ($1.72) |
| 75 | ($1.72) | $25 | ($30) | ($6.72) |

3(b).

Breakeven points are $51.72 and $68.28. Maximum profit occurs at $60.

3(c). The user of this position is betting on low volatility (that prices will stay between breakeven points). The holder has limited liability for substantial price declines and unlimited liability for substantial price increases.

4. Consider the following put option transactions: (i) long one put #1; (ii) short two puts #2, and (iii) long one put #3. The net initial cost of this set of transactions is $0.83 (= 1.70 + 6.47 - 3.67 - 3.67) and its terminal payoffs for a variety of potential expiration date SAS stock prices are:

| SAS Price (Expiration) | Value of Put #1 | Value of Put #2 | Value of Put #3 | Cost of Options | Net Profit |
|---|---|---|---|---|---|
| 20 | 15.00 | -40.00 | 25.00 | 0.83 | -0.83 |
| 25 | 10.00 | -30.00 | 20.00 | 0.83 | -0.83 |
| 30 | 5.00 | -20.00 | 15.00 | 0.83 | -0.83 |
| 35 | 0.00 | -10.00 | 10.00 | 0.83 | -0.83 |
| 40 | 0.00 | 0.00 | 5.00 | 0.83 | 4.17 |
| 45 | 0.00 | 0.00 | 0.00 | 0.83 | -0.83 |
| 50 | 0.00 | 0.00 | 0.00 | 0.83 | -0.83 |
| 55 | 0.00 | 0.00 | 0.00 | 0.83 | -0.83 |
| 60 | 0.00 | 0.00 | 0.00 | 0.83 | -0.83 |

Graphing these payoffs would lead to the same illustration as shown in Figure 24.9.

5(a).

$$\text{Hedge ratio} = \frac{C_u - C_d}{uS - dS} = \frac{20 - 0}{120 - 80} = 0.5$$

$$\text{Implied probability (p)} = \frac{(1+r) - d}{u - d} = \frac{(1.1) - 0.8}{1.2 - 0.8} = 0.75$$

$$\text{Call value} = \frac{pC_u + (1-p)C_d}{1+r} = \frac{.75(20) + .25(0)}{1.1} = 13.6$$

**_OR_**

<u>Step 1</u>

Set up binomial tree and calculate the option values at expiration for each ending stock price.

<u>Step 2</u>

Solve for the amount to invest in the stock and the amount to borrow in order to replicate the option given its value in the up state and its value in the down state. Solve these equations simultaneously.

<u>Step 3</u>

Use the values derived in Step 2 to solve for the value of the option at the beginning of the period.

**<u>OR</u>**

<u>Step 1</u>

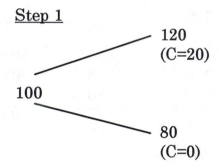

<u>Step 2</u>

20 = 120*D - 1.1*B
 0 =  80*D - 1.1*B

$$D = \frac{-1.1(20) - (-1.1)0}{120(-1.1) - 80(-1.1)} = \frac{-22}{-44} = 0.5$$

C = 80(.5) - 1.1*B

O = 80(.5) - 1.1 *B

24 - 12

B = 40/1.1 - 36.4

Step 3

C = 50 - 36.4 = 13.6

5(b).  The binomial option pricing model is a discrete version of the continuous time Black-Scholes option pricing model. As the number of intervals in the binomial model approaches infinity, the option value derived from this model approaches the option value derived from the Black-Scholes model.

The binomial model is more flexible than the Black-Scholes model because it does not require one to assume constant interest rates and constant variance throughout the horizon. These values can be changed at any of the nodes in the binomial tree. However, the binomial model is more cumbersome to use since accuracy requires that the tree include many nodes.

6(a).  An individual put will hedge an amount of the underlying stock index equal to the underlying value of the put, which in each case here is the respective stock index times $100.

Also, due to the differing betas, the portfolio and the stock indexes are expected to produce gains or losses in proportion to their respective betas. Thus the number of puts required to hedge the portfolio must be adjusted for the betas of the respective stock indexes relative to the beta of the portfolio.

The number and cost of protective puts could be calculated indirectly or directly.

Indirect method:

$$\left(\beta_{port}\right)\left(V_{port}\right) = \left(\beta_{GAC}\right)\left(V_{GAC}\right) = \left(\beta_{opt}\right)\left(V_{opt}\right)$$

The indirect method is based on the fact that an overall portfolio's beta is equal to the weighted average of its component betas. Since we are seeking a zero beta portfolio, the left hand side of the equation can be set to zero.

For the S&P 100:

$$0 = -(1.05)(7,761,700) = (0.95)(V_{opt})$$

$$V_{opt} = -(1.05/0.95)(7,761,700)$$

$$V_{opt} = -8,578,721$$

Number of puts = $8,578,721/(365*100) = 235$

Cost of puts = $235 * \$10.25 * 100 = \$240,875$

For the S&P 500:

$$0 = (1.05)(7,761,700) = (1.00)(V_{opt})$$

$$V_{opt} = -(1.05/1.00)(7,761,700)$$

$$V_{opt} = -8,149,785$$

Number of puts = $8,149,785/(390*100) = 209$

Cost of puts = $209 * \$11.00 * 100 = \$229,900$

For the NYSE:

$$0 = (1.05)(7,761,700) = (1.03)(V_{opt})$$

$$V_{opt} = -(1.05/1.03)(7,761,700)$$

$$V_{opt} = -7,912,413$$

Number of puts = $7,912,413/(215*100) = 368$

Cost of puts = $368 * \$6.25 * 100 = \$230,000$

<u>Direct method:</u>

The direct method calculates the number of puts by utilizing the hedge ratio (HR).

24 - 14

HR = volatility of hedged security / volatility of hedging instrument

Beta, which measures the movement in a security relative to the S&P 500, serve as a measure of volatility.

For the S&P 100:

Number of puts = (1.05/0.95)(7,761,700)/(365*100) = 235

Cost of puts = 235 * $10.25 * 100 = $240,875

For the S&P 500:

Number of puts = (1.05/1.00)(7,761,700)/(390*100) = 209

Cost of puts = 209 * $11.00 * 100 = $229,900

For the NYSE:

Number of puts = (1.05/1.03)(7,761,700)/(215*100) = 368

Cost of puts = 368 * $6.25 * 100 = $230,000

6(b). The cost of the S&P 500 and NYSE puts are essentially the same and less than the cost of the S&P 100 puts; other relevant factors in the decision are correlation and liquidity.

While the hedge calculated in Part A is intended to protect GAC's portfolio from a decline, the portfolio does not replicate any of the indices. The hedge could be less than perfect if the price movement of GAC's portfolio does not track the index movement. In this context, the index which has the highest correlation with GAC's portfolio (the S&P 500, 0.95) would be most preferred, while the index exhibiting the lowest correlation with GAC (the S&P 100, 0.86) would be least preferred.

The hedge should be implemented with a minimum of market impact thus another consideration is liquidity. If the hedge transaction represents a disproportionate share of average daily trading volume, the market could move adversely, increasing the cost of the hedge. The required put position represent 2.4% (235/10,000) of average daily trading volume for the S&P 100, 5.2% (209/4,000) for the S&P 500, and 36.8% (368/1,000) for the NYSE. Thus based on trading volume and likely market impact, the S&P 100 would be most preferred, with the S&P 500 also acceptable; the NYSE transaction would clearly be least desirable.

The S&P 500 options would appear to be the preferred protective position, offering the best combination of cost, hedging ability (correlation), and liquidity; the S&P 100 is a relatively costly position and the NYS position is relatively illiquid.

6(c).    The scenario in Part A used options with strike prices equal to the current index value (i.e. "at the money"). Such options have no intrinsic value (the difference between the index value and the strike price) and contain only a time premium. Buying the put at-the-money will enable a hedge of the portfolio with no loss from current levels assuming that the betas used in the GAC hedge are stationary; then decreases in the portfolio value will be offset exactly by increases in the put option value.

As the relationship between the strike price and the index value changes, however, a trade-off enters into the investment decision. If the strike price is below the current index value, then the puts are "out of the money." These options will be less expensive than "at the money" or "in the money" puts; however they expose the portfolio to potential loss, with the difference between the index value and strike price being analogous to the deductible on an insurance policy. For example, if the S&P 500 index is at 400 and the strike price at 390, then GAC's portfolio would be unprotected for the 10 point difference. The portfolio value will decline by 2.5 (10/400) if the index drops to 390 or lower. However, an index value between 390 and 400 at option expiration will not provide any offset to a portfolio decline. The portfolio would have incurred the cost of the option, only to have it expire worthless at expiration.

If the strike price is above the current index value, then the puts are "in the money. These puts will be most expensive, since they include both intrinsic value and a time premium. Buying  "in the money" puts is analogous to selling the portfolio at the strike price and owning a call option. If the S&P 500 index is 390 and the strike price is 400, then the portfolio is assured of a 2.6% (10/390) gain (ignoring the cost of the option).

In summary, the protective put strategy will prove a floor value for the portfolio. However, the various index options will each have strike prices different from their respective current index values. Thus the portfolio manager must weigh the trade-off between the cost of the put option (the higher the strike price, the higher the put premium) and the degree of protection sought (level of assured portfolio value).

6(d).  An option pricing model, such as the Black-Scholes or binomial approaches, can be used to establish the fair value of an option and to facilitate value comparisons across different strike prices, different times to expiration, and different stock index options. To the extent that mispricings can be identified, arbitrage opportunities may be exploited.

The Black-Scholes formula utilizes the current index price and strike price, in conjunction with the risk-free interest rate, the time to expiration, and return volatility, to establish a fair option price. Alternatively, prevailing option prices may used in the model to calculate implied volatility and to facilitate volatility comparisons across strike prices and times to expiration; this also enables assessment of option premiums against implied risk levels. The model can also be used to calculate hedge ratios, the change in portfolio value for a $1 change in index price.

In summary, option pricing models allow the portfolio manager to quantify the relative pricing of options to determine which option gives the most efficient portfolio protection per dollar of cost.

7(a).  We need to calculate the following parameters, option values, and hedge ratios at each node.

U=42/40=1.05
D=38.4/40=.96
R = 1.06$^{1/3}$ = 1.01961
rf=1.961% per period
Pu = (R-D)/(U-D) = (1.01467-.96)/(1.05-.96) = .607

(i).    S = 40.32

If the stock moves up the option will be worth $4.34 ($C_{udu}$); if the stock moves down the option will be worth $.71 ($C_{udd}$). The value of the option and hedge ratio at this node is

$$C_{ud} = \frac{.607(4.34) + (1-.607)(.71)}{1.01961} = 2.86$$

$$HR_{ud} = \frac{4.34 - .71}{(1.05 - .96) * 40.32} = 1.00$$

(ii).    S = 42

If the stock moves up the option will be worth $6.62 ($C_{uu}$); if the stock moves down the option will be worth $2.86 ($C_{ud}$). The value of the option and hedge ratio at this node is

$$C_u = \frac{.607(6.62) + (1-.607)(2.86)}{1.01961} = 5.05$$

$$HR_u = \frac{6.62 - 2.86}{(1.05 - .96) * 42} = 1.00$$

Note:

$$C_{uu} = \frac{.607(8.31) + (1-.607)(4.34)}{1.01961} = 6.62$$

(iii).    S = 40

If the stock moves up the option will be worth $5.05 ($C_{uu}$); if the stock moves down the option will be worth $1.87. The value of the option and hedge ratio at this node is

$$C = \frac{.607(5.05) + (1-.607)(1.87)}{1.01961} = 3.72$$

$$HR = \frac{5.05 - 1.87}{(1.05 - .96) * 40} = 0.8333$$

Note:

$$C_d = \frac{.607^2(4.34) + 2*(1-.607)(.71)}{1.0196^2} = 1.87$$

So the riskless portfolio will initially contain 1 call option and be short 0.8833 shares of stock. Since after an initial up move to 42.00 the option can only finish in-the-money, the hedge ratio is 1.00.

7(b).

| Ending Price | Number of Paths | Path Probability | Total Probability |
|---|---|---|---|
| $46.31 | 1 | $.6075^3 = .2242$ | .2242 |
| $42.34 | 3 | $.6075^2 * .3925^1 = .1449$ | .4346 |
| $38.71 | 3 | $.6075^1 * .3925^2 = .1449$ | .2808 |
| $35.39 | 1 | $.3925^3 = .0604$ | .0604 |

7(c).

$$C = \frac{.607^3(8.31) + 3*.607^2*(1-.607)(4.34) + 3*.607*(1-.607)^2(.71)}{1.06} = 3.72$$

7(d).

$$P = \frac{(1-.607)^3(2.61)}{1.06} = 0.15$$

Check with put call parity. Does the following hold true:

C-P = S-PV(K)
3.72 - .15 = 40 - 38/1.06
3.57 ≠ 4.15
Put-call parity does NOT hold exactly.

8(a). One way is to calculate approximate dividend yield:
approximate annual dividend yield = 8/75 = .1067

| Asset Price | Strike | Volatility | T | R(f) | Div. Yield | Put/Call |
|---|---|---|---|---|---|---|
| **75.00** | **70.00** | 0.2000 | **0.25** | **0.0900** | **0.1067** | **1** |
| B-S Value | | | Delta | Gamma | $\phi X(1)$ | $\phi X(2)$ |
| 5.68424 | | | 0.6798 | 0.0406 | 0.6982 | 0.5982 |

Or we could calculate the value exdividend: 75 - 2 = 73

| Asset Price | Strike | Volatility | T | R(f) | Div. Yield | Put/Call |
|---|---|---|---|---|---|---|
| **73.00** | **70.00** | 0.2000 | **0.25** | **0.0900** | **0.000** | **1** |
| B-S Value | | | Delta | Gamma | $\phi X(1)$ | $\phi X(2)$ |
| 5.66469 | | | 0.6946 | 0.0429 | 0.6946 | 0.5946 |

The difference in price is less than 2 cents, much less than the bid-ask spread.

8(b). Using put call parity

$$P = C - S + PV(D) + PV(K)$$
$$P = 5.68 - 75 + (70+2)*\exp(-.09*.25)$$
$$P = 1.08$$

8(c).

| Asset Price | Strike | Volatility | T | R(f) | Div. Yield | Put/Call |
|---|---|---|---|---|---|---|
| **75.00** | **70.00** | 0.2000 | **0.25** | **0.0900** | **0.1067** | **1** |
| B-S Value | | | Delta | Gamma | $\phi X(1)$ | $\phi X(2)$ |
| 7.25695 | | | 0.9649 | 0.0334 | 0.9649 | 0.8649 |

So the price would increase: $1.57

8(d). An increase in the volatility to 30% would increase the call's value. A decrease in the risk-free rate to 8% would decrease the call's value.

9(a). Call:

| Futures Price | Strike | Volatility | T | R(f) | Div. Yield | Put/Call |
|---|---|---|---|---|---|---|
| **46.50** | **46.50** | 0.2300 | **0.50** | **0.0545** | **0.000** | 1 |
| Future Option | | | Delta | Gamma | d(1) | d(2) |
| 4.14286 | | | 0.1150 | 0.0524 | 0.1150 | -0.1150 |

Put:

| Futures Price | Strike | Volatility | T | R(f) | Div. Yield | Put/Call |
|---|---|---|---|---|---|---|
| **46.50** | **46.50** | 0.2300 | **0.50** | **0.0545** | **0.000** | -1 |
| Future Option | | | Delta | Gamma | d(1) | d(2) |
| 4.14286 | | | -0.1150 | 0.0524 | 0.1150 | -0.1150 |

9(b). You have created a long forward on a future. An investor that is bullish on the futures price would take a long position in this synthetic forward.

10(a).

| Asset Price | Strike | Volatility | T | R(f) | Div. Yield | Put/Call |
|---|---|---|---|---|---|---|
| **653.50** | **670.00** | 0.1600 | **0.25** | **0.0550** | **0.0280** | 1 |
| B-S Value | | | Delta | Gamma | $\phi X(1)$ | $\phi X(2)$ |
| 15.48 | | | -0.1860 | 0.0074 | -0.1873 | -0.2673 |

10(b).

| Asset Price | Strike | Volatility | T | R(f) | Div. Yield | Put/Call |
|---|---|---|---|---|---|---|
| **653.50** | **670.00** | 0.1751 | **0.25** | **0.0550** | **0.0280** | 1 |
| B-S Value | Market Price | | | | | |
| | Price | Difference | Delta | Gamma | $\phi X(1)$ | $\phi X(2)$ |
| 17.40 | 17.400 | 0.00 | -0.1628 | 0.0068 | -0.1640 | -0.2515 |

24 - 21

So, the option has an implied volatility of 17.51%.

10(c). The market price may differ from the estimated price for the following reasons:

1. The quote may be stale. That is the market maker may not have adjusted the price to reflect new market conditions.
2. Is this a bid or ask price? The ask price will have a higher implied volatility than the bid price or the midpoint.
3. We are making the assumption that dividends are paid continuously, when in fact they are clumped together. So our estimate of the effective dividend yield may be incorrect.
4. Black-Scholes model may not be the correct pricing model.

11(a). The volatility estimates are calculated as:

Period A    0.2708
Period B    0.2570

11(b).

| Asset Price | Strike | Volatility | T | R(f) | Div. Yield | Put/Call |
|---|---|---|---|---|---|---|
| **120.63** | **115.00** | 0.2570 | **0.17** | **0.0742** | **0.0365** | 1 |
| B-S Value | Market Price | Difference | Delta | Gamma | $\phi X(1)$ | $\phi X(2)$ |
| 8.72 | 12.250 | 3.53 | 0.5608 | 0.0265 | 0.5643 | 0.4583 |

The market price is much higher than the calculated BS price. This implies that if all of the other parameters of the model are correct, the implied BS volatility is much higher than the historical volatility. This could be because of recent developments in the stock. Another more controversial explanation is that implied volatilities have a risk-premium built into them such that implied volatilities are on average higher than realized historical volatilities.

# CHAPTER 25

# Swap Contracts, Convertible Securities, and Other Embedded Derivatives

# Answers to Questions

1(a). An interest rate swap is a customized risk-management vehicle. In a pension portfolio (i.e., investment) context, an interest rate swap would be represented by an agreement between two parties to exchange a series of interest money cash flows for a certain period of time (term) based on a stated (notional) amount of principal. For example, one party will agree to make a series of floating-rate coupon payments to another party in exchange for receipt of a series of fixed-rate coupon payments (or vice versa, in which case the swap would work in reverse). No exchange of principal payments is made.

1(b). Strategies using interest rate swaps to affect duration or improve return in a domestic fixed-income portfolio can be divided into two categories:

*Duration modification.* Swapping floating- for fixed-rate interest payments increases portfolio duration (and vice versa, decreases duration when the portfolio is the floating-rate recipient). This method of modifying duration can be used either to control risk (e.g., keep it within policy guidelines/ranges) or to enhance return (e.g., to profit from a rate anticipation bet while remaining within an allowed range).

*Seeking profit opportunities in the swap market.* Opportunities occur in the swap market, as in the cash markets, to profit from temporary disequilibrium between demand and supply. If, in the process of exploiting such opportunities, portfolio duration would be moved beyond a policy guideline/range, it can be controlled by using bond futures contracts or by making appropriate cash-market transactions.

If a strategy calls for a large-scale reorientation of the portfolio's characteristics in a manner that swaps could achieve, their use for implementation of the strategy would act to reduce transaction costs (thus improving portfolio return) and might also permit transactions to be effected more quickly or completely than through conventional trading mechanisms.

2. An interest rate swap is an agreement to exchange a series of cash flows based on the difference between a fixed interest rate and a floating interest rate on some notional amount. A fixed rate receiver would get the difference between a fixed rate and a floating rate if the fixed rate was above the floating rate, and pay the difference if floating was above fixed. The fixed rate is set so that no cash changes hands upon initiation of the deal. This can be thought of as:

   i. A series of forward contracts on the floating rate because forward contracts also have no initial cash flow and will net the difference between the floating rate and the forward rate (which acts like a fixed rate). To make the analogy precise, only one forward rate is chosen but it is chosen such that the sum of the values of all the contracts are zero. The fixed rate receiver is like the short position in the interest rate forwards, because if interest rates go up, she loses.

   ii. A pair of bonds, one with a floating-rate coupon the other with a fixed-rate coupon (both selling at par with the same face value and maturity). Being the fixed-rate receiver in the swap is the same as being long the fixed-rate bond and short the floating-rate bond. As long as the floating rate is less than the fixed rate, the coupon payment from the fixed-rate bond will cover the interest due on the floating rate bond and the difference is profit. If the floating rate is above the fixed rate then the fixed-rate receiver must make up the difference. Since the bonds are of the same face amount, there is no net cash flow at the beginning or end of the agreement.

3. To have zero value at origination, the present vale of the expected cash flows from the swap must be zero. This implies that if there is an upward sloping yield curve, the expected cash flows to the floating payer will come at the beginning of the swap and be offset by expected payments by the floating payer at the end of the swap. The only way this is possible is if the fixed rate is somewhere between the current floating rate (low) and the implied floating rate later in the contract (high).

4. You are essentially holding a two-year swap agreement that requires you to pay 7% in exchange for floating. Since the market rate for the same swap is 6.5%, if your counterparty defaulted you would be able to replace the swap at

a lower rate. Thus, it would be to your benefit for your counterparty to default, and you would realize an economic gain.

5. You have created an off-market swap where you are paying a fixed rate of 7%. This is seen by analyzing the portfolio of long a 7% cap and short a 7% floor. If interest rates are above 7%, then the cap pays the difference between 7% and the floating rate, and the floor is out-of-the money. If interest rates are below 7%, then you must pay the difference between floating and 7%, and the cap is out-of-the-money. Since the market rate is a fixed rate of 8% for the same maturity and you only have to pay 7%, you will have to pay money up-front to get the cap and floor. In other words, the cap costs more than you will get from selling the floor.

6(a). The purchase of an interest rate receiver's swaption would modify (1) the risk characteristics of a fixed-income portfolio and (2) the return characteristics of a fixed-income portfolio, in the following manner:

   (1). The interest rate receiver's side of the swaption provides the right to receive a fixed interest rate and pay a variable rate. The swaption behaves as a call option on a bond with leverage arising from paying the variable rate. The transaction increases the duration of the portfolio, but because of the option aspect, convexity would be greater for an interest rate decrease than for an interest rate increase. Risk increases but not symmetrically.

   (2). If interest rates rise, the option will not be exercised and the loss will be limited to the premium paid to enter the swaption. That is, the effect of a rate rise is the loss of the premium. Downside risk is limited. If interest rates decline, the option will be exercised and the portfolio's return enhanced. The return is enhanced because it receives the higher interest rates (strike rates) instead of the lower prevailing market rates, which offsets reinvestment rate risk in a declining interest rate environment. Overall, the larger the decline in rates, the larger the return enhancement effect.

6(b). The following are major disadvantages of using swaptions to help manage risk in a fixed-income Portfolio:

   (1). Swaptions are illiquid instruments whose use incurs transaction costs. Because transaction costs are measured by the bid-ask spread employed by the counterparty, the more custom-made the swaption the larger the spread and the larger the transaction cost if the instrument is not held to term.

(2).   Swaptions have a credit risk that can be much higher than that of exchange-traded securities such as futures contracts or standard options. Because owning the instruments can be highly profitable to buyers if interest rates decline, swaptions can also be very costly to sellers. Hence, the importance of controlling credit risk is increased.

(3).   A swaption purchase imposes a return-reducing cost on the portfolio (the premium).

The following are minor disadvantages:

1. As with most derivative instruments, using swaptions complicates performance measurement. This disadvantage is not directly related to risk control or portfolio management.

2. Because no standard contracts exist for swaptions, they are subject to legal risks (e.g., a party may be able to nullify a contract or be forced into litigation before honoring a contract).

3. Swaptions potentially introduce accounting risk. Financial Accounting Standards Board standards continue to evolve. Issues such as the validity of treating swaptions as a form of off-balance-sheet financing must also be considered.

4. Using a derivative based on a yield set in the swap market to hedge against a yield set in the capital market exposes the portfolio to the potential for basis risk.

7(a).  The problem here is to sell equities and reinvest the proceeds with the skilled fixed-income manager, without changing the split between the existing allocations to the two asset classes. The solution is to turn to derivative financial instruments as the means to the end: selling enough of the existing fixed-income exposure and bringing in enough of the equity exposure to get the desired mix result.

The following are distinct derivatives strategies that the board could use to increase the Fund's allocation to the fixed-income manager without changing the present fixed-income/equity proportions:

**Strategy 1.** **Use futures**. One strategy would be to sell futures on a fixed-income index and buy futures on an equity index.

Selling the futures eliminates the fixed-income index return and risk, while keeping the skilled fixed-income manager's extra return. By being long the equity index, the portfolio obtains the index return and risk, keeping its exposure to the equity market.

**Strategy 2.** **Use swaps**. A second strategy would be to use over-the-counter (OTC) swaps.

BI would swap a fixed-income index return for an equity index return in a notional amount large enough to keep the skilled manager's extra return while eliminating the fixed-income market return and replacing it with the equity market return.

**Strategy 3.** **Use option combinations**. A third strategy would use put and call options to create futures-like securities.

Buying put options and selling call options on a fixed-income index, while selling put options and buying call options on a stock index, would achieve the same result as the appropriate futures position.

7(b). The following are advantages and disadvantages of each strategy identified and explained in Part A:

**Strategy 1.** **Use futures**

*Advantages:*

1. Futures contracts are liquid instruments.
2. Transaction costs are low.
3. Credit risk is negligible because the securities are marked to market daily.

25 - 7

*Disadvantages:*

1. If the holding period is long, rollover (transaction) costs are incurred.
2. Standard contract forms are limited, so contracts may not exist on the index or instrument needed. Tracking errors may create basis risk between the index and the performance benchmark.

## Strategy 2.   Use swaps

*Advantages:*

1. Swaps can be tailored to fit the desired investment horizon, eliminating (or reducing) rollover costs.
2. Swaps can be contracted for a specific index (like the performance benchmark) even if there is no futures contract on it.
3. The desired adjustment goal can be accomplished through a single transaction.

*Disadvantages:*

1. A counterparty credit risk is created that can be much larger than with other types of instruments.
2. Swap agreements are illiquid instruments, and disposals can be both difficult and expensive.
3. Transaction costs are large because of typical "tailoring" of a given swap.

## Strategy 3.   Use option combinations
Buying put and call options on fixed income index (synthetic short position) and buying call and selling puts on stock index (synthetic long position)

*Advantages:*

1. Transaction costs are low.
2. Credit risks are small.

*Disadvantages:*

1. Rollover(s) may be necessary.
2. The "right" option may not be available when needed or at all.
3. Holders may exercise the put option and end the hedge.

A generic disadvantage of any strategy is that returns are automatically eroded by the costs of establishing and maintaining the strategies, of meeting margin requirements, if any, and of unwinding them, if necessary.

8(i).  From BI's perspective, the major risk it would eliminate under this transaction is represented by participation in the EAFE Index (to the extent that this participation has been reduced), the return on which is now being paid to the counterparty bank.

BI has reduced its international equity exposure. The market risk, formerly present in that part of the total participation that has now been swapped out in exchange for S&P Index exposure, has been eliminated.

8(ii).  From BI's perspective, the major risk that is retained after this transaction (i.e., not eliminated) is the risk of tracking error between BI's international equity portfolio and the EAFE Index. This potential tracking error arises from differences between the portfolio and the index in terms of country weights and security selection. Thus, as the correlation coefficient between BI's portfolio and the index is probably less than 1.0, a basis risk is retained.

To the extent that significant differences in composition now exist (either in terms of country weights or security selection), BI's return experience could be quite different from that expected when the decision to change the exposure was made. In effect, the transaction is a bet that U.S. stocks will outperform EAFE stocks in U.S. return terms. The market risks inherent in all such exposures still apply, including exposure to global equity markets. Because the EAFE return is dollar denominated, the BI international equity portfolio is still exposed to currency risk either hedged or unhedged.

8(iii).  From BI's perspective, risks created under this transaction include:

**1.  Counterparty credit risks**. BI now has contractual relationships with two banks that it did not have before, creating a new risk dimension that will require monitoring and ongoing evaluation. This credit risk is, in effect, an added element of cost and uncertainty that must be considered in assessing the cost/benefit outcomes expected to result from the transaction.

**2.  Return risks arising from spread changes between LIBOR and T-bill rates.**  If the initial or expected spread between these two markets moves against BI, it will find its realized return to be different from its expected return. This will, in effect, increase the cost of the move and reduce its efficacy.

**3. Return risks arising from differential S&P 500 Index and EAFE Index performance.** Future relative performance levels are uncertain. Thus, BI's new risks include not only a spread risk in terms of the S&P Index (added) versus the EAFE Index (reduced) but also spread risk between the actual portfolio and the index portfolios.

**4. Risk related to the one-year term of the transaction.** If BI wants to reverse or modify the original move away from international to U.S. equity exposure or to change the LIBOR/T-bill markers, new complications arise. Liquidity risk is now present. Changing or undoing the contracts with the counterparty banks may be impossible or unduly costly. A risk of being "frozen-in-place" and being unable to take advantage of new circumstances or avoid new dangers has been introduced. A corollary risk is that the one-year term does not equate with the "temporary" reduction intent of the bond's proviso. A risk of overstaying a temporary reduction has been introduced and may manifest itself in liquidity or additional expense terms.

**5. Rollover risk.** BI may be unable to renew the contracts on satisfactory terms if the board wants to do so at the expiration of the original one-year term.

**6. Lower diversification.** BI has temporarily reduced its diversification because it has decreased its international equity exposure and increased its domestic equity exposure.

**7. Risk of mismatched notional amounts.** If the swaps have variable notional amounts, there is risk that the notional amounts upon which the swap payments are based may become mismatched as the return experience of the EAFE and S&P 500 indexes diverge.

**8. Regulatory, legal, or accounting risk.** BI has added the risk that the regulatory, legal, or accounting treatment of these swaps may be changed unfavorably during the term of the contracts.

**9. Benchmark measurement.** The benchmark should measure the portfolio manager's execution of the strategies for which he or she is responsible. If the board changes the strategy, it may need to change the benchmark.

9. The difference between warrants and regular options comes from the difference in issuer. Unlike a regular call option, when a warrant is exercised the shares purchased are new shares created by the company. Since the shares have identical rights as existing shares and have been purchased at a discount to existing shares (otherwise the warrants wouldn't be exercised) the value of existing shares is watered down. This depresses the value of the stock. Consequently warrants are less valuable than regular options since regular options have no affect on the capital structure of the firm.

Firm's may wish to issue warrants if the floatation costs are lower or if they are worried about not being able to sell enough new stock. Warrants can be used to "force" the issuance of new shares.

10. Convertible bonds and preferred stock are both very similar to an ordinary bond (or perpetuity) and a call option on the firm's common stock. This is because these instruments give the holder the option but not the obligation to trade in the existing asset for common stock, much the way a call option gives its holder the right but not the obligation to purchase shares at a prespecified price. Since call options have upside potential and a limited downside, these traits are passed on to the convertible bonds and preferred stock. The pricing of these securities must take into account the optionality embedded in the issue.

11. Structured notes must satisfy several criteria to be successfully issued. Most important is that the payoff structure be one that appeals to investors. Perhaps it helps get around some legal restrictions or provides a payoff that is not available in other traded securities. Investors will not take on the additional hassle of owning structured notes unless there is some benefit to them. It must also be the case that the payoff of the note is well defined. It must be based on an easily measured index or price that is not subject to interpretation or manipulation. You will never see a structured note whose payoff depends on the number of "nice days" in New York or the price of an illiquid stock or commodity.

Issuers usually rely on investment banks to know what the needs or preferences of prospective investors are. Frequently, investment banks will know that a client wants a certain type of structured note and will approach prospective issuers to put the deal together.

# Answers to Problems

1. The fixed-rate receiver will receive 5.48%.

| Date | Fixed-Rate | LIBOR | Converted FR-LIBOR (-1) | Net Cash Flows |
|------|-----------|-------|-------------------------|----------------|
| 3/1/96 | 5.48% | 5.30% | | |
| 9/1/96 | 5.48% | 5.60% | 0.11% | $11,968.75 |
| 3/1/97 | 5.48% | 6.15% | -0.20% | ($22,250,000) |
| 9/1/97 | 5.48% | 6.30% | -0.76% | ($84,984.37) |
| 3/1/98 | 5.48% | 5.90% | -0.91% | ($102,093.75) |

2(a). Company W will want to enter into a receive-fixed pay floating swap with semiannual payments for 5 years with a notional principal of USD 35M. The current quote on this swap is 5.95%. Company X will want to enter into a pay-fixed receive floating swap with semi-annual payments for 4 years with a notional principal of USD 50M. The current quote on this swap is 5.86%.

2(b). The two swaps are not matched perfectly. The first mismatch is the size of the notional principal. Since Company W's swap is for USD 15M less than Company X's the dealer is exposed to a USD 15M receive-fixed swap for the first four years. The second mismatch is maturity. Company W's swap is one year longer, so after four years, the dealer will be exposed to a USD 35M pay-fixed swap.

3. The key is to recognize that the combination of buying the cap and writing a floor at the same strike rate generates the same settlement cash flows as a pay-fixed swap. The fixed rate on the swap would equal the strike rate on the cap and floor.

   Consider first the 8 percent cap-floor combination. The treasurer could buy the cap for 413 basis points (the market maker's offer) and sell the floor for 401 basis points (the market maker's bid). The net is an up-front outflow of 12 basis points (times the notional principal). Because the 8 percent pay-

25 - 13

fixed swap would not entail an initial payment, the 8 percent cap-floor combination can be rejected.

Consider next the 7 percent cap-floor combination. The treasurer could buy the cap for 597 basis points and sell the floor for 320 basis points, resulting in a net up-front outflow of 277 basis points. The fixed rate on the synthetic swap would be 7 percent however, not 8 percent. The attraction of the cap-floor alternative turns on the trade-off of a present value of 277 basis points versus a three-year annuity of 100 basis points (actually a 12-period annuity of 25 basis points per quarterly period). Using the three-year fixed rate of .20 percent, the present value of the savings is 263.57 basis points; that is,

$$\sum_{t=1}^{12} \frac{25}{\left(1+\dfrac{00820}{4}\right)^t} = 263.57$$

Because the 263.57 basis points is less than the up-front cost of 277 basis points, the 7 percent cap-floor combination can be rejected as well.

Consider finally the 9 percent cap-floor combination. The treasurer could buy the cap for 220 basis points and sell the floor for 502 basis points, resulting in a net up-front inflow of 282 basis points. The fixed rate on the synthetic swap would be 9 percent. Because the initial receipt exceeds the present value of the higher swap coupon (i.e. 282 > 263.57), this combination should be considered. Is it definitely better? Perhaps so in terms of cash flow and the time value of money, but the treasurer would also have to consider the tax and accounting treatment of the difference in the options premiums to confirm the benefit.

4(a).  Issue the Traditional FRN and enter <u>one pay-fixed</u> swap:


[(LIBOR + 0.25%) x (365/360)] + [9.20% - (LIBOR x 365/360)] = 9.20% + (0.25% x 365/360) = 9.4535% (sabb)

Issue the Bull Floater and enter <u>one receive-fixed</u> swap:

$$[(18.40\% - \text{LIBOR}) \times (365/360)] + [(\text{LIBOR} \times 365/360) - 9.10\%)] =$$
$$(18.40\% \times 365/360) - 9.10\% = 9.5556\% \text{ (sabb)}$$

Issue the Bear Floater and enter <u>two pay-fixed</u> swaps (or one with twice the notional principal):

$$[(2 \times \text{LIBOR} - 9.10\%) \times (365/360)] + [2 \times \{9.20\% - (\text{LIBOR} \times 365/360)\}] =$$
$$(2 \times 9.20\%) - (9.10\% \times 365/360) = 9.1736\% \text{ (sabb)}$$

Note that the Bull/swap combination is fixed only for LIBOR < 18.40%, since the coupon on the Bull Floater would be zero if LIBOR > 18.40% while the net settlement payout on the swap increases. The Bear/swap combination is fixed only for LIBOR 2 4.55%. If LIBOR < 4.55%, the coupon of the Bear Floater remains zero while the net settlement payout on the swap increases.

4(b).   Issue one $25 million tranche as a Traditional FRN and a second $25 million tranche as a Bull Floater:

$$(1/2) [(\text{LIBOR} + 0.25\%) \times 365/360] + (1/2) [(18.40\% - \text{LIBOR}) \times (365/360)] =$$
$$(1/2) (0.25\% \times 365/360) + (1/2) (18.40\% \times 365/360) = 9.4545\%$$

4(c).   Student exercise.

4(d).   As suggested by its name, investors in a Bull Floater are "bullish" on bonds, expecting bond prices to rise. Since the coupon rate on the Bull Floater is inversely related to LIBOR, these investors must expect the future path for LIBOR to be steady or falling.

4(e).   Investors in a Bear Floater are "bearish" on bonds, expecting bond prices to be falling. So, as market rates (and LIBOR) rise, the coupon rate on the Bear Floater rises even faster, in fact, at twice the rate. An investor who buys the Bear Floater as a hedge must be exposed to higher levels for LIBOR.

| Event | Exposure | Hedge (Buy Bear Floater) |
|-------|----------|--------------------------|
| LIBOR rises | Lose | Gain |
| LIBOR falls | Gain | Lose |

This could occur, for instance, if the investor had long-term, fixed-rate assets funded by short-term or variable-rate liabilities. The duration gap would be positive.

5.    First of all, recognize that at the current exchange rates, USD 25 million translates in JPY 3,186,750,000 (the product of USD 25,000,000 and JPY 127.47/USD) and GBP 12,736,264 (USD 25,000 divided by USD 1.82/GBP). These become the principal amounts governing the transaction.  Then:

5(a).  The desired swap could be accomplished by combining the following transactions:
- "pay 4.92% Japanese yen, receive US dollar LIBOR" currency swap
- "receive 9.83% British sterling, pay US dollar LIBOR" currency swap, resulting in a "pay 4.92% yen, receive 9.83% sterling," which represents your offer swap rate in yen and your bid rate in sterling.

5(b).  After swapping principal amounts at the origination date, the cash flow exchanges on first settlement date from the counterparty's standpoint are calculated as follows:

Yen payment =  $(0.0492) \times (183/365) \times (JPY\ 3,186,750,000) = JPY\ 78,608,828$

and

Pound receipt =  $(0.0983) \times (183/365) \times (GBP\ 13,736,264) = GBP\ 686,390$

The full set of cash exchanges, which will be known at the inception of the deal, is:

| Settlement Date | Days in Settlement | Payments (Millions) | Receipts (Millions) |
|---|---|---|---|
| Initial | -- | GBP 13.736 | JPY 3,186.75 |
| 1 | 183 | JPY 78.61 | GBP 0.69 |
| 2 | 182 | JPY 78.18 | GBP 0.68 |
| 3 | 183 | JPY 78.61 | GBP 0.69 |
| 4 | 182 | JPY 78.18 | GBP 0.68 |
| 5 | 183 | JPY 78.61 | GBP 0.69 |
| Final | 182 | JPY 3,186.75 and JPY 78.18 | GBP 13.736 and GBP 0.68 |

6(a). The MTM value of the swap was the present value of the dollar inflows converted to francs at the spot rate, less the present value of the franc outflows. The reduction in the dollar interest rate from 12.72 percent to 10.20 percent raised the value of the swap (and the default loss), and the reduction in the franc rate from 14.88 percent to 12.78 percent lowered the value. Adding the appreciation in the dollar relative to the franc from FRF 8.4435/USD to FRF 9.4829/USD suggests that the net effect should have been a positive MTM value. This result is confirmed by the following calculations:

$$PV_{USD} = \frac{USD12,720,000}{1.1020} + \frac{USD112,720,00}{(1.1020)^2} = USD10,361,84$$

$$PV_{FRF} = \frac{FRF125,639,280}{1.1278} + \frac{FRF969,989,280}{(1.1278)^2} = FRF874,012,546$$

$$Value = \frac{USD104,361,843}{USD0.105453/FRF} - FRF874,012,546 = FRF115,640,124$$

The default by the counterparty caused the French corporation to lose FRF 115,640,124, the market value of the swap that had become an asset.

6(b). The at-market, plain vanilla currency swaps that were available in the market on April 15, 1988, were priced such that the French corporation could receive a fixed rate of 10.20 percent in dollars and pay a fixed rate of 12.78 percent in francs. If the corporation wanted an off-market swap to receive

12.72 percent (an additional 252 basis points in dollars), it would need to pay a higher rate in francs. First calculate the value in francs of 252 basis points in dollars:

$$\frac{\text{252 bps}}{1.1020} + \frac{\text{252 bps}}{(1.1020)^2} = \frac{x}{1.1278} + \frac{x}{(1.1278)^2}$$

or, $x = 260.7375$ bps.

The off-market swap fixed rates would be 12.72 percent in dollars versus 15.387375 percent in francs (15.387375 percent = 12.78 percent + 2.607375 percent). The principal on the swap would be USD 100 million = FRF 948,290,000.

The scheduled cash flows on the two-year swap from the perspective of the French corporation would be:

| Date | Receive | Pay |
| --- | --- | --- |
| April 15, 1989 | USD 12,720,000 | FRF 145,916,938 |
| April 15, 1990 | 112,720,000 | 1,094.206.938 |

The MTM value of the currency swap can also be measured as the present value of the lost (or gained) cash flows from entering into a replacement swap at current rates. Because the remaining scheduled and replacement cash receipts are the same, the value of the swap is the difference between the payments. Those differences are FRF 20,277,658 on April 15,1989, and FRF 124,217,658 on April 15, 1990. Discounting those amounts by 12.78 percent provides the value of the swap.

$$\text{MTM Value} = \frac{\text{FRF20,277,658}}{1.1278} + \frac{\text{FRF 124,217,658}}{(1.1278)^2} = \text{FRF 115,640,383.}$$

Note that the value of the swap obtained by the replacement swap method is virtually identical to the more direct mark-to-market method (differing only because of rounding).

7(a).   With these estimates, the settlement payments can be calculated as follows:

*March 2:*
Floating-rate payment =
(0.0350 - 0.0010) x ($50,000,000) x (90/360) = $425.000

Equity-index receipt =
[(477.51 - 463.11)/463.111 x ($50,000,000) = $1,554,706.

So the *net receipt* the fund expects would be ($1,554,706 - $425,000) = $1,129,706.

*June 2:*
Floating-rate payment =
(0.0325 - 0.0010) x ($50,000,000) x (92/360) = $402,500

Equity-index receipt =
[(464.74 - 477.51)/477.51] x ($50,000,000) = -$1,337,145.

So the *net payment* the fund owes would be ($1,337,145 + $402,500) = $1,739,645.

*September 2:*
Floating-rate payment =
(0.0375 - 0.0010) x ($50,000,000) x (92/360) = $466.389

Equity-index receipt =
[(480.86 - 464.74)/464.74] x ($50,000,000) = $1,734,303.

So the *net receipt* the fund expects would be ($1,734,303 - $466,389) = $1,267,914.

*December 2:*
Floating-rate payment =
(0.0400 - 0.0010) x ($50,000,000) x (91/360) = $492,917

Equity-index receipt =
[(482.59 - 480.86)/480.86] x ($50,000,000) = $179,886.

So the *net payment* the fund owes would be ($492,917 - $179,886) = $313,031.

7(b).   It is also quite common for equity swaps to be based on a notional principal amount that varies directly with the level of the underlying index. If, for instance, the swap participants had agreed to let the initial notional principal of $50 million vary over time, it would have been adjusted up on March 2 to $51.555 million. This adjustment is calculated as ($50 million 11 + [(477.51 - 463.11)/463.11]). That is, each settlement date, the notional principal is adjusted up (down) by the percentage of capital appreciation (depreciation) in the starting level of the index. This adjustment process, which is equivalent to adding the gross equity settlement payment to the initial notional principal, simulates the return that investors with direct stock positions would obtain inasmuch as their actual equity exposure would rise or fall with market conditions. In contrast, a fixed notional principal in an equity swap is equivalent to an asset allocation strategy by which the equity exposure is kept constant.

8(a).   To achieve Ames' goal, HSF would enter into a two-year swap agreement as the fixed rate payer. In return for agreeing to make quarterly cash flow payments based on the two-year swap fixed rate of 5.5%, HSF would receive a cash flow based on the three-month LIBOR that prevailed at the beginning of the settlement period. Each quarterly swap settlement payment would be made on a *net* basis, the direction of which would depend on the difference between that period's LIBOR and 5.5%. There would be no exchange of (notional) principal.

8(b).   If the candidate uses the interest rate information provided in the question, the amount of the cash flow would be the difference in the fixed rate and the Eurodollar rate multiplied times the notional amount times the fraction of annual time period. The calculation would be (.055 - .051) x $10,000,000 x 1/4 = $10,000. The direction: the endowment pays this cash flow at the end of the first period.

[NOTE: Candidates may use different practices in calculating the holding period of the swap (e.g., 92 days/360 or 365 days) which may produce slightly different solutions.]

[IMPORTANT NOTE: Technically, insufficient information was provided in order to answer this question. Swap settlement practices follow the debt market convention of determining LIBOR at the *start* of the settlement period but paying the cash flow at the end. Thus, the September 30, 1996 settlement payment will be based on the three-month spot LIBOR that prevailed on June 30, 1996. The September 1996 Eurodollar futures rate of 5.1% (as established on June 30, 1996) will be floating rate for the second swap settlement payment, which will be made on December 30, 1996. Since the problem does not provide the current (i.e., June 30, 1996) three-month LIBOR, there is no way to answer the question correctly as it is written.]

8(c). A pay-fixed swap can be viewed as either: (1) lengthening the duration of a floating rate liability, or (2) shortening the duration of a fixed-rate asset. In HFS's case, the second interpretation is appropriate. By reducing asset duration, HFS has moved to a more defensive posture against the anticipated increase in short-term rates. Said differently, by converting its fixed-rate asset into a synthetic floating-rate note, HFS is now in a position to receive larger coupon cash flows if Ames' interest rate forecast is correct.

8(d). A plain vanilla interest rate swap is an agreement that requires two counterparties to exchange cash flows on a periodic basis, with one of these cash flows based on a fixed interest rate and the other tied to a variable (i.e., floating) reference rate index. In general, the cash flow for either side of the swap on a given settlement date is calculated as [(Rate) x (Notional Principal) x (% of Year covered by Settlement Period)]. For two risk-neutral counterparties to agree to such an exchange without requiring (or being willing to make) a front-end premium payment, the sum of the discounted expected values of these cash flow streams must be equal.

Although all but the first floating-rate cash flow settlement payment on the swap will not be known at the time the agreement is originated, they can be locked in using a strip of Eurodollar futures contracts. For a two-year, quarterly settlement swap negotiated in June 1996, which has a total of eight settlement dates, the following sequence of LIBOR can be established: Payment #1: three-month spot LBOR in June 1996; Payment #2: September 1996 Eurodollar futures rate, as established in June 1996; Payment #3: December 1996 Eurodollar futures rate, as established in June 1996; etc. Thus, the floating rate side of the swap contract can be fully hedged in June

25 - 21

1996 with Eurodollar futures positions extending out to the March 1998 contract.

With these future LIBOR levels established, the swap fixed rate can then be calculated as the time-weighted average of this sequence. That is, the fixed rate can be thought of as the yield that generates an annuity equal (in present value terms) to the variable cash flows associated with the future LBOR payments tied to the strip of Eurodollar futures contracts. (By way of an analogy, the swap fixed rate is to the strip of forward LIBOR what a bond's yield-to-maturity is to the underlying term structure of zero-coupon discount rates.)

8(e).    HFS's pay-fixed swap position (with a fixed rate of 5.5%) could be replicated with an interest rate collar by: (1) purchasing an interest rate cap, which can be viewed as a portfolio of European-style call options on LIBOR, at a strike rate of 5.5%; and (2) selling an interest rate floor, which is a portfolio of European-style put options on LIBOR, at the same strike rate. If, on a given settlement date, LIBOR is above 5.5%, HFS will receive a settlement check from the cap seller. Conversely, if LIBOR is less than 5%, HFS will have to make a settlement payment to the floor buyer. If the cap sell/floor buyer is the same company, these arc the identical settlement exchanges that would occur on a swap with a fixed rate of 5.5%.

In general any "long cap, short floor" combination (i.e., collar) done with the same strike rate, maturity date, and settlement terms will recreate a pay-fixed swap under those same conditions. However, only when that common strike rate is equal to the prevailing swap fixed rate will the collar have no net front-end cost to either counterparty. This result is the swap equivalent of the put-call parity condition.

9.    The Spanish pension fund would buy El Oso Grande, enter three swaps (each for a notional principal equal to the par value of the FRN or, equivalently, one swap with three times the notional value) to receive the fixed rate of 13.35 percent and write three floors at a strike rate of 8 percent (or, again, one with three times the notional amount).

The role of the floors is to create a fixed-rate asset even when LIBOR is less than 8 percent. Neglecting the floors, if LIBOR $\geq$ 8 percent, the return will be (3 x LIBOR - 24 percent) + (3 x 13.35 percent - 3 x LIBOR). The LIBOR flows net out by design, and the return is 16.05 percent. If LIBOR < 8 percent, the return will be (3 x 13.35 percent - 3 x LIBOR) > 16.05 percent. Writing the floors in effect sells off the potential for a higher return if LIBOR is low. The receipt of 420 basis points (3 x 140 basis points for each floor) raises the fixed rate of return above 16.05 percent.

The net cost of the position is only 95.8 percent of par, the cost of the FRN less the premium received on writing the floors. So the all-in, semiannual fixed rate of return is 17.34 percent, calculated as

$$95.80 = \sum_{t=1}^{10} \frac{8.025}{(1+y/2)^t} + \frac{100}{(1+y/2)^{10}}.$$

Payoff to EOG is,
Coupon = max(0, 3*LIBOR - 24%)

So the bondholder's exposure is the equivalent of long 3 floaters and long a floor. We can rewrite the payoff as
Coupon = max[0, 3*(LIBOR - 8%)]
Coupon = 3*max[0, LIBOR - 8%]

So to convert this to straight fixed, the fund would need to undertake 3 receive fixed swaps and sell 3 floors at 8%.

This gives a new coupon of (where AFP = amortized floor premium)
New Coupon = 3*max[0, LIBOR - 8%] + 3*13.35 - 3*LIBOR + 3* min[0,LIBOR-8%] + AFP
New Coupon = 3*[LIBOR - 8%] + 3*13.35 - 3*LIBOR +AFP
New Coupon = 3*LIBOR - 24% + 3*13.35 - 3*LIBOR +AFP
New Coupon = 16.05% + AFP

PVFA(AFP,13.5%) = 140
AFP = 40bp

New Coupon = 16.05% + .40% = 16.45%

10(a). The bond's cash flows can be broken down depending on two mutually exclusive possibilities; either the NYSE index exceeds 166 after three years or it does not:

| NYSE Index | CF1 | CF2 | CF3 |
|---|---|---|---|
| < or = 166 | 3 | 3 | 103 + 0 |
| > 166 | 3 | 3 | 103 + [100 x (NY$_3$ -166) / 166] |

Thus, you receive the same cash flows as a straight bond which pays a 3% coupon and is redeemable at par plus the additional cash flows associated with 0.60241 (=100/166) units of a call option on the NYSE index which pays a dollar for each point the index exceeds 166 at maturity.

10(b). A regular bond without the embedded index option would have to sell for 71.65% , or:

$$P = \left[3/(1.0765)\right] + \left[3/(1.0765)^2\right] + \left[103/(1.0765)^3\right] = \$87.94$$

Guinness was able to sell the SPEL for 100.625, meaning that the value of the option feature must satisfy:

100.625 = 87.94 + (Bond's Option Value)

so that the bond's option feature is worth $12.685. (Recall that this represents only about 60% of a regular NYSE index call option struck at 166.) The bond's option value is purely a time premium since the option is currently out of the money (i.e., the index value of 134 is less than the exercise price of 166).

11(a).

$$d_1 = \frac{\ln(35/50) + \left[.052 + \left(.34^2/2\right)\right]5}{.34\sqrt{5}} = .25$$

$$d_2 = .25 - .35\sqrt{5} = -.51$$

$$N(.25) = .5987$$

$$N(-.51) = .3050$$

$$c(t) = 35(.5987) - 50e^{-.052(5)}(.3050) = 9.196$$

$$q = \frac{10,000}{100,000} = 0.1$$

$$w(t) = \frac{9.196}{1.1} = 8.36$$

11(b). Since the stock price before exercise must be $5,200,000/100,000 = $52, then all warrants will be exercised. Then the warrant holder will purchase 10,000 shares at $50 per share, thus injecting $500,000 of new capital into the firm. Then the firm will be worth $5,700,000/10,000 = $51.82.

11(c). The warrant was originally worth $8.36. At expiration, the warrant was only 2 points in-the-money and with the dilution effect, it was worth only 2/1.1 = 1.82. This is a percentage decrease in value of (1.82/8.36) - 1 = -0.7823. Meanwhile the stock price increased from $35 to $52, an increase of $8.57. Obviously, the warrant lost considerable value even though the stock price gained significantly in value. The reason is that when the warrant was purchased all of its price was its time value (it was not in-the-money). During the life of any warrant or option, it will lose all of its time value. The large time value reflects the volatility and long time to expiration. Ultimately at expiration, the warrant finished barely in-the-money. The warrant holder gained a little in intrinsic value but lost so much time value because the stock price, in spite of its large percentage move, still did not change by enough over the warrant's life.

# CHAPTER 26

# Investment Companies

# Answers to Questions

1.  After the initial public sale of the investment company, the open-end fund will continue to sell new shares to the public at the NAV with or without a sales charge and will redeem (buy back) shares of the fund at the NAV. In contrast, the closed-end fund does not buy or sell shares once the original issue is sold. Therefore, the purchase price or sales price for a closed-end fund is determined in the secondary market.

2.  The first is the NAV which is computed the same as any open-end fund. The second is the current market price of the shares as determined in the secondary market (e.g., the NYSE). In the majority of cases, the shares are selling at a discount to NAV of about 15-20 percent – i.e., the current market price is 15-20 percent below the NAV.

3.  The load fund charges a sales commission of about $7^{1/2}$ - 8 percent when you buy the fund shares. Therefore, when you buy the shares, you only get stock worth about 92-93 percent of what you invest. In contrast, with a noload fund, you pay only the NAV (i.e., there is no sales commission). Notably, in order to purchase a no-load fund, it is necessary to directly contact the fund to buy or sell shares.

4.  A common stock fund only invests in common stock and typically will not acquire any bonds with the possible exception of convertible bonds. A balanced fund will invest in stocks **and** in bonds in various proportions, depending upon their outlook for the market. Because of the combination of stocks and bonds, you would expect the balanced fund to have lower risk and return than a pure common stock fund.

5.  You definitely should care. One of the major advantages of a mutual fund is instant diversification, so it is important. Given the CAPM, it is known that the market only pays for systematic risk so it is important to eliminate unsystematic risk, which is the purpose of diversification. A portfolio that is completely diversified will be perfectly correlated with the market portfolio ($R^2 = + 1.00$).

6.  Risk stability is important because an investor will often select a fund on the basis of her risk preference and it is important to know that the fund will remain in the same risk class over time. The empirical results are generally quite encouraging – funds typically have high correlation of their beta coefficients over time. Therefore, it is possible that historical risk classes can be used for future investment decisions. Also, there tends to be a relationship between the return and risk for alternative funds.

7.  They should be judged on a risk-adjusted basis because it is easy to get high return by simply investing in a portfolio of high beta stocks. Assuming investors are risk-averse, it is obviously necessary to consider return **and** risk. You can envision an example where two funds have a small difference in return that is more than compensated by risk differenc3es – e.g., Fund A: Return = 11.5%; Beta = 1.5. Fund B: Return = 11.0%; Beta = 0.9. Fund A has a higher return by **much** higher risk.

8.  The net return for a fund is the return after all research and management costs. The gross return is before these expenses. The net return is the return reported to the stockholder since all expenses have been allowed for in the NAV. To compute the gross return, it is necessary to compute the expenses of the fund and **add these back** to the ending NAV and compute the returns with these expenses added back. Typically, the average difference in return is about one percent a year, but this varies by fund. As an investor, it is the net return that is important because these are the returns that you derive.

9.  To determine whether the manager is better than average in selecting stocks or at market timing, you should examine **gross** returns that do no include his expenses. Assuming the gross returns will indicate superior management ability, the **net** returns will indicate whether the managers are superior enough to cover the expenses involved.

10. Just because only half do better than buy-and-hold on the basis of risk-adjusted return does not mean you ignore them, because there are other functions that investment companies perform that are important. These other functions include diversification, flexibility, and record keeping. To derive these other advantages, it may be necessary to give up some of the return.

11. It is questionable whether good performance will continue during two successive short-term periods, because in many cases, it could be a random

26 - 4

event of a couple of winners that are not repeated. Empirically, such superior performance has **not** been consistent beyond what you would expect by chance.

12. The poor performance can be more consistent because it can be caused by poor analysts or because of excess expenses which tend to be more permanent. Again, the empirical evidence indicates more consistency for **inferior** funds.

13(a). To derive a quick view of recent performance, you can look at a recent quarterly review in *Barron's*; the monthly performance listing in the *United Mutual Fund Selector*, or the annual *Forbes* review.

13(b). The long-run analysis and address for the funds are best derived from the Weisenberger *Investment Company* book.

# Answers to Problems

1.  Shares = $50,000 / ($8.00/share) = 6,250

    NAV = $75,800 / 6,250 = $12.13

2.  Load Fund = ($1,000 - 90) x 1.15 = $1,046.50
    Represents a 4.65% in growth.

    No load Fund = ($1,000 x 1.12) - 11.20 = $1,08.80
    Represents a 10.88% growth.

    The no load fund offers an extra $62.30 over the load fund for a $1,00
    investments held over a one-year time period.  The difference in percent
    growth is 6.23%.

3.  Student Exercise.

# CHAPTER 27

# Evaluation Of Portfolio Performance

# Answers to Questions

1. The two major factors would be: (1) attempt to derive risk-adjusted returns that exceed a naïve buy-and-hold policy and (2) completely diversify – i.e., eliminated all unsystematic risk from the portfolio. A portfolio manager can do one or both of two things to derive superior risk-adjusted returns. The first is to have **superior timing** regarding market cycles and adjust your portfolio accordingly. Alternatively, one can consistently **select under-valued stocks**. As long as you do not make major mistakes with the rest of the portfolio, these actions should result in superior risk-adjusted returns.

2. Treynor (1965) divided a fund's excess return (return "less" risk-free rate) by its beta. For a fund not completely diversified, Treynor's "T" value will understate risk and overstate performance. Sharpe (1966) divided a fund's excess return by its standard deviation. Sharpe's "S" Value will produce evaluations very similar to Treynor's for funds that are well diversified. Jensen (1968) measures performance as the difference between a fund's actual and required returns. Since the latter return is based on the CAPM and a fund's beta, Jensen makes the same implicit assumptions as Treynor – namely, that funds are completely diversified.

3. For portfolios with $R^2$ values noticeably less than 1.0, it would make sense to compute both measures. Differences in the rankings generated by the two measures would suggest less-than-complete diversification by some funds – specifically, those that were ranked higher by Treynor than by Sharpe.

4. As suggested above, Jensen defines superior (inferior) performance as a positive (negative) difference between a manager's actual return and his CAPM-based required return. For poorly-diversified funds, Jensen's rankings would more closely resemble Treynor's For well-diversified funds, Jensen's rankings would follow those of both Treynor and Sharpe. By replacing the CAPM with the APT, differences between funds' actual and required returns (or "alphas") could provide fresh evaluations of funds.

5. Since the return for selectivity is the difference between overall performance and the required return for risk, if the overall performance exceeds the

required return for risk, the portfolio experiences a positive return for selectivity. In the example, the required return would have to be less than -0.50 in order to experience a positive selectivity value. Common sense tells us that a negative required return for assuming risk is not realistic.

6. A high $R^2$ value of .95 implies that the portfolio is highly diversified and, thus, the diversification term will be minimal. By definition, if we have a selectivity value of a positive 2.5 percent and a minimal diversification term, net selectivity will be a positive value.

7(a). The returns of a well-diversified portfolio (within an asset class) are highly correlated with the returns of the asset class itself. Over time, diversified portfolios of securities within an asset class tend to produce similar returns. In contrast, returns between different asset classes are often much less correlated, and over time, different asset classes are very likely to produce quite different returns. This expected difference in returns arising from differences in asset class exposures (i.e., from differences in asset allocation) is, thus, the key performance variable.

7(b). Three reasons why successful implementation of asset allocation decisions is more difficult in practice than in theory are:

A. Transaction Costs - investing or rebalancing a portfolio to reflect a chosen asset allocation is not cost-free; expected benefits are reduced by the costs of implementation.

B. Changes in Economic and Market Factors - changing economic backgrounds, changing market price levels and changing relationships within and across asset classes all act to reduce the optimality of a given allocation decision and to create requirements for eventual rebalancing. Changes in economic and market factors change the expected risk/reward relationships of the allocation on a continuing basis.

C. Changes in Investor Factors - the passage of time often gives rise to changes in investor needs, circumstances or preferences which, in turn, give rise to the need to reallocate, with the attendant costs of doing so.

In summary, even the "perfect" asset allocation is altered by the very act of implementation, due to transaction costs and/or changes in the original economic/market conditions and, as time passes, changes in the investor's situation. These impediments to successful implementation are inherent in the process, mandating ongoing monitoring of the relevant input factors. In practice, the fact of change in one or more of these factors is a "given;" constant attention of the degree and the importance of the effects required.

8. The difference by which a manager's overall actual return beats his/her overall benchmark return is termed the total value-added return and decomposes into an allocation effect and a selection effect. The former effect measures differences in weights assigned by the actual and benchmark portfolios to stocks, bonds and cash "times" the respective differences between market-specific benchmark returns and the overall benchmark return. The latter effect focuses on the market-specific actual returns "less" the corresponding market-specific benchmark returns "times" the weights assigned to each market by the actual portfolio. Of course, the foregoing analysis implicitly assumes that the actual and benchmark market-specific portfolios (e.g., stocks) are risk-equivalent. To be otherwise would invalidate this analysis.

9. Use of a "benchmark portfolio" has been proposed as a potential solution to the difficulty of distinguishing real active management skill from mere random results. By identifying the investment style, an appropriate benchmark can be developed which provides a reference point by which to judge the active management results. An appropriate benchmark would represent the characteristics that the manager's portfolio would exhibit in the absence of active investment management; i.e., a passive representation of a money manager's investment process.

A benchmark which serves as an effective tool for investment performance evaluation possesses the following characteristics:

Unambiguous - the names and weights of securities comprising the benchmark are clearly delineated.

Investable - the option is available to forgo active management and simply hold the benchmark as a representation of the style.

27 - 5

<u>Measurable</u> - it is possible to readily calculate the benchmark's return on a reasonably frequent basis.

<u>Appropriate</u> - the benchmark is consistent with the manager's investment style or biases.

<u>Reflective of current investment opinions</u> - the manager has current knowledge of the securities which make up the benchmark.

<u>Specified in advance</u> - the benchmark is constructed prior to the start of an evaluation period.

The "median manager" approach is an example of a commonly used benchmark whose value is seriously compromised as a measurement tool due to its lack of the above-listed characteristics. While the median-manager result is capable of being measured, most critically the median manager benchmark is not specified in advance. The median manager is identified only ex post.

Because the median manager is not known in advance, neither the manager being evaluated nor the client has the option to invest in the median manager's portfolio. Further, the median manager is ambiguous in that the portfolio composition is unavailable for inspection before or after the evaluation period.

In addition, the median manager's portfolio most likely contains securities of which the manager being evaluated has no current investment knowledge. Finally, the median manager benchmark is unlikely to be appropriate because of the high probability that the median manager's investment style will not be identical to that of the manager being evaluated.

Other factors favoring benchmark portfolios over the median manager approach are their ability to be used as the basis of performance fees and calculation of various risk-adjusted performance measures (Sharpe ratio, Treynor value, Jensen ratio, etc.). Moreover, benchmark portfolios do not suffer the "survivorship bias" of the median manager approach.

10(a). The basic procedure in portfolio evaluation is to compare the return on a managed portfolio to the return expected on an unmanaged portfolio having the same risk, via use of the CAPM. That is, expected return (Ep) is calculated from:

$$E_p = E_f + \left(E_m - B_p\right)$$

Where $E_f$ is the risk-free rate, $E_m$ is the unmanaged portfolio or the market return and $B_p$ is the beta coefficient or systematic risk of the managed portfolio. The benchmark of performance then is the unmanaged portfolio. The typical proxy for this unmanaged portfolio is some aggregate stock market index such as the S&P 500.

10(b). The benchmark error often occurs because the unmanaged portfolio used in the evaluation process is not "optimized." That is, market indices, such as the S&P 500, chosen as benchmarks are not on the evaluator's **ex ante** mean/variance efficient frontier. Benchmark error may also occur because of an error in the estimation of the risk free return. Together, these two sources of error will cause the implied Security Market Line (SML) to be mispositioned.

10(c). The main ingredients are that the true risk-free rate is lower than the measured risk-free rate and the true market is above the measured market. The result is under-performance relative to the true SML rather than superior performance relative to the measured SML.

10(d). The fact that the portfolio manager has been judged superior based on several different benchmarks should not make me feel any more comfortable because all the benchmarks could have errors, which means that you are simply computing different errors. It is shown by Roll that if the various indexes are perfectly correlated, a proportionate difference will exist in the error. Notably, all of these indexes are very highly correlated.

10(e). All of the discussion by Roll is **not** directed against the CAPM theory, but is concerned with a **measurement problem** involved in finding a valid benchmark, i.e., an unmanaged portfolio that is mean/variance efficient. The theory is correct and valid. The problem is implementing the theory in the real world where it is difficult to construct a true "market portfolio."

11. When measuring the performance of an equity portfolio manager, overall returns can be related to a common total risk or systematic risk. Factors influencing the returns achieved by the bond portfolio manager are more

complex. In order to evaluate performance based on a common risk measure (i.e., market index), four components must be considered that differentiate the individual portfolio from the market index. These components include: (1) a **policy effect**, (2) a **rate anticipation effect**, (3) an **analysis effect**, and (4) a **trading effect**. Decision variables involved include the impact of duration decisions, anticipation of sector/quality factors, and the impact of individual bond selection.

12(a). **Yield-to-maturity**. This is the expected return on the bond based upon the beginning price. Assuming no changes in the market, it is made up of the accrued coupon payments; an expected price change to amortize the differ e between par and the beginning market price' and the "roll effect," which is due to changes in yield-to-maturity due to the slope of the yield curve and the fact that the bond's maturity declined during the holding period.

12(b). The **interest rate effect** is an analysis of what happened to the bond's price due to a change in market interest rates during the period. Specifically, the analysis involves relating what should have happened to the price of the portfolio bond taking into account the change in yields for treasury securities of a comparable maturity and assuming the same spread as at the beginning of the period .

12(c). The **sector/quality effect** examines what should have happened to returns based upon changes in sector/quality differentials during the period. You begin with a matrix of differential returns for the bonds in different sectors (corporates, utilities, financial, telephone) and quality (Aaa, Aa, Baa) relative to the returns for Treasury bonds of the same maturity. As an example, the matrix will indicate that the return difference for an Aa corporate bond during the period was one percent more or less than a similar maturity Treasury bond. Put another way, it indicates what happened to bonds of this quality and sector during this period relative to Treasury bonds.

12(d). The **residual return** is what is left of total return after taking account of yield to maturity, the interest rate effect, and the sector/quality effect. It is as follows:

**Total Return =
Yield to Maturity + Interest Rate Effect +
Sector / Quality Effect + Residual Return**

# Answers to Problems

1(a).  The risk adjusted returns of the two equity portfolios are computed as follows:

$$\text{Risk Adj Returns} = \frac{(\text{Realized returns} - \text{risk free rate})}{\text{beta}} + \text{risk free rate}$$

Good Samaritan Equity Portfolio:

$$\frac{11.8\% - 7.8\%}{1.20} + 7.8\% = 3.3\% + 7.8\% = 11.1\%$$

Mrs. Atkins' Equity Portfolio:

$$\frac{10.7\% - 7.8\%}{1.05} + 7.8\% = 2.8\% + 7.8\% = 10.6\%$$

Both portfolios outperformed the S&P 500 both on an absolute basis and on a risk adjusted basis. The Good Samaritan portfolio outperformed Mrs. Atkins' portfolio by more than a full percentage point before risk adjustment, but by only one-half percentage point after risk adjustment. These differences are small enough to be within the range of normal statistical variation and are therefore not meaningful in judging performance.

1(b).  Factors which could account for the differences in *total account performance* would include the following:

*Different asset mixes between stocks, bonds, and short term reserves.* Clearly, a higher proportion of equity investments would have improved the total portfolio return for Mrs. Atkins.

*The use of taxable bonds versus tax exempt bonds.* Since Mrs. Atkins' bonds were tax exempt whereas the Good Samaritan bonds were undoubtedly taxable, Mrs. Atkins' portfolio return would be adversely affected unless an adjustment were made for *after-tax* returns.

Mrs. Atkins' portfolio is *not well-diversified*, since it contains only eight equity issues (other than Merit Enterprises). This creates a higher potential for specific risk to affect the portfolio return in any given year.

The *objectives and constraints* under which the two portfolios are operating are probably *quite different*. The higher beta of the Good Samaritan portfolio suggests that it may have been managed with less restrictive constraints than Mrs. Atkins' portfolio.

The relatively short *time period* (i.e., twelve months) *is too short* to make a truly meaningful evaluation of relative performance of the two portfolios. A complete market cycle would be more appropriate.

2(a). 
$$S_P = (.15 - .07)/.05 = 1.60 \; (\#2)$$
$$S_Q = (.20 - .07)/.10 = 1.30 \; (\#4)$$
$$S_R = (.10 - .07)/.03 = 1.00 \; (\#5)$$
$$S_S = (.17 - .07)/.06 = 1.67 \; (\#1)$$
$$S_M = (.13 - .07)/.04 = 1.50 \; (\#3)$$

2(b). 
$$T_P = (.15 - .07)/1.0 = 0.080 \; (\#3)$$
$$T_Q = (.20 - .07)/1.5 = 0.087 \; (\#2)$$
$$T_R = (.10 - .07)/0.6 = 0.050 \; (\#5)$$
$$T_S = (.17 - .07)/1.1 = 0.091 \; (\#1)$$
$$T_M = (.13 - .07)/1.0 = 1.060 \; (\#4)$$

2(c). It is apparent from the rankings above that Portfolio Q was poorly diversified since Treynor ranked it #2 and Sharpe ranked it #4. Otherwise, the rankings are similar.

3(a). The Treynor measure (T) relates the rate of return earned above the risk-free rate to the portfolio beta during the period under consideration. Therefore, the Treynor measure shows the risk premium (excess return) earned per unit of systematic risk:

$$T_i = \frac{R_i - R_f}{\beta_i},$$

where
$R_i$, = average rate of return for portfolio i during the specified period,
$R_f$ = average rate of return- on a risk-free investment during the specified period, and
$\beta_i$ = beta of portfolio i during the specified period.

| Treynor Measure | Performance Relative to the Market (S&P 500) |
|---|---|

$$T = \frac{10\% - 6\%}{0.60} = 6.7\% \quad \text{Outperformed}$$

Market (S&P 500)

$$T_M = \frac{12\% - 6\%}{1.00} = 6.0\%$$

The Treynor measure examines portfolio performance in relation to the security market line (SML). Because the portfolio would plot above the SML, it outperformed the S&P 500 Index. Because T was greater than $T_M$, 6.7 percent versus 6.0 percent, respectively, the portfolio clearly outperformed the market index.

The Sharpe measure (S) relates the rate of return earned above the risk free rate to the total risk of a portfolio by including the standard deviation of returns. Therefore, the Sharpe measure indicates the risk premium (excess return) per unit of total risk:

$$S_i = \frac{R_i - R_f}{\sigma_i},$$

where
$R_i$ = average rate of return for portfolio i during the specified period,
$R_f$ = average rate of return on a risk-free investment during the specified period, and
$\sigma_i$ = standard deviation of the rate of return for portfolio i during the specified period.

<u>Sharpe Measure</u>                    <u>Performance Relative to the Market (S&P 500)</u>

$$S = \frac{10\% - 6\%}{18\%} = 0.222\%$$        *Underperformed*

<u>Market (S&P 500)</u>

$$S_M = \frac{12\% - 6\%}{13\%} = 0.462\%$$

The Sharpe measure uses total risk to compare portfolios with the capital market line (CML). The portfolio would plot below the CML, indicating that it underperformed the market. Because S was less than $S_M$, 0.222 versus 0.462, respectively, the portfolio underperformed the market.

3(b).   The Treynor measure assumes that the appropriate risk measure for a portfolio is its systematic risk, or beta. Hence, the Treynor measure implicitly assumes that the portfolio being measured is fully diversified. The Sharpe measure is similar to the Treynor measure except that the excess return on a portfolio is divided by the standard deviation of the portfolio.

For perfectly diversified portfolios (that is, those without any unsystematic or specific risk), the Treynor and Sharpe measures would give consistent results relative to the market index because the total variance of the portfolio would be the same as its systematic variance (beta). A poorly diversified portfolio could show better performance relative to the market if the Treynor measure is used but lower performance relative to the market if the Sharpe measure is used. Any difference between the two measures relative to the markets would come directly from a difference in diversification.

In particular, Portfolio X outperformed the market if measured by the Treynor measure but did not perform as well as the market using the Sharpe measure. The reason is that Portfolio X has a large amount of unsystematic risk. Such risk is not a factor in determining the value of the Treynor measure for the portfolio, because the Treynor measure considers only systematic risk. The Sharpe measure, however, considers total risk (that is,

27 - 12

both systematic and unsystematic risk). Portfolio X, which has a low amount of systematic risk, could have a high amount of total risk, because of its lack of diversification. Hence, Portfolio X would have a high Treynor measure (because of low systematic risk) and a low Sharpe measure (because of high total risk).

4(a).  Portfolio MNO enjoyed the highest degree of diversification since it had the highest $R^2$ (94.8%). The statistical logic behind this conclusion comes from the CAPM which says that all fully diversified portfolios should be priced along the security market line. $R^2$ is a measure of how well assets conform to the security market line, so $R^2$ is also a measure of diversification.

4(b).

| Fund | Treynor | Sharpe | Jensen |
|------|---------|--------|--------|
| ABC | 0.975 (4) | 0.857(4) | 0.192(4) |
| DEF | 0.715(5) | 0.619(5) | -0.053(5) |
| GHI | 1.574(1) | 1.179(1) | 0.463(1) |
| JKL | 1.262(2) | 0.915(3) | 0.355(2) |
| MNO | 1.134(3) | 1.000(2) | 0.296(3) |

4(c).

| Fund | t(alpha) |
|------|----------|
| ABC | 1.7455(3) |
| DEF | -0.2789(5) |
| GHI | 2.4368(1) |
| JKL | 1.6136(4) |
| MNO | 2.1143(2) |

Only GHI and MNO have significantly positive alphas.

5(a).

5(b). Overall Performance $= R_a - R_f = .15 - .05 = .10$

5(c). Selectivity $= R_a - R_a (B_a) = .15 - .11 = .04$

5(d). Risk $= [R_x (B_a) - R_f] = .11 - .05 = .06$
where $R_x (B_a) = .05 + 1.2 (.10 - .05) = .111$

6(a). The following briefly describes one strength and one weakness of each manager.

    1.    **Manager A**

**Strength.** Although Manager A's one-year total return was slightly below the EAFE Index return (.0 percent versus -5.0 percent, respectively), this manager apparently has some country/security return expertise. This large local market return advantage of 2.0 percent exceeds the 0.2 percent return for the EAFE Index.

**Weakness.** Manager A has an obvious weakness in the currency management area. This manager experienced a marked currency return shortfall compared with the EAFE Index of 8.0 percent versus -5.2 percent, respectively.

    2.    **Manager B**

**Strength.** Manager B's total return slightly exceeded that of the index, with a marked positive increment apparent in the currency return. Manager B had a -1.0 percent currency return versus a -5.2 percent currency return on the EAFE index. Based on this outcome, Manager B's strength appears to be some expertise in the currency selection area.

**Weakness.** Manager B had a marked shortfall in local market return. Manager B's country/security return was -1.0 percent versus 0.2 percent on the EAFE Index. Therefore, Manager B appears to be weak in security/market selection ability.

6(b).   The following strategies would enable the Fund to take advantage of the strengths of the two managers and simultaneously minimize their weaknesses.

1.   **Recommendation**: One strategy would be to direct Manager A to make no currency bets relative to the EAFE Index and to direct Manager B to make only currency decisions, and no active country or security selection bets.

   **Justification**: This strategy would mitigate Manager A's weakness by hedging all currency exposures into index-like weights. This would allow capture of Manager A's country and stock selection skills while avoiding losses from poor currency management. This strategy would also mitigate Manager B's weakness, leaving an index-like portfolio construct and capitalizing on the apparent skill in currency management.

2.   **Recommendation**: Another strategy would be to combine the portfolios of Manager A and Manager B, with Manager A making country exposure and security selection decisions and Manager B managing the currency exposures created by Manager A's decisions (providing a "currency overlay").

   **Justification**: This recommendation would capture the strengths of both Manager A and Manager B and would minimize their collective weaknesses.

7(a).   (i)   $.6(-5) + .3(-3.5) + .1(0.3) = -4.02\%$
        (ii)   $.5(-4) + .2(-2.5) + .3(0.3) = -2.41\%$
        (iii)   $.3(-5) + .4(-3.5) + .3(0.3) = -2.81\%$

   Manager A outperformed the benchmark fund by 161 basis points while Manager B beat the benchmark fund by 121 basis points.

7(b).   (i)   $[.5(-4 + 5) + .2(-2.5 + 3.5) + .3(.3 - .3)] = 0.70\%$

        (ii)   $[(.3 - .6)(-5 + 4.02) + (.4 - .3)(-3.5 + 4.02) + (.3 - .1)$
        $(.3 + 4.02)] = 1.21\%$

27 - 15

Manager A added value through her selection skills (70 of 161 basis points) and her allocation skills (71 of 161 basis points). Manager B added value totally through his allocation skills (121 of 121 basis points).

8(a). Overall, both managers added value by mitigating the currency effects present in the Index. Both exhibited an ability to "pick stocks" in the markets they chose to be in (Manager B in particular). Manager B used his opportunities not to be in stocks quite effectively (via the cash/bond contribution to return), but neither of them matched the passive index in picking the country markets in which to be invested (Manager B in particular).

|  | Manager A | Manager B |
|---|---|---|
| Strengths | Currency Management<br>Stock Selection | Currency Management<br>Stock Selection<br>Use of Cash/Bond Flexibility |
| Weaknesses | Country Selection<br>(to a limited degree) | Country Selection |

8(b). The column reveals the effect on performance in local currency terms after adjustment for movements in the U.S. dollar and, therefore, the effect on the portfolio. Currency gains/losses arise from translating changes in currency exchange rates versus the U.S. dollar over the measuring period (3 years in this case) into U.S. dollars for the U.S. pension plan. The Index mix lost 12.9% to the dollar reducing what would otherwise have been a very favorable return from the various country markets of 19.9% to a net return of only 7.0%.

9. $\Pi = E + U - 11 = 10 + U.$   Therefore, U. = 1

| | 10-Year AA Bonds | 5-Year A Bonds | 25-Year B Bonds |
|---|---|---|---|
| M | 1.50 | 1.00 | 3.00 |
| S | -0..40 | -0.60 | -1.20 |
| B | .25 | .50 | .75 |
| C | 1.35 | .90 | 2.55 |
| I | 11.00 | 11.00 | 11.00 |
| R | 12.35 | 11.90 | 13.55 |

where

| | S | |
|---|---|---|
| AAA | - | .2 |
| AA | - | .4 |
| A | - | .6 |
| BBB | - | .8 |
| BB | - | 1.0 |
| B | - | 1.2 |

and

$M = .2 \times 5 + .1 \times 5 = 1.50$ (10 Yr.)
$M = .2 \times 5 + .1 \times 0 = 1.00$ ( 5 Yr.)
$M = .2 \times 5 + .1 \times 20 = 3.00$ (25 Yr.)

10(a). Evaluation begins with selection of the appropriate benchmark against which to measure the firms' results:

*Firm A.* The Aggregate Index and "Managers using the Aggregate Index" benchmark are appropriate here, because Firm A maintains marketlike sector exposures. Performance has been strong; Firm A outperformed the Aggregate Index by 50 basis points and placed in the first quartile of managers' results.

*Firm B.* Firm B does not use mortgages; therefore, the Government/Corporate for both index and universe comparisons would be the appropriate benchmark. Although Firm B produced the highest absolute performance (9.3 percent), it did not perform up to either the Index (9.5 percent) or other managers investing only in the Government/Corporate sectors (third quartile).

*Firm C.* Like Firm A, this firm maintains broad market exposures and should be compared with the Aggregate Index for both index and universe comparisons. Performance has been good (30 basis points ahead of the index and in the second quartile of manager results) but not as good as Firm A's showing during this relatively short measurement period.

10(b). Firm A does not show an observable degree of security selection skill (-10 basis points); nor does it appear to be managing in line with its stated marketlike approach. Some large nonmarketlike bets are driving return production (e.g., duration bets, +100 basis points; yield curve bets, +30 basis points; and sector-weighting bets, -70 basis points) and account for its +50 basis-point better-than-benchmark total return.

Firm C's ability to anticipate shifts in the yield curve correctly is confirmed by the analysis (its +30 basis points accounts for all of its observed better than-benchmark outcome). In addition, its claim n to maintain marketlike exposures is also confirmed (e.g., the nominal differences from benchmark in the other three attribution areas).

10(c). Firm C produced the best results because its style and its expertise were confirmed by the analysis; Firm A's were not.